Preaching the Whole Bible as Christian Scripture

*The Application of Biblical Theology
to Expository Preaching*

Graeme Goldsworthy

WILLIAM B. EERDMANS PUBLISHING COMPANY
GRAND RAPIDS, MICHIGAN / CAMBRIDGE, U.K.

Wm. B. Eerdmans Publishing Co.
2140 Oak Industrial Drive N.E., Grand Rapids, Michigan 49505 /
P.O. Box 163, Cambridge CB3 9PU U.K.
www.eerdmans.com

Printed in the United States of America

12 11 10 09 08 07 06   13 12 11 10 9 8 7 6

Library of Congress Cataloging-in-Publication Data

Goldsworthy, Graeme.
Preaching the whole Bible as Christian scripture: the application of biblical
theology to expository preaching / Graeme Goldsworthy.
p.   cm.
Includes bibliographical references (p.) and indexes.
ISBN-10: 0-8028-4730-7
ISBN-13: 978-0-8028-4730-0 (pbk. : alk. paper)
1. Bible — Homiletical use. 2. Preaching.   I. Title.
BS534.5 .G65   2000
251 — dc21
00-035429

PREACHING THE WHOLE BIBLE
AS CHRISTIAN SCRIPTURE

Contents

PART 2:
THE PRACTICAL APPLICATION
OF BIBLICAL THEOLOGY TO PREACHING

Foreword

I have come to the discipline of biblical theology late in my ministry. I remember reading Graeme Goldsworthy's *Gospel and Kingdom* in 1981, and it was the dawning of a new day. I had always known that the story of David and Goliath was not really about me facing the "giant problems" in my life, but what it had to do with Jesus and salvation eluded me. For much of my ministry the Old Testament was not given its rightful place in my preaching because I was uneasy about its Christian meaning. I knew that it was the word of God, and I knew that it had integrity of its own. However, I also knew that if a Jew, or even a Muslim, was happy with my interpretation of some passage, then it could not be Christian.

This book is a fine addition to the work that the author has already done in this field. It will encourage preachers to deal with both the Old and the New Testaments in a way that gives recognition that Christ is the fulfillment of all things.

In the two Bible colleges at which I teach, I hear students preach regularly. Without a doubt their hardest exercise is to relate the Old Testament to the gospel in a way that flows from the text of Scripture and isn't just some appendage that is tacked on to the end to make it Christian. This book will help them preach from the Old Testament with confidence and accuracy.

I was given a "state-of-the-art" CD player for my sixtieth birthday. It was a surprise — a very pleasant one! The eight-year-old who lives next door to me was delighted. He had it playing music before I had read the first page of the instructions. If we can encourage preachers to deal with the Scriptures in the way this book suggests, then within a generation every Sunday School child will be able to understand how the exodus of Israel from Egypt and the exodus that Jesus brought to pass in Jerusalem mesh together in a unity. They will be able to "play music" with their Bibles while many others are still fumbling with the instructions.

I have friends who are not Christian. From time to time they will accept my invitation to come to church with me. However, they are erratic, and I am never sure if they will turn up. When they do, I am delighted. It doesn't seem unreasonable for me to hope that they will hear the gospel when they do come. It may not be the major part of the sermon. However, if they listen, they should have a clear idea about that which is at the center of our faith.

You will imagine my delight when I read in chapter 9 the following:

> Sermons preached in church are delivered inevitably to a more float-ing congregation. There will be the staunch regulars who can be de-pended on to be there every Sunday except when they are sick or away on holidays. There will be those who consider "regular" atten-dance to mean once a month. There will be those whose attachment to church-going is fairly loose, who will go when the weather is good and if they feel like it. Then there are those who have no real attach-ment to any church or particular congregation, and who are brought as a one-time venture by friends, or who just turn up. As a colleague of mine puts it, those who just happen to be there once ought to at least have the opportunity to hear what we are really on about.

There is no doubt that this book will help us all to show how every part of the Scriptures contributes to our understanding of the gospel. It is my prayer that this will happen.

Sydney, Australia   *John C. Chapman*
May 1999

Preface

The aim of this book is to provide a handbook for preachers that will help them apply a consistently Christ-centered approach to their sermons. While the main readership is theologically trained pastors, I am aware that there is a considerable body of lay preachers who may have had little or no formal training. I am therefore aiming to keep technical language fairly muted while at the same time providing necessary references and technical comments in footnotes.

While focusing on biblical theology I do not want merely to repeat what I've already published on the subject. Nevertheless, some basic exposition of what I understand the biblical-theological method to be and to yield must be included in order to give coherence to the book. In this regard I provide a number of diagrams to aid in conceptualizing the structure of revelation in the Bible. In part 1 my aim is to stand where the evangelical pastor-preacher stands and to ask the sort of questions that the preacher would ask about the Bible, biblical theology, and preaching. In part 2 I seek to apply the biblical theological method to the various genres of biblical literature, all the time with the preaching task in mind.

Among evangelicals there is a strange neglect of biblical theology even though it is, to my way of thinking, one obvious implication of the evangelical view of the Bible. Books on preaching abound, even books on "expository" preaching. Yet, apart from a few scattered references, there seems to be very little that takes up the function of biblical theology in the process of moving from the text to the hearer.

In the early 1970s I was a visiting lecturer in Biblical Theology at Moore Theological College. Upon the urging of my students, I wrote up the course into an introductory handbook for Christian teachers and preachers on applying the Old Testament. The fact that the resulting book, *Gospel and*

Kingdom: A Christian Interpretation of the Old Testament (Carlisle: Paternoster, 1981), has been continuously in print since then indicates to me that a real need exists for some basic biblical theology of a nontechnical kind.

At the beginning of 1995 I returned to a full-time position on the faculty of Moore College to teach Biblical Theology and Hermeneutics. I am grateful to the Principal and the College Council for granting me special leave during 1999 to write this book. Much of the stimulus for the book has come from the opportunity to teach these subjects and from interaction with faculty and students. A number of our students have come from overseas, including Britain and the U.S.A., to study with us because of our emphasis on biblical theology. I count it a great privilege to be part of the ministry team at Moore College, which, from its small beginnings in 1856 as a place for the training of clergy for the Anglican Diocese of Sydney, has now become an international center for Reformed and evangelical theology.

John Chapman, better known to his acquaintances as "Chappo," has been to me a spiritual mentor, friend, and colleague since my conversion in 1950. He has had a wide-ranging and fruitful evangelistic and preaching ministry throughout Australia and in many countries overseas. He graciously consented to write the Foreword for this book.

Moore Theological College
Sydney, Australia
May 1999

INTRODUCTION

Jesus and the Koala

The Predictable "Jesus Bit"

There is a story told about an Australian Sunday School teacher who felt that her approach to teaching was in need of some remedial action. She thought she was altogether too predictable and the children were becoming bored with her story-telling and questioning of the class about what they had learned. She decided on a new tack to try to rectify matters. The next Sunday, once the preliminaries were over, she stood before the class of five-year-olds and asked, "Who can tell me what is gray and furry and lives in a Gum tree[1]?" The children were completely taken by surprise by this totally unexpected and new approach. They thought there must be a catch and stared blankly at the teacher. "Come on," she coaxed, "someone must know. What is gray, furry, lives in a Gum tree — has a black leathery nose and beady eyes?" Still no answer. "Oh, surely you know." She was nonplussed by this reticence. "It lives in a Gum tree; eats Gum leaves; it has big beady eyes and furry ears." Silence. She was about to switch tactics and to go on to something else when a small girl gradually raised her hand in the air with much hesitation. Delighted, the teacher asked, "Yes, Suzie?" The child replied, "I know it's Jesus, but it sounds like a Koala!"

Such predictability is, hopefully, a bit of a caricature. Yet, at a more sophisticated level it can exist. Some of the students that I teach at Moore Theological College discussed their concerns with me about listening to preachers who deal with the Old Testament in such a way that the students were moved to think, in the course of the sermon, "Ho hum! now here comes the Jesus bit." These preachers were attempting to avoid an exposition of the

1. The common name for any variety of the eucalypts.

Old Testament without Christ, which so often leads to a moralizing approach. Obviously a preacher needs to have a clear sense of the relationship of Old Testament texts to the person and work of Jesus, but that preacher also needs to be able to communicate this relationship in ways that avoid such stereotyping. It is also obvious that something is very wrong if the preacher's way of relating the text to Jesus is felt to be boring and predictable.

Problems with the Old Testament

My original intention was to deal with the thorny subject of preaching from the Old Testament. There is no doubt in my mind, and clearly in the minds of many, that preaching from the Old Testament presents many problems for the Christian preacher. Having taught Old Testament for a number of years in two theological colleges and a Bible college, I have found that people expect me to be both motivated and experienced in preaching from the Old Testament. Yet, in all the years I have spent in full-time pastoral ministry, I have found a need to be very disciplined in planning a preaching program to include the Old Testament on a regular basis. It is plainly easier as a Christian to preach from the New Testament than from the Old. Some may feel that preaching from the Old Testament is the same in principle as preaching from the New. Of course, if we are diligent in the choice of our texts, that may well appear to be the case. But even at the level of ethical teaching in the prophets, or the praise of God in the Psalms, we instinctively recognize that the material still emanates from the period before Jesus came into the world. How much more, then, is the gap obvious when we deal with some ceremonial prescriptions in the law of Moses.

The Separation of the Testaments

However, other considerations lead me to take up a more general approach to preaching and biblical theology. The first of these is that the separation of biblical studies and biblical theology into the two specialized areas of Old Testament and New Testament, however necessary at the formal and academic level, has led to an extremely costly separation of the Testaments. There are obvious distinctions between the Testaments that make such separation seem logical and even necessary. But the Christian Church has received one canon of Scripture and has always recognized both the distinctions between the Testaments and their essential unity. This particular problem has many expressions, but we need note only two. First, in academic curricula established in theological and Bible colleges the division between the Testaments tends to be fairly rigidly maintained. This has repercussions for the way pastors preach and teach, and for the kind of role models they create for their lay preachers and teachers. Furthermore, while the study of the New Testament will inevitably raise questions of the use of the Old Testament in the New, the study of the Old Testament is easily carried on in total isolation from the questions of how this significant body of literature should function as Christian Scripture. Second, in the field of theological writing we notice two major characteristics of literature related to the concern of this study. Biblical theologies are almost entirely either theologies of the Old Testament or theologies of the New Testament. Very few writers have attempted to write a theology of the Bible.[2] In addition, commentaries on the Old Testament rarely take up the question of the Christian significance of the Old Testament text. Even some series of Old Testament commentaries emanating from evangelical publishers tend to be very coy about raising the questions about how the texts can be related to the concerns that might figure in a Sunday sermon. Perhaps it could be said with some justification that the question of Christian application is not the concern of commentaries. Unfortunately it does not appear to be the concern of any other major body of literature either.

Problems with the New Testament

There is another related problem that affects the way we deal with the New Testament, a problem that also exists for the preacher of texts from both Testaments. Its specifics may differ because of the distinctions between the two Testaments, but the nature of the problem is the same: What is the relationship of this text to the person and work of Jesus of Nazareth? Let me be a little more specific. Preachers with a concern for expository preaching are predisposed to developing a preaching program in which a series of expositions from one particular book is given. In my experience the preaching of a series of sermons, say, from an epistle, easily leads the preacher to fragmentation because, while the epistle was written as a single letter to be read at one time,

---

2. More academically oriented scholarship tends to regard the task too large for one person to attempt to write a theology of the whole Bible. Some theologians seem to be driven by a sense of the overwhelming distinctions between the Testaments and to regard the task as impossible. One exception is the work of Brevard Childs, *Biblical Theology of the Old and New Testaments* (London: SCM, 1992). Evangelical writers have been less inhibited about the task, but also have tended to produce works that are more oriented to the nontechnical reader.

it is often divided up so that it is dealt with in Sunday sermons over a period of several weeks. There is nothing wrong with that as such, provided we recognize the changed dynamics. Thus, Paul may expound the gospel in the first part of the letter, and then go on to spell out some ethical and pastoral implications. When the preacher finally gets to deal with the latter, it is possibly a couple of weeks or more since the gospel exposition has happened, and the connection between the gospel and behavior, very closely related in the epistle, can be lost. The result is that the exhortations and commands are no longer seen to arise out of the good news of God's grace in the gospel but as simple imperatives of Christian behavior; as naked law.[3]

The relationship between what is and what ought to be, that is, the relationship between the finished work of Christ and the task of the believers, is often well flagged in the text. Paul, for example, frequently indicates the relationship by using the word "therefore" or a similar indicator of consequence. If we were to preach a series on Philippians, an obvious unit for one sermon would be the servant passage in Philippians 2:1-11 in which the saving work of Christ for us is clearly expounded. The following Sunday might feature the next part of the chapter, say vv. 12-18. How easy it is to ignore the "therefore" and to see the injunctions and exhortations of this passage as standing alone and not, as Paul expounds them, as the implications of the grace of God in Christ.[4] A regular attender who is fairly well informed may make the connection. But a newcomer, or someone who missed the previous Sunday, could gain the impression that the essence of Christianity is a matter of keeping the rules.

There are also broader questions of the relationship of the modern Christian to the contents of the ancient text. Does a saying of Jesus, for example, the Sermon on the Mount, have enduring significance as a direct word to Christians today? What are the interpretative matters that face us in the four Gospels, which relate a situation that no longer exists, namely, Jesus' presence in the flesh? Or again, in what way can the narrative material in Acts be the norm for the life of the modern church? A description of an event involving the apostles or the primitive church does not necessary stand as the pattern for all time. We recognize the existence of elements of discontinuity between us and the Old Testament, but we do not so readily recognize those that exist between us and the New Testament.

---

3. I will consider the way Old Testament law is shaped by the grace of God in chapter 11.
4. As the saying goes, "When we see a *therefore,* we should ask what it is there for."

Every One Is an Interpreter:
Every One Should Be a Biblical Theologian

These are some of the issues that the preacher faces, like it or not. They can not be avoided on the grounds of a simplistic assertion about the clarity of Scripture. The preacher is an interpreter of Scripture, as is every Christian who reads the Bible and seeks to make sense of its application to our daily lives. There are some basic principles that stem from the nature of the Bible that we need to be clear about. We also recognize that our assessment of the nature of the Bible involves certain basic assumptions or presuppositions that should be owned. It is vital for us to remember that our reference point is Jesus of Nazareth as he is testified to by Holy Scripture. The apostolic testimony to him shapes our approach to the Bible as a whole. This testimony necessitates the self-conscious formation of a biblical-theological approach to the unity and diversity of the Bible.

In this study, I approach the subject with certain presuppositions that were initially shaped by my conversion as a teenager under an evangelical ministry, and by my theological training at Moore Theological College. Graduate theological studies at the University of Cambridge and at Union Theological Seminary in Virginia forced me to examine carefully my presuppositions and my reasons for holding to them. Some of my earlier assumptions have undergone a measure of modification as I have gained what I think is a better grasp of the overall message of the Bible. Notwithstanding the need to mature, I have, for better or worse, come to the conviction that the position of traditional historical Christianity is the most consistent.[5] My position is one of reformed and evangelical theology.[6] On this basis I seek to establish my biblical theology as a primary hermeneutic tool for understanding the significance of the biblical text and as a vital expository tool for preaching. While I think it important to make clear my own presuppositions, I do not thereby imply that the matters raised in this book are relevant only to those who agree in every detail with my presuppositions. It is my hope that any preacher or teacher who wants to expound the Scriptures as the word of God will find encouragement in these pages for that most noble task.

---

5. I have raised the subject of presuppositions in my book *According to Plan: The Unfolding Revelation of God in the Bible* (Leicester: IVP, 1991) and in " 'Thus Says the Lord,' the Dogmatic Basis of Biblical Theology," in *God Who Is Rich in Mercy: Essays Presented to Dr. D. B. Knox,* ed. P. T. O'Brien and D. G. Peterson (Homebush West, Sydney: Lancer, 1986). The subject is ably dealt with by Carl F. H. Henry, *Toward a Recovery of Christian Belief* (Wheaton: Crossway, 1990).

6. I hope thus to remain consistent with the position of Christian theism.

CHAPTER 1

Nothing but Christ and Him Crucified

The Preacher's Dilemma

Evangelical preachers have an agenda. We want to proclaim Christ in the most effective way possible. We want to see people converted and established in the Christian life on the surest foundation — the word of God. We want to see people grow in their spiritual understanding and in godliness. We want to see churches grow, mature, and serve the world by reaching out to it with the gospel and with works of compassion. We want to impact our local communities through evangelism and ministries of caring. We want to strengthen our families and to nurture the children in the gospel. And at the heart of this agenda is the conviction that God has charged us with the ministry of preaching and teaching the Bible as a prime means of achieving these goals. Evangelical preachers stand in a long and venerable tradition going back to the apostles. It is a tradition of the centrality of the preached word in the life of the Christian congregation. We believe that preaching is not some peripheral item in the program of the local church, but that it lies at the very heart of what it is to be the people of God. We understand the activity of preaching as the primary way in which the congregations of God's people express their submission to his word. Of course the sermon in the church service is not the only way that the word of God comes to us. We encourage people to study the Bible in the privacy of their homes, to attend small group Bible studies, and even to undertake some more formal training in Bible and theology. But none of these things, important as they are, should detract from the primacy of preaching. In chapter 4 I will consider the question of the essential nature of preaching.

What did Paul mean when he wrote 1 Corinthians 2:2, "I decided to know nothing among you except Jesus Christ, and him crucified"? It is clear

I

that he wrote in all his epistles about a great deal more than the death of Jesus Christ. It is also clear that the main subject of all his writings is the person and work of Jesus. Yet he also writes about matters concerning his personal life and the lives of his fellow Christians. This particular passage in 1 Corinthians is a useful place to start our investigation, for in it Paul repudiates the worldview of the pagan, the philosopher, and even the Jew who attempts to get a handle on reality apart from the truth that is in Christ. "We proclaim Christ crucified, a stumbling block to Jews and foolishness to gentiles, but to those who are the called, both Jews and Greeks, Christ the power of God and the wisdom of God" (1 Cor. 1:23-24). The reason for this Christ-centeredness is so that the faith of his readers "might not rest on human wisdom but on the power of God" (1 Cor. 2:5). This means that the only appropriate way to respond to God's revealed power and wisdom is by being focused on the person of Christ. Elsewhere Paul defines the power of God as Christ and his gospel.[1] We will need, therefore, to take up the question later in this study of what the gospel is.[2]

The problem we face as preachers is not a new one. Throughout the ages Christian preachers have struggled with the question of the centrality of Christ and how this affects the way we handle the text of the Bible. It is an obvious problem for the preaching of the Old Testament, but, in a more subtle way, it also exists for the preacher of the New Testament. If a passage is not directly about the gospel events of the life, death, and resurrection of Jesus, to what extent are we obliged to make the connection? Would Paul really have us preach sermons in which we end up making the same platitudinous remarks about Jesus dying for our sins? Can the Old Testament speak to us from within itself and without any attempt being made to connect it to the gospel?

There is no doubt that many Christian preachers, in effect, do preach from the Old Testament about God in the Psalms, or the life of faith exhibited by one or other of the heroes of Israel, without connecting it specifically to the person and work of Christ. Furthermore, it is not only in the more academic books of theology or biblical studies that the Old Testament is dealt with in isolation from the New. Many books and inductive Bible study guides are written specifically to edify Christians from the Old Testament but without any explicit Christian content. A number of factors seem to be at work here, particularly among evangelical writers. There is, first, the correct assumption that the Old Testament is Christian Scripture and that, despite the difficulties in doing so, it must be appropriated for Christian people. Second, there is the recognition that the people of the Old Testament believed in the same God that we as Christians acknowledge. But then there is also the questionable assumption that the peo-

---

1. 1 Cor. 1:17, 24; Rom. 1:16.
2. See chapters 6 and 7.

ple of the Old Testament primarily function to provide patterns of faith and behavior for us to imitate or, conversely, to avoid.

There is often a failure to think through how the link between the people
and events of the Old Testament are to be made with us as, presumably, New
Testament people. This failure leads to some major defects in preaching, not
the least of which is the tendency to moralize on Old Testament events, or simply to find pious examples to imitate. But, as Edmund Clowney puts it,

> preaching which ignores the *historia revelationis,* which "again and
> again equates Abraham and us, Moses' struggle and ours, Peter's de-
> nial and our unfaithfulness; which proceeds only illustratively, does
> not bring the Word of God and does not permit the church to see the
> glory of the work of God; it only preaches man, the sinful, the sought,
> the redeemed, the pious man, but not Jesus Christ."[3]

Clowney also rightly points out that we have to be very selective in the
way we find examples to follow in the Old Testament saints.[4] After all, we
know how the Old Testament has always been an embarrassment to some because much of what are regarded as pious deeds in ancient Israel would simply not pass muster today. This raises the related issue of moral problems in
the Bible. The Old Testament is the source of many such moral problems for
those who would treat it seriously. Death and destruction, slaughter and pil-
lage, are standard fare in the narratives of Israel's conquest of Canaan. What
do we learn from such situations? If the narratives of Elijah teach us to "walk
close to the Lord" as I heard one speaker put it, what are the implications for
this walk with God of Elijah's command to slay all the prophets of Baal?
Most of us have worked out some way around these moral dilemmas created
by the Old Testament. An evangelical is not likely to feel at home with the assessment of old liberalism that the Old Testament depicts a primitive and,
therefore, substandard form of religion. But, the problem remains. What, for
example, can we say about the imprecations of Psalm 137, which are approv-
ing of those who take Babylonian babies and dash them against a rock![5]

---

3. Edmund P. Clowney, *Preaching and Biblical Theology* (London: Tyndale Press, 1962;
Grand Rapids: Eerdmans, 1961), p. 78, n. 9, quoting from Karl Dijk, *De Dienst der Prediking*
(1955), p. 109.
    4. Clowney, *Preaching,* pp. 79-82.
    5. Ps. 137:9. In the metrical version of Ps. 137, the Christian Reformed Church has man-
aged to soften the blow by making it more impersonal:

> God give you evil for reward,
> Blest be the one who brings your fall,
> Babylon great — your seed be smashed!
> Vengeance shall come from God our Lord.
> > *Psalter Hymnal* (Grand Rapids: CRC Publications, 1987)

Inductive Bible study books[6] are a prime source of the problem, not because there is anything wrong with applying this technique to the study of the Bible as such, but because this method alone is insufficient. If we give a group of Christians the task of reading a portion of the Old Testament in conjunction with some prescribed questions aimed at getting them to look carefully at the text in order to be able to understand what is being said, this is good as far as it goes. But the technique either makes enormous assumptions about the ability of people to see how this portion of text actually fits into the total unity of Scripture and, thus, how it relates to Christ, or else ignores the necessity to do so. Many people would not find that a problem. Parallels between the people of the Old Testament and ourselves are all that some readers need to be able feel deeply that this is the word of God to us today. I have to say that I do find it a problem, not because I am uninterested in what the Bible has to say to us, but precisely because I am interested. The burning question is whether the predominant attention given to the examples of faith and unbelief in the Bible is really focusing on what God primarily is wanting to say to us.

The point can be illustrated from a more obvious area of biblical teaching. It is quite clear that the New Testament shows us that the person of Jesus Christ is worthy of imitating. In fact the imitation of Christ is an important dimension in the teaching about the Christian disciple's existence. Yet, most Christians would understand that the imitation of Christ is not the center of the teaching of the New Testament. We are saved and made into the image of Christ not by our efforts to imitate him. Such an idea reduces the gospel to ethical effort. We recognize that the gospel tells us of the absolutely unique work of Christ, both in his living and his dying, by which we are saved through faith. We cannot imitate or live the gospel event as such. We can only believe it. We cannot work our way to heaven by moral endeavor. We can only depend on the finished work of Christ for us. We cannot command other people to live or do the gospel. We must proclaim the message of what God has done for them in Christ. We follow the New Testament in calling on people to live out the implications of the gospel, but we cannot urge people to actually live the gospel, for that was the unique work of Christ. This distinction between the gospel and its fruit in our lives is crucial. If we reject the notions of liberal Christianity that reduced the work of Jesus to ethical example, the implications are far-reaching for the way we handle the Bible. It is clear from the New Testament that the ethical example of Christ is secondary to and dependent upon the primary and unique work of Christ for us. Yet this does not seem to be clear to many when it

6. By which I refer to the many series of studies available that use the inductive method (i.e., moving from the particular text to a general application). The portion of text is read and considered for the specific information it can yield. From this the applications are generalized to the reader and to all Christians. Frequently the approach is to pose a number of questions calculated to get the reader to think analytically about the portion of the Bible text.

comes to the Old Testament. The message of the Old Testament is too easily reduced to the imitation of godly example and the avoidance of the ungodly example. This raises the questions of the nature of the Bible's unity, the relationship of the Testaments. To these we must turn later.

The Centrality of the Gospel

The central message of the New Testament concerns God incarnate, Jesus of Nazareth, who did for us what we could not do for ourselves, in order to bring us, a lost people, back to God. The whole of Scripture is filled with the sense of the divine initiative in salvation. In the Old Testament the sin of Adam and Eve, which brings the judgment of God, is not the end of the story because God has a plan of mercy and grace. The narratives of Noah and Abraham are eloquent of the sovereign work of God to bring rebellious humanity back from the brink of destruction. The covenant of God made with a chosen people is before all else a covenant of grace. God elects his people, makes significant promises to them, and acts to bring about the fulfillment of these promises. Only after the great redemptive act in the exodus from Egypt is Israel given the code of conduct in the law of Sinai: "I am the Lord your God, who brought you out of the land of Egypt, out of the house of bondage" (Exod. 20:2). They are already his people through what he has done in the past. They could not save themselves from Egypt and from their bondage to foreign gods; they could only stand still and see the salvation that God would achieve for them (Exod. 14:13-14). Then, having been saved by grace, they are bonded to their God in the covenant of Sinai. This primacy of grace, which is at work all the way through the Old Testament, points us to the centrality and primacy of the gospel of grace in the New Testament.

The nature of the relationship between the salvation revealed in the Old Testament and the gospel of Jesus Christ is something that we strive to understand on the basis of our biblical theology. This is not an easy task, and it is one that is readily shelved in favor of a more platitudinous and moralizing approach to the meaning of the Old Testament for us. The consistently Christian and biblical approach is to start with the New Testament and, specifically, with the gospel.

First, the gospel is central to our thinking in an experiential sense. Through the gospel we are brought to acknowledge the lordship of Christ, our need, and his grace to save all who believe in him. We may have had a lot of information about the contents of the Bible, and even have entertained sincerely religious thoughts before we believed the gospel. But the gospel is our means of contact with the truth about God. Indeed, the message about Christ

5

is the point of turning. Conversion, whether gradual or sudden, is a turning from a worldview and personal commitment in which we ourselves are at the center. For the secular mind, conversion is the point when all facts in our universe cease to be marshaled against the God of the Bible and are seen to testify to his reality. The gospel is the starting point for our eternal life with God. It is the means of becoming reconciled to God so that we have assurance of God's favor and of the gift of eternal life. It is the means by which we are born again and know the indwelling of God's Holy Spirit.[7]

Second, the gospel is central theologically. Though we have already touched upon the matter, we must never forget that, in both Testaments, what the people of God are called upon to do is always based upon what has already been done. Jesus is presented in the New Testament as the one who fulfills the promises of God by achieving for humankind the salvation that is otherwise beyond our reach. Against the backdrop of the complexity of the history and prophetic expectations of the Old Testament, Jesus proclaims himself to be the goal of all the purposes and promises of God. Where the Old Testament describes the goal of God's work in terms of a remnant of the chosen people, the promised land, the temple, the Davidic prince, and a whole range of images and metaphors, the New Testament claims simply that the death and resurrection of Jesus fulfills them all. The mighty acts of God, interpreted by his prophetic word, and by which he revealed his nature, are declared by the preaching of Jesus and his apostles to be preparatory for the person and work of Jesus. The God who acts in the Old Testament is the God who becomes flesh in the New Testament in order to achieve the definitive saving work in the world.

At the heart of this saving work is not the ethical teachings of Jesus, but his obedient life and death, his glorious resurrection and his ascension to the right hand of God on high. In a remarkable way the resurrection is portrayed as the event that encapsulates and fulfills all the theological themes of the Old Testament. This is not in any sense to denigrate the ethical dimension. The Bible shows us that God is lawful and that the freedom we have in Christ is not lawlessness. It is a matter of perspective, as I will say in a number of ways in this study. So often distortions of Christianity come about not by introducing totally foreign elements but by getting certain elements that are manifestly biblical out of perspective. The ethics of the Bible are put out of perspective when they are given exclusive or prior claim over the grace of God. To put it another way, the gift of God is always prior to and the basis of the task we are given, to live godly lives.

---

7. This is not the place for a discussion about whether faith or regeneration comes first. I suspect some of the arguments about this are misplaced. It is true that the sinner, being dead in trespasses and sins, cannot turn of his own accord to believe the gospel without the grace of the Holy Spirit. It is also true that the New Testament teaches that the word and Spirit go together.

Preaching and Biblical Theology

In the course of writing this book I have consulted a wide range of books on preaching. A survey of the history of preaching would show us that the nature of preaching has undergone many changes. The place and nature of the sermon have, from time to time, been under attack from various quarters and in different ways. Most preachers today will have access to the contemporary literature, but few would have the inclination or the resources to examine the development of preaching over the centuries. As evangelicals we will have some notion of apostolic preaching drawn from the New Testament. Beyond that, unless we have a special interest in patristics, or medieval preaching, or in some other historical period, we will probably confine our reading and understanding to some of the many available contributions to the literature of our time. My own impression of the modern literature is that it is predominantly weighted towards matters of effective communication and methods of sermon preparation. I find that questions regarding the nature of Scripture, which provide us with the principles of interpretation and application, are not so prominent.

It is here that biblical theology comes into its own. Much of the literature on preaching either ignores biblical theology completely or makes only a passing reference to it. Assumptions are made about the application of the results of careful exegesis, but the principles for making the connection between the ancient text and the contemporary hearers are not always so clearly dealt with. In asserting that biblical theology is the way forward, I am not thereby seeking to ride some hobbyhorse or to provide some brilliant revelation that no one else ever thought of. I am simply saying that the way the Bible presents its message, a message that reaches its climax in the person and work of Jesus of Nazareth, provides us with the principles we need. Biblical theology is nothing more nor less than allowing the Bible to speak as a whole: as the one word of the one God about the one way of salvation.

In the pages that follow I take up a number of pertinent questions that any evangelical preacher might ask about the assumptions we make, the method we use, and the applications that we can draw in our preparation of expository sermons. By this means I hope to clarify the role of biblical theology, not as an optional extra, but as the heart of the process of bringing the word of God to the contemporary hearer. The last part of the book explores the application of biblical theology to the various genres or characteristic types of material that go to make up the incredible diversity within the unity of the Bible.

PART 1

BASIC QUESTIONS WE ASK ABOUT PREACHING AND THE BIBLE

CHAPTER 2

What Is the Bible?

Evangelicals Are Bible People

Much has been written about what makes evangelicals distinctive. The term "evangelical" has become somewhat rubbery and hard to pin down, but it behooves us to try to define it. I would suggest that the bottom line in the definition is this: an evangelical is one who maintains adherence to the conviction of the final authority of the Bible as God's word written. We can also define an evangelical by stating qualifications to certain emphases: an evangelical values the traditions of the Church but subordinates them to the Bible. An evangelical believes in the gift of human reason but understands it to be subject to the ultimate truth revealed by God, who alone determines what is reasonable. An evangelical believes in the gracious work of the Holy Spirit in the believer but asserts that the Spirit does not work apart from or against the word of the Bible. Thus, an evangelical repudiates the oft-stated belief that Christians have a threefold authority: Scripture, tradition, and reason. This belief is rejected because it is as unworkable as it is unrealistic. Furthermore, it is misleading for it suggests that these three authorities are equal. As soon as there is a clash between any of them, one will take over as supreme. Once we accept the supreme authority of Scripture, the importance of tradition and reason are not in question. The importance of tradition for evangelicals can be seen in the strategy of the Reformers who constantly argued their position as the truly catholic one attested to by the church fathers. Evangelicalism, despite the emergence of the self-conscious movement in comparatively recent times, sees itself as authentic, historic, and in that sense traditional, Christianity.

The name "evangelical," of course, means a gospel person. Because nearly every person of whatever persuasion who claims to be a Christian appeals to the Bible and the gospel, we have to be more discerning. The gospel needs to be defined as to its content and effects, and the Bible needs to be asserted as to its nature and authority. Evangelicals have often dealt with the latter concern by affirming their sense of the authority of the Bible in terms of its inspiration, infallibility, and inerrancy. I do not propose to enter into that discussion here except to say that I understand all these properties to stem from, and to be rightly understood in the light of, the nature of the gospel and the relationship of the Bible to Jesus Christ.

To claim the name "evangelical" does not necessarily mean that we always understand its implications or are consistent in the way we carry them out in our lives or in our preaching. The understanding may be rather unformed and basically negative. This carries the ever-present danger of pharisaism: "I thank God that I am not like these Catholics, Liberals, and Charismatics; I read my Bible every day; I accept only the Bible as my authority." The conviction may be a "feel-good" thing that somehow relates religious experience to some vague convictions about the Bible being the authority that authenticates this experience. The danger here is that as long as what we do makes us feel good, we are content to accept that it is biblical without necessarily examining the Scriptures to see if it really is. This good feeling may be some undefined inner warmth or simply the recognition that our ministerial strategies are working. People are attending our meetings; many express how they have been helped by the teaching; and so on. One does not want to be critical of fellow evangelicals, but it has to be said that sometimes there is little in common between various groups or individuals who claim the name. It is easy to claim to be biblical, but much harder to translate that into the way we read the Bible and shape our thoughts, lives, and ministries. All of us must be thoughtful and prayerfully vigilant in our endeavors to be biblical.

If we evangelicals are Bible people, then we have to be diligent in working out our understanding of the message of the Bible and of its effects in the way we perceive the world and seek to live in it as God's people. The main purpose of this chapter is not so much to define evangelicalism as to attempt to understand what evangelical belief implies about the nature of the Bible. As evangelical preachers we will need to work very hard to ensure that the nature of our preaching is truly biblical. Using Bible texts, focusing on biblical characters, or using well-worn clichés that are asserted as biblical are not in themselves a guarantee that our preaching is essentially biblical. My hope is that this study in the application of biblical theology to preaching will assist us to be more biblical in our preaching.

The Bible Is the Word of the *One God*

A basic assumption in the evangelical view of the Bible is that there is one God who has revealed himself to us by his word. Here the supreme authority of God is in view, for he alone is God. This one God is consistent in his character and in his adherence to the truth of which he is the author. There is no room for relativism in evangelical faith because God is God alone. No other scenario could account for the nature of the biblical message. Furthermore, this scenario includes the authority of God as the author of all things. The only thing that relativizes the truth is our sinful repression of it. This is not to suggest that, if sinless, we could understand all truth. But it must be asserted that God has made us able to have knowledge, if not exhaustively, then truly.[1]

We should also remind ourselves of some relevant aspects of the biblical teaching. The one God has made all things, and the evidence of his being is everywhere in creation. The human race was created in the image of God and thus with a knowledge of the fact that every aspect of creation witnesses to the Creator's being and power. Humankind has rebelled against its Creator and suppressed the knowledge of the truth. But, in love and mercy God has acted to redeem a people for himself. The word that he now speaks to the world is a redemptive word, and its authenticity is established by the Spirit of God as he takes from us our rebellious spirit and gives us a heart of faith.

God is one, and his plan of salvation embraces the whole of humankind. There is no place here for the kind of relativism that places all gods and all religions on the same level. The unique character of God rules this out since he is holy and perfect in a way no other supposed deities are. The plan of salvation revealed in the Bible is consistent only with a God who alone is God. It is a comprehensive plan that reflects the unity and uniqueness of God. The preacher who does not have confidence in these teachings cannot preach according to the Bible. In the face of postmodern rejection of absolutes and of the prevailing relativism, we must be bold to assert the oneness of God and the absolute nature of his authority. Truth is absolute and coherent because it is the truth of an absolute and coherent God. Postmodernism and popular relativism are expressions of ideological atheism that must be resisted. The ultimate form of relativism is the theory that the universe has come about by chance rather than by creative design. In such a universe, even knowing, or thinking that we know, is a chance event. Evangelical preaching affirms the worldview of Christian theism. We acknowledge that the universe

---

1. This distinction between exhaustive and true knowledge is a feature of the epistemology of Christian theism as set out by Cornelius Van Til. One implication is that in heaven we will not know everything, for only God has that kind of exhaustive knowledge.

is the creation of one God and that it is meaningful and orderly. Only sin and the consequent judgment of God confuse that orderliness.

The Bible Is the *One Word* of God

We have considered the oneness and uniqueness of God as the baseline for our understanding of authority. The Bible has a number of metaphors to thrust home the point, not least that of the potter and the clay.[2] The very notion of author carries with it as a derivative, linguistically and actually, the notion of authority. The supreme Author who has made all things has the authority to rule all things. As we come to consider the word of this one God we recognize the importance given to it in creation and redemption. Why does the Genesis creation account stress that "God said, let there be . . . and there was"? Could not God have (metaphorically) snapped his fingers, or simply thought the idea of creation? Are we here dealing with a primitive anthropomorphic story that conceives of God as human and transfers a human mode of acting to the event? Hardly! You and I don't make things by saying "Let there be." We might say "I think I'll make a stool (or a batch of scones)." But then we get on and do it using our hands and tools to fashion already existing raw materials. The creation account is no anthropomorphic story; it is utterly unique. God speaks a word and the whole universe, including everything in it, comes to be. Everything out of nothing. No raw materials, no tools. Only God and his powerful word. This word becomes central to our understanding of preaching, and we will consider it again when we look at the nature of preaching.

The oneness of the word of God follows from the oneness of God. There are those who would say that Christianity is a Western cultural phenomenon, a curious assertion given its Eastern origins. It is seen to be Western because it was mostly Western Christians who brought the Christian faith into Africa, Asia, and the Americas. Sometimes they did it very badly or insensitively as they gave the impression that Christianity and Western civilization were the same thing. It has to be said that Christianity was indeed a dominant force in the shaping of Western civilization, but there were many other forces behind Western cultural developments that had little or nothing to do with Christianity. These included the corrupt imperialism of the church and the state as well as the secularism born of the Enlightenment.

The postcolonial world has seen a resurgence of self-conscious ethnicity particularly among indigenous peoples of former colonial states. One re-

2. Isa. 29:16; 41:25; 45:9; 64:8; Jer. 18:6, 11; Rom. 9:21.

sult is that there are many impulses to relativism and syncretism challenging the uniqueness of the gospel and of the teaching of the Bible. But such moves can only succeed if the Bible is not allowed to speak with its own self-authenticating authority as the word of God. Cultural relativism soon develops into ideological and theological relativism. To give an example, on a televised documentary about indigenous Christians in Canada, a tribal Native American who was also a Roman Catholic nun gave the ultimate expression to the relativism that the Second Vatican Council has allowed when she defended the syncretistic mixing of "indigenous spirituality and traditional religious practices" with Catholicism. She explained that if Jesus had been born as one of them (a Native American) instead of as a Jew, Christianity would be very different. There was in this explanation a total lack of the sense of the sovereignty of God in the outworking of salvation in history. There certainly was no place given to the biblical picture of the way God would bring people from all nations into blessing as promised to Abraham. The spirit of Christ, the Jew, was put on the same level as the spirits worshiped by the pre-Christian tribal Native Americans.

The unity of the Bible has been under attack since the Enlightenment in the eighteenth century rejected the notion that God, if such a being existed, had anything to do with the production of the Bible. It was asserted that the Bible consequently must be treated like any other humanly produced book. Historical criticism has radically changed the way people understand the unity of the Bible. With the One Author out of the way, the unity is dissolved, leaving us with a collection of disparate documents only loosely connected ideologically with one another. I am certainly not suggesting that we reject out of hand all the critical methods and their findings, for the incarnation of Jesus reminds us that the word of God is both a divine and a human word. Biblical criticism when rightly pursued is a theological task seeking to understand how the divine and the human relate in the word of the Bible. The problem is not critical study but the unbiblical and humanistic presuppositions that are applied in so much critical assessment of the text.[3]

Countering the deliberate attacks on the unity of the Bible mounted by humanistic criticism is one task that we must undertake. In addition, we must also recognize that the unity of the Bible has suffered by default in the evangelical camp. This is nowhere more clearly evident than in the way the Bible is preached by many evangelicals. Texts are taken out of context; and applications are made without due concern for what the biblical author, which is ultimately the Holy Spirit, is seeking to convey by the text. Problem-centered and topical

---

3. An excellent treatment of the Enlightenment and the development of the historical-critical method can be found in Roy A. Harrisville and Walter Sundberg, *The Bible in Modern Culture* (Grand Rapids: Eerdmans, 1995).

preaching become the norm, and character studies treat the heroes and heroines of the Bible as isolated examples of how to live. The old adage about a text without its context being a pretext needs reexamination. It is stating an important truth, but it urges upon us the question of what the context of any text is that stops it from becoming a pretext. The answer is not simple, but the bottom line is undoubtedly that the text is part of one unified word from God. The whole Bible is the context of the text. Practically speaking, this does not mean that we have to laboriously go through the entire biblical story every time we preach. It does mean that we must strive to understand the tried and true Reformation principle of the analogy of Scripture, the truth that Scripture interprets Scripture. The meaning of any text is related to the meaning of all other texts. The thing that makes this task manageable is the principle that I will be at pains to emphasize in this study: that the center and reference point for the meaning of all Scripture is the person and work of Jesus of Nazareth, the Christ of God.

While the most destructive aspects of the historical-critical method and its developments have undermined the sense of the unity of Scripture, biblical theology has done much to preserve it. Now it must be recognized that many biblical theologians have taken on board the presuppositions of the Enlightenment, and thus the theology they produce is, from an evangelical perspective, lacking. I will seek to show that a biblical theology consistent with evangelical presuppositions has great explanatory power and preserves the sense of the unity of Scripture while also recognizing the great diversity that is there.

The Bible Is the Word of God
about the *One Way of Salvation*

Evangelicals are committed to the uniqueness of Christ.[4] We reject the notion that all roads lead to God, for the simple reason that the Bible expressly rejects it. The idea that different cultures should be encouraged to develop their own non-Christian or syncretistic spirituality is quite foreign to the Bible. Religion does not consist in human beings seeking after God, as is popularly stated. Rather the biblical picture is of God's revealed truth being challenged by idolatry. It would appear from Paul's treatment of the subject in Romans 1:18-32 that religion is in fact the ultimate human endeavor to avoid the truth of God that is everywhere evident in us and all around us.

If all religions are thought to lead to God, then there is simply no point

4. See, for example, John McIntosh, "Biblical Exclusivism: Towards a Reformed Approach to the Uniqueness of Christ," *Reformed Theological Review* 53.1 (1994).

in preaching from the Bible. Such religious relativism is usually accompanied by some form of universalism. This means that the religious views of the atheist who creates a god in his own image are as acceptable as those of the Christian theist. The Christian and the atheist both have the same destiny, and the only possible difference is in the present quality of life that each set of convictions produces. We cannot accept this state of affairs. For some evangelicals there is uncertainty about the fate of those who have never heard the gospel, but this, I suggest, is not simply a matter of opinion but one of assessing the biblical evidence. It is a feature of evangelical faith that eternal destiny is at stake, and it is eternal destiny that gives preaching its urgency. As Bernard Ramm states, "The absolute distinction between saved and lost still governs the thinking and theology of the evangelical."[5]

Once again it is a biblical-theological perspective that strengthens our conviction of the one way of salvation. Biblical theology should assist us in avoiding the worst kinds of ecumenical and interfaith relativism. But, closer to home, it should energize our preaching with a greater zeal for evangelism and for sound doctrine as the means of establishing people in the faith and leading them to maturity. The great strength of biblical theology is that it uncovers the massive inner coherence of the divine plot in salvation history. This is an aspect of its apologetic strength in the defense of Christianity. The complexity of the interrelationships of biblical themes and doctrines can often elude us when we allow our preaching to become focused on the practical situations and problems in the hope of being known as a relevant preacher. The danger is that relevance becomes a subjective judgment rather than one based on the biblical analysis of things. After all, God is the most qualified to say what is relevant.

Among those features of the biblical way of salvation that stand out as presenting an utterly unique program for the rescue of the world of sinners is the characteristic of divine grace. Religions, along with humanistic altruism, present programs of works and human effort as the means of reaching the desired destiny. Christianity presents a unique picture that is so out of step with the secular way of thinking that it has to be constantly argued and defended even within the pages of Scripture. Abraham is called to leave a world of paganism in order to be the one through whose descendants God intends blessing for all the nations of the earth (Gen. 12:1-3). Israel is called out of Egypt so that its thraldom to Egyptian powers can be set aside and so that it may become a nation free to serve the one true and living God. Whenever syncretism or, as it is sometimes called today, interfaith dialogue[6] emerges in the

---

5. Bernard Ramm, *The Evangelical Heritage* (Waco: Word, 1973), p. 148.

6. Modern interfaith dialogue that aims at greater understanding of other peoples of different religions is not in question. The religious relativism of some who promote it, however, cannot remain unchallenged.

life of Israel, it is in direct contravention of the divine ordinances. It inevitably leads to disaster. There is only one way the nations will find God, and that is through the salvation of Israel, which is set to be a light to the nations.

The Bible Is the *One Written Word of God* about the Way of Salvation

God is one and there is one mediator between God and man, the man Christ Jesus. So wrote Paul to Timothy in the context of his stated concern for the nations of the world.[7] We have spoken of the oneness of God and of his plan of salvation. Now we need to remind ourselves of the importance of the Bible as the written word of God. We cannot do this without coming to the uniqueness of Jesus as the Word incarnate and the only mediator between God and mankind. The evangelical preacher stands by the conviction that the Bible has a very high dignity. God has spoken to humankind, and he has not left us, who come after, without a witness. The Holy Spirit, the promised Paraclete,[8] has exercised his gracious ministry in such a way that the God-breathed Scriptures have been given to us as the true and faithful record of the way God has spoken and acted in history for our salvation.

This sacred activity of writing down what God has said is not confined to the apostles and New Testament authors. Many critics doubt the traditions about Moses having written the Pentateuch, the first five books of the Old Testament. Be that as it may, the basis for such a tradition is there in the text itself: Moses was instructed to write certain things down; others were written by the finger of God; and there is a record of Moses having written much more.[9] This precedent was continued by Joshua[10] and the prophets.[11] The same principle emerges in the New Testament. Not only does the record of the earthly life and death of Jesus find expression in a new and unique literary genre, the Gospel, but the majority of the New Testament documents originated as letters written to various Christian churches facing a variety of challenges and needs.

A matter we will have to take up in more detail is the relationship of the Bible to the person of Jesus Christ. The question arises for at least two rea-

---

7. 1 Tim. 2:5. The context is Paul's exhortation for prayer to be made for everyone. He refers to this principle of the mediatorship of Jesus, which has much wider ramifications than the immediate context.

8. John 14:15-17, 26; 15:26; 16:13-14.

9. Exod. 17:14; 24:4; 34:1, 28; Deut. 4:13; 5:22; 9:10; 10:2, 4; 27:3, 8; 31:9, 19.

10. Josh. 8:32; 24:26.

11. Isa. 30:8; Jer. 30:2; 36:2, 17, 28.

sons. The first is the recorded conviction of the central character, Jesus, that he himself sums up and fulfills all that has gone before in the Old Testament Scriptures. The second is the common designation given to both Jesus and the Scriptures: the word of God.

Let us for the moment note one of the most important implications of the nature of reality as presented by the Bible. God is there and he is not silent.[12] He has spoken, and he has done so in a way that both reflects reality and is understandable by human beings as thinking, reasoning creatures. Whereas modern thinkers asked what the meaning of a text was, postmodern thinkers question whether a text has any meaning at all.[13] The evangelical preacher must accept that a text has meaning because meaning is established by the Creator of all things and he has communicated with us on the basis that he determines meaning and that we are creatures who are able to receive his communication. The question of our sinful repression of this communicated truth is dealt with in the Bible, as is the redemptive solution involving the gospel, which is applied to us by the Holy Spirit. God has shone into our darkness with the light of Christ. On this basis we preach with confidence that God's gospel is powerful and the Spirit is active to apply it.

The Bible Is Therefore a Book about Christ

It does not take much to demonstrate that the New Testament documents all focus in various ways on Jesus of Nazareth in his life, death, and resurrection. When the historical events as such are not the emphasis, they are the presupposition for the concern for doctrine and the nature of Christian existence. No New Testament document makes sense apart from the central affirmation that Jesus Christ has come among us as the bringer of salvation. Though a composite of twenty-seven distinct documents, the New Testament is unified as a book about Jesus who is the Savior who came to live, die, and rise again; who comes among his people now through his word and Spirit; and who will come again in great glory to judge the living and the dead.

As simple as it is to state this central fact about the New Testament, the

12. This reflects the title of an important book by Francis Schaeffer, *He Is There and He Is Not Silent* (London: Hodder and Stoughton, 1972), which deals with the reason why we can be confident that we can know what is real and true.

13. A comprehensive treatment of the subject by an evangelical scholar is to be found in Kevin Vanhoozer, *Is There a Meaning in This Text?* (Grand Rapids: Zondervan, 1998). See also a defense of biblical realism in Royce Gruenler, *Meaning and Understanding,* Foundations of Contemporary Interpretation 2 (Grand Rapids: Zondervan, 1991).

practicalities, as I have already indicated, are sometimes much harder to implement. There are important, and sometimes quite complex, matters of interpretation of New Testament texts that will be the subject of more intense scrutiny in the second part of this book.[14] One aspect of such misuse that should concern us all is the propensity we have to separate the matters of ethics and godly living from their roots in the gospel. To give a couple of examples of what I mean I refer to sermons I have listened to in church. The first example involved a series on "the marks of the mature church." From memory, there was nothing unbiblical in the exegesis of the texts, but it was the overall focus and the implication of it that disturbed me. Various qualities were set forth as what one should expect to find in the truly mature church. It was like describing what a healthy oak tree should be. The implication was that we as a congregation needed to be more diligent in producing these marks of maturity. What was missing was the way these texts belonged in the New Testament context of the exposition of the gospel. The primary focus became law, not gospel. To take up the oak tree analogy again, describing a healthy tree doesn't help us grow one, it only enables us to recognize one if we should see it. To grow one we need to know about the soil, the seed, and the forces that actually produce such a tree. Without the gospel all the exhortations of the New Testament become not just law, but legalistic.

The second example involved a sermon I heard on the exhortations to fathers in Ephesians 6:4. The theme was specifically Christian fatherhood. Again there was a careful exegesis of the immediate text, and the points raised were pertinent. But there were two things missing. First, it was not made clear that what Paul was saying was an implication of his prior exposition of the gospel. Second, and as a result, there was no comfort in it for fathers who realized that they had failed to live up to this high standard — no grace for failed fathers. Good exegesis of a limited text without its wider context turned the text into law without any visible grace.

When it comes to the Old Testament the task is even more challenging. At this point I want only to emphasize a basic principle that will be examined later in more detail. It needs to be stressed, contemplated, worried through, analyzed, and acted upon if we want our preaching from the Old Testament to be Christian. The principle is simply this: Jesus says that the Old Testament is a book about him. In my introduction I referred to the problem of the predictability of the "Jesus bit" when we try to do the right thing and make Old Testament sermons explicitly Christian. Let me put it another way. Jesus said to the crowds that witnessed his healing of a lame man, "You search the

---

14. The ease with which cults have misread the Bible is dealt with in James W. Sire, *Scripture Twisting* (Downers Grove: IVP, 1980). A more recent treatment of commonly practiced fallacies in preaching is found in Donald A. Carson, *Exegetical Fallacies* (Grand Rapids: Baker, 1984).

scriptures (the Old Testament) because you think that in them you have eternal life; and it is they that testify of me. Yet you refuse to come to me to have life" (John 5:39-40). And again, "If you believed Moses, you would believe me, for he wrote about me" (John 5:46). Luke records for us the extraordinary claim of the risen Christ that he is the subject of all the Scriptures (Luke 24:27, 44-45). These passages along with a much broader range of evidence point us to the essential relationship of all biblical texts to the central theme: the life, death, and resurrection of Jesus of Nazareth, the savior of the world.

To the evangelical preacher, then, I would address one simple but pointed question, a question every one of us should ask ourselves as we prepare to preach (and certainly the answer should be crystal clear in our minds before we get up to preach): How does this passage of Scripture, and consequently my sermon, testify to Christ? There are two main grounds for this question. The first, as stated above, is that Jesus claims to be the subject of all Scripture. The second is the overall structure of biblical revelation, which finds its coherence only in the person and work of Christ. To these we could add a third: it is no accident that the Christian Church has come to understand the Bible to be the word of God, while at the same time acknowledging that this title also belongs to Jesus (John 1:1-14).

Given these considerations of the nature of the Bible, I can think of no more challenging question for the preacher's self-evaluation than to ask whether the sermon was a faithful exposition of the way the text testifies to Christ.

CHAPTER 3

What Is Biblical Theology?

Getting the Big Picture

Geerhardus Vos defines biblical theology as "that branch of exegetical theology which deals with the process of the self-revelation of God deposited in the Bible."[1] He stresses the fact that God's revelation is embedded in history and involves a historic progressiveness. This is the basis of a truly evangelical biblical theology. What, then, does the term "biblical theology" convey? From the evangelical preacher's point of view, biblical theology involves the quest for the big picture, or the overview, of biblical revelation. It is of the nature of biblical revelation that it tells a story rather than sets out timeless principles in abstract. It does contain many timeless principles, but not in abstract. They are given in an historical context of progressive revelation. If we allow the Bible to tell its own story, we find a coherent and meaningful whole. To understand this meaningful whole we have to allow the Bible to stand as it is: a remarkable complexity yet a brilliant unity, which tells the story of the creation and the saving plan of God. Preaching, to be true to God's plan and purpose, should constantly call people back to this perspective. If God has given us a single picture of reality, albeit full of texture and variety, a picture spanning the ages, then our preaching must reflect the reality that is thus presented.

One aspect of this that causes contention even among evangelicals is the matter of the nature of the unity of the Bible. The influence of the Enlightenment on biblical criticism has sometimes rubbed off on those who claim an evangelical position. An empiricist approach is adopted in that the

---

1. Geerhardus Vos, *Biblical Theology: Old and New Testaments* (Grand Rapids: Eerdmans, 1948), p. 13.

apparent disunity in the biblical records, rather than their diversity, is accepted as a fact. It should be asserted that such empiricism is not consistent with an evangelical approach. The unity of the Bible is matter of revelation, not of empirical investigation. Put simply, I believe that the Bible gives me a single, accurate, and coherent picture of reality principally because Jesus tells me that it does. The unity of the Bible is an article of faith before ever it is arrived at empirically. The empirical discovery of the unity is governed by the presupposition of divine revelation. If I have difficulty in understanding how that unity exists in the face of certain phenomena, or apparent phenomena, that is a problem in my understanding, not in the biblical text. Furthermore, I know it will not always be a simple matter to show how every text in the Bible speaks of the Christ, but that does not alter the fact that he says it does. I am encouraged in the task by the exciting gains and insights that the simple application of the method of an evangelical biblical theology gives me.

This unified view of revelation is an implication of the principles dealt with in the previous chapter on the nature of the Bible. There is a curious assumption that liberal and neo-orthodox theologians seem to make, namely, that God simply was not up to the task of saying what he wanted to say accurately and coherently in a way that human beings can understand. Biblical criticism, or the historical-critical method, as important as some aspects of this pursuit are, led the scholarly world up a blind alley to the point where commentaries on the text could no longer address the spiritual issues of God and his saving grace in the lives of his people. The biblical story was refracted through the assumptions of evolutionary theory and anti-supernaturalism. The result was a fragmentation and a de-spiritualizing that destroyed the message of the one word of God.

One attempt to redress this situation was seen in the biblical theology of the twentieth century. Brevard Childs has written about this in his *Biblical Theology in Crisis.*[2] While Childs rightly recognizes the problem of the critical dead end, his own biblical theology fails to come to grips with the matter of biblical authority. His book is important for its analysis of the failure of biblical theology, particularly the American form of it, to break the impasse created by the old criticisms. While Childs is far more sympathetic to an evangelical way of thinking than the radical critics, his own massive contribution to the writing of biblical theologies does not, in my opinion, succeed in presenting a truly biblical theology.[3] He is still tied to unbiblical presuppositions in his use of critical method.

---

2. Brevard Childs, *Biblical Theology in Crisis* (Philadelphia: Westminster, 1970).
3. Brevard Childs, *Biblical Theology of the Old and New Testaments* (London: SCM, 1992).

The unified picture, then, involves the biblical perspective that moves from creation to new creation with extensions into eternity in both directions. This is not the place to take up the vexed question of the relationship of time to eternity, but it needs to be acknowledged that the Bible presents a picture of time-relatedness.[4] This means that the big picture is one that is essentially historical. But it is not merely historical. I find it disappointing that so often outlines or introductions to the Old Testament contain little more than a kind of historical summary of the events recorded in the text. Few would treat the New Testament in such a fashion because of the obvious significance of Jesus. But, when it comes to the Old Testament, the notion of its theological content is often strangely ignored. The fact is that the whole Bible presents its message as theology within a framework of history.

Didn't a Man Named Gabler Invent Biblical Theology?

In March 1787, Johann Philipp Gabler gave his inaugural lecture as professor of theology at the University of Altdorf in Germany. The Latin title of his lecture translates roughly as, "A discourse on the proper distinction between biblical and dogmatic theology and the correct defining of their boundaries."[5] Gabler was not the first to use the term "biblical theology," but his *Oratio* was important for attempting to define a way of doing theology that was significantly different from the dogmatics of the post-Reformation period. Prior to Gabler some German theologians of the seventeenth century used the term "biblical theology" in the titles of their works.[6] Gabler's concern seems to have been more to preserve the integrity of dogmatic theology than to establish a new approach to biblical studies.[7] The history of biblical theology should not be equated with the history of the use of a particular name or term. Without taking away from the importance of the distinction to which Gabler drew attention, we have to say that the history of biblical theology must be sought in the type of theological activity rather than in the use of a name. Furthermore, it cannot be granted that what Gabler designated as

---

4. A significant contribution to this discussion, though not without its critics, is Oscar Cullmann's *Christ and Time* (London: SCM, 1951).

5. "Oratio de justo discrimine theologiae biblicae et dogmaticae regundisque recte utriusque finibus."

6. According to Hans-Joachim Kraus, *Die Biblische Theologie: Ihre Geschichte und Problematik* (Neukirchen-Vluyn: Neukirchener Verlag, 1970), pp. 19-20, these were Wolfgang Jacob Christmann (1629), Henricus Diest (1643), and Sebastian Schmidt (1671).

7. See J. Sandys-Wunsch and L. Eldredge, "J. P. Gabler and the Distinction between Biblical and Dogmatic Theology: Translation, Commentary, and Discussion of His Originality," *Scottish Journal of Theology* 33 (1980): 133-58.

biblical theology, and distinguished from dogmatic theology, is in every way what we now understand by that term. It is certainly not the case that he was the first to engage in biblical theology as we know it. Our starting point for the defining of biblical theology must be the Bible itself.[8]

Of more significance than Gabler's distinction, in my view, is the point made by Hans-Joachim Kraus that the Reformation's return to, and defining of, the doctrine of *sola scriptura* (Scripture alone) lies in the background to biblical theology.[9] For biblical theology to operate as it should we need to be willing to submit to the supreme authority of the Bible and to allow the revelation of the Bible to shape our presuppositions. Historically, then, we can observe how a truly biblical theology is an implication of a Reformed evangelical way of understanding the nature and authority of the Bible. Modern biblical theology has often been diverted from this path, and this is a matter of some regret to the evangelical pastor and preacher. As a result we should be grasping every opportunity to regain this important aspect of our evangelical heritage.

Theology That Is Biblical

Since biblical theology is, at least in part, a descriptive discipline, its method is mainly dictated by the shape of the Bible itself. A truly biblical theology accepts the biblical view of revelation. However, there are different approaches to the material even when there is agreement as to the general nature and authority of the Bible. The soundest methodological starting point is the gospel since the person of Jesus is proclaimed as the final and fullest expression of God's revelation of his kingdom.[10] Jesus is the goal and fulfillment of the whole Old Testament and, as the embodiment of the truth of God, he is the interpretative key to the Bible. Another reason for beginning with Jesus Christ is that that is where our faith journey begins. We probably have all had some exposure to the Bible before conversion, but when we are converted to Christ everything changes for us, including our view of the Bible. Whereas we may have regarded it as a fallible, human book, full of contradictions and reasons for not believing, we now see it as God's word of truth through which we gain a grasp on reality that is totally new and comprehensive.

8. I have dealt with this in my essay, "Is Biblical Theology Viable?" in *Interpreting God's Plan: Biblical Theology and the Pastor,* ed. R. J. Gibson, Explorations 11 (Carlisle: Paternoster, 1997).

9. Kraus, *Die Biblische Theologie,* p. 17.

10. This subject is expounded in detail in Graeme Goldsworthy, *According to Plan: The Unfolding Revelation of God in the Bible* (Leicester: IVP, 1991).

Theology as the Bible Presents It

The name "biblical theology" is often misunderstood because it is not always appreciated that it is a technical term that refers to a particular way of doing theology. Thus some evangelicals will speak of biblical theology as that which contrasts with unbiblical or liberal theology. Therefore it needs to be stressed that we use the term formally to designate theology, not as a statement of what Christians believe now about any given topics (Christian doctrine), but theology understood from the perspective of the biblical writers within their own historical context. While systematic theology or, as it is sometimes called, dogmatic theology is concerned with establishing the Christian doctrine of any given topic of the Bible, biblical theology is concerned with how the revelation of God was understood in its time, and what the total picture is that was built up over the whole historical process. The preacher needs to understand the function of both biblical and systematic theology. The former focuses on the context of the text in the whole of biblical revelation; the latter focuses on the significance of texts in the contemporary context of Christian doctrine as it applies to us now.[11]

One approach to biblical theology concentrates on the theological content of each of the biblical books or, perhaps, corpora. Thus we arrive at the theology of the Pentateuch, the Former Prophets, the different prophetic books, and so on. Some biblical theologies of the New Testament will deal with the Synoptic Gospels, the Johannine literature (which may or may not include Revelation), Paul, and the Catholic Epistles. Such an analytical approach is valid and necessary, but it needs to be linked with a synthetic perspective that relates each individual part to the whole. The way biblical theologies are organized can radically affect the outcome. And the organization of a theology, in turn, usually will betray the author's understanding of the nature of the Bible. A purely analytical approach very easily leads to the fragmentation of the Bible that distorts the unity created by the divine Author. A purely synthetic approach may impose a simplistic unity that overlooks much of the diversity in the Bible. Biblical theology requires an amalgam of two

---

11. Some biblical theologies, particularly earlier ones, were really systematic theologies based on one or the other of the Testaments. Differences in method can often be seen simply by looking at the tables of contents and observing the way the material is organized. For example, Paul Heinisch, *Theology of the Old Testament* (Collegeville: Liturgical Press, 1955), divides his biblical theology into four parts: God, creation, human acts, and life after death. Other works that are topical in their approach include Edmund Jacob, *Theology of the Old Testament* (London: Hodder and Stoughton, 1955); and Alan Richardson, *An Introduction to the Theology of the New Testament* (London: SCM, 1958). This topical approach was rejected by Gerhard von Rad, *Old Testament Theology* (Edinburgh: Oliver and Boyd, 1965), who dealt with the material under the headings: a history of Yahwism, the theology of Israel's historical traditions, and prophecy.

perspectives on the biblical material. The first is the analytic, or synchronic approach, which concentrates on the details of revelation at any given point.[12] The second is the synthetic, or diachronic approach, in which the details are put together in sequence to form the big picture.[13] We need both because we must accurately describe the details and at the same time allow the big picture to contextualize the details. A synchronic approach consists of a series of still shots; the pause button is pressed so that we can examine the theological understanding at a given point in the flow of biblical history. The diachronic approach views the moving picture in its dynamic entirety as biblical history moves through time.

The History of Redemption (Salvation History)

An evangelical biblical theology expresses confidence in the integrity of the biblical text and its historical perspective. Taken at face value the Bible presents a picture of universal history that spans a period of time as yet undetermined by human historians but clearly determined by God. It stretches from the creation "in the beginning" to the new creation of the new heavens and the new earth. This of course breaks through the normal canons of secular historicism and history writing in that there is no known documentary evidence for much of the account beyond the biblical revelation itself, and there is no secular precedent for real history writing before the event. Yet it is clear that prophecy in the Old Testament and the eschatology of Jesus and the apostles is presented as a real projection of history in the future. Secular history presupposes human observers of events and evidences; biblical history presupposes the revelation of the divine ordering of events.

"Salvation history" is a term that has come to be used in relation to a certain perspective in doing biblical theology, one that recognizes a specific history as the framework within which God has worked, is now working, and will work in the future. The idea of salvation history, like that of biblical theology, needs to be distinguished from the delineation of the term in modern biblical studies. Some scholars, like the Lutheran scholar J. C. K. von Hofmann, who pioneered the use of the term, were seeking to describe a biblical phenomenon and the perspective of the biblical authors themselves. There was a reaction here on the one hand to the historical skepticism of nineteenth-century historical criticism, and on the other hand to the rigid dogmat-

---

12. "Synchronic" is the technical term applied to the examination of what happens at any given point in time.

13. "Diachronic" is the technical term applied to the process of revelation through time.

ics of Protestant scholasticism. I suspect that both protests still need to be made along with others against prevailing approaches to the biblical text that undermine the sense of the unity of God's revelation.

Salvation history implies a recognition that Yahweh, the God of Israel, and the God and Father of our Lord Jesus Christ, is the Lord of history. History happens because of his decrees. Furthermore, history is meaningful because it involves the infallible working out of these divine decrees. This being the case, the real meaning of history is only discernible to those who accept the word of the one who gives history its meaning. History is complex, as we know from even a cursory look at the evidences for the world's many peoples and cultures. Yet history has an overriding unity because, according to the Bible, it serves God's purposes and moves inexorably to the fulfillment of them. Postmodernists talk about the end of history, by which they do not suggest that nothing happens, but rather that there is no determined meaning that can be assigned to anything that does happen. This is a form of historical atheism, which refuses to accept that there is a God who governs events and their outcomes.

Postmodern relativism is ruled out by the "catholic" perspective of the Bible. Our catholic faith concerns the universal significance of the biblical events.[14] The biblical story begins with the creation of all things, including the progenitors of the entire human race. After the fall the whole human race remains in view in the account leading up to the flood and beyond it. When the father of Israel, Abraham, is called to leave his pagan homeland, the promises made to him include the purpose of God to bring blessing through Abraham's descendants to all the nations of the earth (Gen. 12:3). Biblical universalism, in the sense that the purposes of God being worked out among one group of people have universal significance, makes religious relativism untenable. The method of salvation history never loses sight of this comprehensive perspective as it moves through the story of Israel to the advent of Jesus Christ. This salvation history is the context within which we understand the significance of Jesus' coming while, at the same time, it is the coming of Jesus that shows us what salvation history is all about. To this aspect of the biblical perspective we will return later.

Salvation history, then, points us to the three dimensions of the Bible that our preaching needs to take account of: literature, history, and theology. We have the task of expounding the biblical text and so we must understand how the literature of the Bible works to convey its message. The message involves history, but this is not simply a string of unrelated historical events. There is a unity to the history, and within it appears the revelation of God and

---

14. The word "catholic" is derived from the Greek words *kata* (in respect to, according to) and *holos* (the whole).

his saving purposes. The literature points us to history and to the theological interpretation of that history. An evangelical position rejects the view that the history, as mere events, constitutes the revelation, a position that is taken in various ways by neo-orthodox and liberal theologians. It was a position that made the American biblical theology movement finally impotent to deal with biblical revelation.[15] The evangelical position stresses that events on their own are not self-explanatory but require the sure word of God to make clear their significance. We see this relationship of word to event over and over again in the Bible. Even the death and resurrection of Jesus require God's word to interpret their significance.

For the preacher, salvation history is an important aspect of the context of any biblical text. It highlights the progressive nature of revelation and the fact that texts do not all bear the same relationship to the gospel and to the Christian church today. We recognize this every time we make allowances for certain aspects of the law of Moses that we no longer observe. We recognize it whenever we deal with an Old Testament passage as relating to ancient Israel in a way that it cannot directly relate to us. But we tend not to be as sensitive to this progressiveness when we enter the New Testament. Often it is assumed that anything in the Gospel narratives applies directly to the contemporary Christian, yet the situation of such events is plainly different from our situation. Whether the difference affects our understanding of the text is something we must work through carefully. Most Gospel texts deal with the period when Jesus was here in the flesh and before his death and resurrection. The perspective of salvation history within biblical theology at least should have us asking the question as to whether the resurrection, the ascension, and Pentecost alter the perspective we have on occurrences prior to these key events. For example, while Jesus frequently used the notion of following him while he was here in the flesh, the concept is not used after Pentecost.[16] Preaching on a passage such as Luke 9:23, "If any want to become my followers, let them deny themselves and take up their cross and follow me," requires us to ask why this concept does not appear after Pentecost and how we should translate it into post-Pentecost terminology.

---

15. A key exponent of this position was George Ernest Wright, *God Who Acts: Biblical Theology as Recital* (London: SCM, 1952).

16. *Theological Dictionary of the New Testament,* vol. 1 (Grand Rapids: Eerdmans, 1964), pp. 213-14.

The Preacher's "Very Present Help in Trouble"!

Biblical theology is the neglected handmaid of the preacher. While it would be facile and misleading to suggest that preaching can ever be an easy task, it is true to say that biblical theology enables the preacher to relate the various parts of the Bible in a way that prevents preaching on a text from becoming a formality or a springboard for a mass of moralizing exhortations. Let me suggest a few ways in which a thoughtful application of biblical theology to the task can assist the preacher to a more effective ministry. Elsewhere I have expanded on the view that biblical theology promotes a high view of the Bible, of Jesus, of the gospel, of the ministerial task, and of the people of God.[17] It does all these things chiefly because of the expansive view of biblical revelation that it enables us to have. By making the valid connections between these dimensions of the biblical message, it shows up the significance of each in important ways. It provides us with a perspective on the grand scale of the plan and purposes of God that is otherwise easily lost in concerns for immediate gratification and "blessings for the day." It shows how the whole of Old Testament revelation stands as the substructure to the revelation of the person and work of Jesus in redeeming a people for himself. I will attempt to spell out some of these gains in the second part of this book as we consider the application of biblical theology to the various literary genres in the Bible.

Biblical theology helps to deliver the preacher from the doldrums of not knowing what to preach about. It is the fitting helper to expository preaching, yet strangely neglected in the literature dealing with that subject. It enables the preacher to declare the whole counsel of God, a somewhat more creative and interesting approach than simply ploughing through book after book as a program of sermonizing. Biblical theology enables those preachers who use various forms of lectionary as the basis for the sermon to show the relationship of every reading to every other reading. Perhaps one of the biggest gains in biblical theology lies in the fact that the Christology of the sermon is immeasurably enriched by showing the various dimensions and the variegated textures that are woven into the New Testament understanding of Christ. When done properly, preaching Christ from every part of the Bible need never degenerate into predictable platitudes about Jesus. The riches in Christ are inexhaustible, and biblical theology is the way to uncover them.

---

17. See Graeme Goldsworthy, "The Pastor as Biblical Theologian," in *Interpreting God's Plan: Biblical Theology and the Pastor,* ed. R. J. Gibson, Explorations 11 (Carlisle: Paternoster, 1997).

CHAPTER 4

What Is Preaching?

Asking the Hard Questions about Preaching

In 1980 Klaas Runia outlined a number of criticisms being leveled at the whole concept and practice of preaching in the church.[1] The attack was seen to be coming from social scientists, communication theorists, and theologians. Runia saw it as warranting a measured response in defense of the traditional practice of proclaiming the word of God. But there are hard questions about preaching that we need to address, for even in evangelical churches the centrality of the sermon, and the method of its delivery, have come in for criticism and much modification. Runia quotes P. T. Forsyth as saying: "It is, perhaps, an overbold beginning, but I will venture to say that with its preaching Christianity stands and falls."[2] There is no doubt that we are faced with the hard questions of the nature of preaching and its importance. Do we capitulate to the modern theorists and theologians, or do we press on and preach the traditional Sunday sermon even if it seems that in numbers of regular listeners we are losing ground? Of course not all congregations are dwindling, and there are always the spectacular success stories to spur us on and to provide us with role models. But how do we determine the nature of success, and what criteria do we use to establish the effectiveness of preaching?

Evangelical Protestants stand in a long and venerable tradition, going back to the Reformation, of the centrality of preaching in the activities of the

---

1. Klaas Runia, *The Sermon Under Attack,* The Moore College Lectures, 1980 (Exeter: Paternoster, 1983).
2. Runia, *The Sermon Under Attack,* p. 1, quoting P. T. Forsyth, *Positive Preaching and the Modern Mind,* The Lyam Beecham Lecture on Preaching, Yale University (London: Hodder and Stoughton, 1907), p. 3.

gathered congregation. We could appeal to the practice of the Reformers, the Puritans, and the leaders of the evangelical revival, not to mention the great preachers of the nineteenth and twentieth centuries. There are stirring accounts of men like John Wesley, George Whitefield, Charles Haddon Spurgeon, and, more recently, Campbell Morgan, D. Martyn Lloyd-Jones, and Billy Graham, whose preaching to thousands was profoundly effective in the conversion and edification of so many. We have to ask about the stimulus for this activity through which multitudes have been converted to Christ. Can it really be simply a passing phenomenon destined to become outdated as we enter a more technologically oriented age of electronic communication media?

One of the real gains of applying the method of biblical theology is that it enables us to understand the biblical teaching on any given topic in a holistic way. We are not dependent on a few proof texts for the establishment of a doctrine or for understanding the nature of some important concept. We can look at what lies behind the developed concept as we may have it in the New Testament, and ask what is really impelling it into the prominence it seems to have. We can observe the various strands that give this doctrine its texture and its richness. We can then better evaluate the importance it should have in the contemporary church.

The standard manuals on preaching rarely deal with the subject from the point of view of biblical theology. There may be many reasons for this, but one of them would be the comparative neglect of biblical theology among evangelicals and the outright suspicion of it among many nonevangelicals. This is a regrettable state of affairs and somewhat hard to understand. After all, the common conviction of evangelicals is that the Bible is the word of God and that we have a commission to proclaim it. Yet for some reason, the obvious perspective of the unity of the Bible, the overall message of biblical revelation, seems to become submerged under a mass of lesser concerns.

Building a Biblical Theology of the Preached Word

It is clear from the New Testament that the primary means by which the church grew was through the preaching of the gospel. The apostle Paul, who wrote to the Corinthians that he was determined to know nothing among them but Christ and him crucified, expressed it simply: "we proclaim Christ crucified, a stumbling block to Jews and foolishness to Gentiles" (1 Cor. 1:23; 2:2). The act of proclaiming, or preaching, was not the giving of opinions or of reinterpreting old religious traditions in new and creative ways. It was proclaiming the word of God. Whatever the form of the proclamation, the content was the gospel of Jesus, and it was by this means alone that peo-

32

ple were added to the church. "Faith comes through what is heard, and what is heard comes through the word of Christ" (Rom. 10:17). We note to begin with that the word of God now attaches to both Jesus and to the testimony about Jesus. It is the latter that extends to apply to the final canon of this testimony, so that we rightly refer to the Bible as the word of God.

In the previous chapter I proposed that the soundest methodological starting point for doing theology is the gospel since the person of Jesus is set forth as the final and fullest expression of God's revelation of his kingdom. Jesus is the goal and fulfillment of the whole Old Testament, and, as the embodiment of the truth of God, he is the interpretive key to the Bible. Another reason for beginning with Jesus Christ is that our encounter with him is where our faith journey begins. When we are converted to Christ everything changes for us, including our view of the Bible. Whereas we may previously have regarded it as a fallible, human book, full of contradictions and reasons for not believing, we now see it as God's word of truth through which we gain a grasp on reality, a perspective that is totally new and comprehensive.

As we saw in chapter 1, all biblical texts testify in some way to Jesus Christ. This makes him the center of biblical revelation and the fixed reference point for understanding everything else in the Bible. Furthermore, as Paul reminds us in Romans 1:16, the gospel is the power of God for salvation for everyone who believes. As we develop a biblical understanding of salvation we recognize that it involves the whole process by which God brings us out of our sinful darkness into the light of Christ, conforms us into his image, and, on the last day, perfects us in his presence for eternity. What is the role of preaching in this grand plan of salvation? In starting with Jesus as we seek to develop a biblical theology of preaching, we note some key assertions. For example, in John 1:1-14 and 14:6, he is the very Word of God that has become flesh and that is the embodiment of truth. Jesus did not come merely to tell us the truth; he is the truth. The implications of these statements for hermeneutics and biblical theology are enormous. Unless we want to maintain that there are two words of God, two different messages, then the very closest relationship is established between Jesus Christ and the Bible. They are not identical, for one is God come in the flesh whom we worship as God; the other is an inspired book that is not God and that we do not worship.[3]

The prologue to John's Gospel reminds us that the divine communication by which the worlds were made is the same word that has taken human flesh in order to dwell among us. This passage alone is sufficient to send us back to the beginning of creation to examine the way the creative word has worked until now. John is telling us that there is a history of the word that is

---

3. The frequent charge against evangelicals of bibliolatry is born of prejudice and does not fit the facts.

part of salvation history, and this climaxes in the event he describes in v. 14 as the word becoming flesh and tabernacling among us. In making the comparison between Moses and Jesus, John does not detract from the ministry of Moses but links it to the greater word of God that brings grace and truth. In describing the incarnation of Jesus as a "tabernacling,"[4] John deliberately links the incarnation to the dwelling of God among his people in the tabernacle as recorded in the Old Testament. This is confirmed by the way he moves very quickly to incorporate the account of the cleansing of the temple in chapter 2. Here the temple of Herod is but a symbol of the true temple that has come with Jesus. Jesus' reference to the destruction of the temple is clearly a reference to his own death, for his claim to rebuild it in three days is interpreted by John as a reference to the resurrection.[5] The effect of John's treatment of the *logos* in this prologue passage is to place the incarnation of the living Word, Jesus, firmly in the context of salvation history in Israel, and to extend the line of this holy history back to the creation and behind that to the preexistence of Christ as the eternal Word of God.

The Word of God That Addresses Us

Given that a biblical theology of preaching is integral to a theology of the word of God, we need to understand the significance of this word in the whole plan and purpose of God. The gospel of the Word who becomes flesh requires us to examine its antecedents in the Old Testament. We will briefly examine the nature of the word of God in creation, judgment, and salvation, as the redemptive history unfolds and moves toward the fulfillment in the gospel. The word of God by which all things were created is the word that establishes a covenant with a people being redeemed, and that finally bursts into our world as the God-man, Immanuel.

1. Creation and Fall

The holy history approach to the word of God in John's prologue suggests a methodology for the development of a biblical-theological overview of the

---

4. Καὶ ὁ λόγος σὰρξ ἐγένετο καὶ ἐσκήνωσεν ἐν ἡμῖν. The use of the verb that means "to take up one's dwelling in a tent" is almost certainly a reference to the tabernacle in the wilderness.

5. This point seems to be missed by those who see the other references of Jesus to the destruction of the temple as primarily pointing to the literal destruction of the building in A.D. 70.

34

subject. John begins his Gospel by recalling the first words of the book of Genesis, but in so doing he identifies the word of God by which creation was effected as the same word that became flesh. The Genesis account tells us that God spoke the universe into being and thus establishes the principle that is developed throughout Scripture that God chooses freely to relate to his creation by his word. In keeping with this is the fact that when he creates the human pair he blesses them by addressing them with a spoken word (Gen. 1:26-30). It is an aspect of their being created in the image of God that he addresses them with words, and that they are able to understand this address.[6] The word that he speaks establishes and interprets the context within which human beings exist and relate to everything else in creation. There is a hierarchy of relationships in which God is sovereign Lord of all and chooses human beings to be his regal representatives by having dominion and authority over the rest of creation.

Genesis 3 tells of the process by which the serpent persuades the humans to doubt the integrity of God's word and to reject its authority. The "fall" is really a failed attempt to leap upward and to wrest authority from God and his word. Despite the awful consequences, the human grab for power is in fact the assertion of the principle of human autonomy and independence from the authority of the Creator's word. Thereafter the question "Has God said?" will characterize the rebellious will of human beings as they seek to escape the implications of the right of the Creator to rule them by his word.

The next stage in the drama is the new word of God spoken to Adam and Eve as a word of judgment that involves the whole of their domain. In effect, since they have chosen to challenge the authority of God's word and rule, the creation that has been subjected to human rule will from now on challenge that rule. The most awful judgment is that their rejection of the life-creating word results now in the sentence of death. However, the grace that, as John reminds us, finds its perfect expression in Jesus is already in evidence. God begins even within the word of judgment to unfold a plan of grace. A redress of the disaster is more than hinted at in Genesis 3:15, and the very fact that the sentence of death is delayed so that life, procreation, and the struggle for subsistence go on indicates a wider plan for the destiny of creation.[7] As that plan unfolds, the word of the Lord is central both in pronouncing judgment on the enemies of the kingdom of God, and in proclaiming the salvation of a people chosen to be the inheritors of the kingdom. A

---

6. A biblical theology of prayer would need to investigate this principle that God first addresses us before ever we can address him.

7. The structure of the revelation of this plan is discussed and outlined in Graeme Goldsworthy, *Gospel and Kingdom: A Christian Interpretation of the Old Testament* (Exeter: Paternoster, 1981), and *According to Plan: The Unfolding Revelation of God in the Bible* (Leicester: IVP, 1991).

biblical theology of preaching is a specific aspect of a broader biblical theology of the word of God, and it will only make sense in that context.

2. The Word of God as the Covenant of Salvation

God's plan of salvation is made known through his word. Even on those occasions when he reveals himself by more visual means, such as dreams and visions, these are interpreted and communicated in words. The predominant emphasis is on God speaking, and when he is said to appear to someone it is usually in order to speak or to reveal his glory.[8] This speaking of God is never mere information giving because it is a word of judgment and of redemption. Those scholars who, like William Temple, have rejected the notion of propositional revelation have often resorted to a false dichotomy between God communicating truth concerning himself and God communicating himself.[9] As is so often the case, we are not faced with an "either-or" decision, but one of "both-and." Knowing God is not some mystical and incommunicable thing. We know him through his acts *and* his word, by which he informs us of his acts and interprets them to us. God's communication of himself through the presence of his Spirit does not happen apart from his communication about himself through his word. Furthermore, we would not know of the presence of his Spirit if it did not please him to tell us about it.

The function of the covenant as the promissory relationship that God graciously establishes with people has been the subject of much scholarly study. It has also provided the structure within which the Christian Church has traditionally understood God's activity.[10] The covenant formula is frequently discussed in terms of ancient treaty forms, and this has been a productive idea.[11] However, we cannot escape the notion of promise as integral to the covenant, that is, a word that God speaks about a future event by which he will fulfill his purpose of restoring his people and, with them, the whole creation. Thus the covenant with Abraham in Genesis 12:1-3 is paradigmatic of salvation history that is to come. It promises a people, a land for them to live in, a blessed relationship with God, and through this elect people a blessing that will spread to all the peoples of the earth. The apparent irony of the biblical story is the way in

8. For example, Gen. 12:7; 26:2, 24; Exod. 3:16; 6:3.

9. This mistaken notion is refuted by Peter Adam, *Speaking God's Words* (Leicester: IVP, 1996), p. 18. See also Leon L. Morris, *I Believe in Revelation* (London: Hodder and Stoughton, 1976), chapter 6.

10. See William J. Dumbrell, *Covenant and Creation: An Old Testament Covenantal Theology* (Exeter: Paternoster, 1984); Thomas Edward McComiskey, *The Covenants of Promise* (Nottingham: IVP, 1984); O. Palmer Robertson, *The Christ of the Covenants* (Phillipsburg: Presbyterian and Reformed, 1980).

11. This will be discussed in more detail in chapter 11.

which these promises are so elusive. The end of the Genesis narrative presents a scenario that in almost every way denies the reality of the covenant promises. They remain just that — promises. A people, few in number, find themselves in a land not promised, and soon there unfolds the horror of the oppression that they will suffer at the hands of the Egyptians.

The covenant word is, however, presented as the authentic word of a gracious God who keeps covenant with his people.[12] On the basis of this covenant word God chooses Moses to go to the enslaved Israelites with a word of salvation (Exod. 2:23-25). He is chosen to be both the mediator of God's saving plan for his people and the prophetic mouthpiece who will speak the word of God to the people. He is commanded to go and to speak to Israel and to Pharaoh. He has a word of promise to Israel; a word of salvation that is accompanied by signs and wonders and, above all, by the mighty acts of God that bring about the release of his people from captivity. Then Moses is called upon to establish the covenant existence of the nation by bringing the word of God to the people at Mount Sinai.

God's address to Israel at Sinai is analogous to his address to Adam and Eve in Eden. There the word prescribed the relationship of the people to God, to each other, and to the creation. Now a newly created nation is given a word that prescribes its relationship to God and to the world around it. It details the relationships that are to exist within the nation and between groups and individuals. In each case the word of God establishes the framework within which people will interpret the universe around them. In each case there is a covenantal element, and in each case the word of the Lord is the focus: God has spoken and the only appropriate response is, "Everything that the Lord has spoken we will do" (Exod. 19:8). The main difference between the word inside Eden and the word outside Eden is that the former is spoken directly by God to his people and the latter is mediated through a human intermediary who acts as God's mouthpiece.

As Adam and Eve were intended to respond with obedience to the creative act of God and his word, so Israel was intended to respond with faith and obedience to the redemptive-creation of the nation in the exodus. It is important that we see the word of God at Sinai in the context of the covenant promise and the redemptive deeds of God in saving his people from Egypt. The giving of the Sinai law begins with "I am Yahweh your God, who brought you out of the land of Egypt, out of the house of slavery" (Exod. 20:2). Most people are familiar with the statement that puts the whole of the law into the context of a people who have been saved by grace and are now

---

12. The Hebrew word חסד *(hesed)* expresses this covenant faithfulness of God and is translated in a variety of ways in the English versions: mercy, loving kindness, steadfast love, and so forth.

commanded to live consistently with that fact. Yet, how easily we transgress that principle by preaching law without the word of the gospel to support it as a word of grace.

3. "Thus Says the Lord": the Beginning of Preaching

For the moment let us concentrate on the biblical emphasis on God speaking or commanding his prophets to speak, and his prophets speaking what they affirm to be the words of God.[13] The pattern of prophetic word that is established in the ministry of Moses becomes the definitive pattern of God speaking to his people. The prophets are also the preachers of the Old Testament. Over four hundred times the phrase "Thus says the Lord" is used in the Old Testament prophets or narratives about the prophetic activity of proclamation in Israel. A variety of words are used to convey the idea of proclaiming the word of the Lord. When it comes to the question of Israel's obedience and faithfulness, it is the prophetic voice that brings the word of judgment because of a broken covenant. At different phases of Israel's history the prophetic ministry fulfills different roles: law giving, king making, indictment of sin, promise of salvation. In each situation it is the word of God that is proclaimed.

The biblical-theological epoch in which Abraham and Moses received the word of God came to a grinding halt after reaching its high point with David and Solomon. As the nation goes into decline, it no longer reflects the saved status of the people of God. During the first stages of the decline the prophetic voice calls the people back to faithfulness to the Sinai covenant. This is predominantly what the ministry of Elijah and Elisha is about. However, as Israel continues down the slippery slope to disaster because of unrepented rebellion against the word of the Lord, a new breed of prophets emerges. These prophets have three basic things to say within the specific context of Israel's sins. They have a word of indictment, a word of judgment, and a word of restoration. Frequently the latter is given in the stereotyped form of what is referred to by form critics as an oracle of salvation.[14] Characteristically it begins with the formula "fear not" or "do not be afraid." It is a word spoken in a situation of impending disaster or judgment and expresses the faithfulness of God to save his people.

13. In the NRSV the phrase "God spoke/said" occurs over 50 times; the phrase "The Lord spoke/said" occurs over 250 times; and the prophetic phrase "Thus says the Lord" occurs over 400 times.

14. This aspect of a biblical theology of preaching is dealt with in Gail O'Day, "Toward a Biblical Theology of Preaching," in *Listening to the Word,* ed. G. O'Day and T. G. Long (Nashville: Abingdon, 1993).

There is one more characteristic to be noted that is crucial to the biblical theology of preaching. In the prophetic word of hope the theme emerges of the future saving work of God, which comes about actually through the proclamation of the word of God. This is not surprising given the function of the word in creation. Thus, as God created by his word, so he will also bring about a new creation by proclaimed word. The difference between the first and new creations is human mediation of the word in the latter. This theme is most notable in the prophecy of Isaiah. We have a prophetic message that doesn't simply promise a future saving act of God but indicates that it will be through proclamation that this salvation will come:

> Go out from Babylon, flee from Chaldea, declare this with a shout of joy, proclaim it, send it forth to the end of the earth; say, "The LORD has redeemed his servant Jacob!" They did not thirst when he led them through the deserts; he made water flow for them from the rock; he split open the rock and the water gushed out. (Isa. 48:20-21)

> Therefore my people shall know my name; therefore in that day they shall know that it is I who speak; here am I. How beautiful upon the mountains are the feet of the messenger who announces peace, who brings good news, who announces salvation, who says to Zion, "Your God reigns." (Isa. 52:6-7)

And the passage that Jesus read in the synagogue at Nazareth (Luke 4:16-30):

> The spirit of the Lord GOD is upon me, because the LORD has anointed me; he has sent me to bring good news to the oppressed, to bind up the brokenhearted, to proclaim liberty to the captives, and release to the prisoners; to proclaim the year of the LORD's favor, and the day of vengeance of our God; to comfort all who mourn. (Isa. 61:1-2)

The theme of a future day of salvation coming with the proclamation of the word of the Lord is repeated many times over in the latter prophets of Israel.[15] I repeat that the prophetic office is directly and theologically connected to the revelation of God as the one who has created by his word. The prophetic proclamation speaks the word of God for salvation. Isaiah 65:17-25 gives us a vision of the new heaven and earth that underpins the notion of new creation in the New Testament:

---

15. For example, Isa. 62:11; Jer. 23:18; 31:7; Nah. 1:15: Zech. 1:17.

> For I am about to create new heavens and a new earth; the former things shall not be remembered or come to mind. But be glad and rejoice forever in what I am creating; for I am about to create Jerusalem as a joy, and its people as a delight. I will rejoice in Jerusalem, and delight in my people; no more shall the sound of weeping be heard in it, or the cry of distress. (Isa. 65:17-19)[16]

The Medium Is the Message

1. Jesus as the God Who Speaks

The phrase "the medium is the message" describes the importance of the medium through which communications are made. This idea is addressed in a well-known book by the Canadian academic Marshall McLuhan in his book *The Medium Is the Massage,* the title of which gives an ironic twist to the common phrase.[17] McLuhan considered the influence of the various media of mass communication to be far greater than the actual messages they conveyed. Thus the medium becomes the real message that shapes our thought. McLuhan's idea could be applied to the gospel, for here the medium, or the mediator, is himself the content of his message. We can go further, for in understanding who Jesus is we begin with the fact that he is God come in the flesh. John's Gospel picks up a number of the implications of this fact, which is the subject of the prologue. The word was God, says John, and everything was made by him.

How do we know God? When Philip asks Jesus to show him the Father he is reminded that to have seen the Son is to have seen the Father (John 14:8-10). This is not a claim to a monistic being of God but an assertion of the unity within God and the exclusive role of Jesus as revealer of the Father. This has some far-reaching implications for preaching, for once again we are faced with the fact that once the Christ has come he is the God who reveals to us the Father. If our congregations would see God, they must see him in and through Christ. This prevents the three letter word G-o-d from becoming an empty frame in which the human mind can construct its own image of God. But, of course, this is true only if the five letter word J-e-s-u-s is filled with content from the biblical witness to Jesus.

---

16. This passage finds many echoes in Rev. 21:1-4.

17. Marshall McLuhan, *The Medium Is the Massage* (Harmondsworth: Penguin, 1967). In this and mamy other books, McLuhan expounded his views that the communication media, rather than the content of the messages they convey, are the real shapers of the way we think.

2. *Jesus as the Word of God Spoken*

When Jesus claims to be the truth he makes himself the arbiter of what is real and the source of all meaning. Here again we see the medium being the message. The prologue to the Epistle to the Hebrews puts Jesus, the Son, as the word that supersedes the word of the prophets:

> Long ago God spoke to our ancestors in many and various ways by the prophets, but in these last days he has spoken to us by a Son, whom he appointed heir of all things, through whom he also created the worlds. He is the reflection of God's glory and the exact imprint of God's very being, and he sustains all things by his powerful word. When he had made purification for sins, he sat down at the right hand of the Majesty on high. (Heb. 1:1-3)

Here Jesus is spoken of as the prophetic word, the creative word, the God-revealing word, the sustaining word, and the redeeming word. The preacher must allow his exegesis to explore the implications of this, and seek to understand what it means for Jesus to be for us the pattern of all truth. A sound Christology becomes a vital part of our theological formation, and without it we will probably become purveyors of sentimental images of Jesus. What Jesus says in the Gospel narratives can never be taken as anything other than an explanation of what he is and what he does. His words are an important part of the message, but they must not be isolated from his deeds. A preacher dealing with the actual sayings of Jesus will find it all too easy to slip into the error of conveying the idea that the essence of Christianity is what Jesus taught. People will soon reduce the notion of the teachings of Jesus to a few ethical generalities or the golden rule. Jesus is left as merely the good teacher. Let the preacher who would preach on the parables of Jesus take heed!

3. *Jesus as the Proclaimer*

There is a clear emphasis in the Gospels on the fact that Jesus taught. He was an itinerant preacher, and many of his sayings are preserved for us in the Gospels. But at the heart of it was his conviction that he fulfilled the Old Testament word, and one such word was the passage from Isaiah 61 that he read in the synagogue at Nazareth. Jesus the preacher is a subject for our consideration, for at the heart of his proclamation is his saving work. The two go together. One of the problems that dogs the preacher of texts from the Gospels is the ease with which it is possible to remove the sayings of Jesus from the wider context of the doings of Jesus. One of the great gains of modern literary criticism has been to refocus attention upon the literary structures of the documents and the strategies of the authors. Yet passages such as the Sermon on the Mount are still taken and used in sermons as self-contained and self-explanatory texts, without any respect for the Gospel's theological concerns. Given the emphasis in all four Gospels on the death and resurrection of Jesus, it is strange that the sayings of Jesus are so frequently used merely as ethical guidelines.

Jesus as the preacher stands as the fulfillment of all Old Testament prophesying. In Deuteronomy 18:15, Moses, the first and definitive Old Testament prophet, promised Israel a new prophet. Many such prophets arose, but none perfectly fulfilled the prophetic role to the degree that Jesus did. The mark of a true prophet in the Old Testament was difficult to define in objective terms. Even the passage referred to (Deut. 18:20-22) indicates how to identify the false prophet rather than the true one. Of the true prophet it is said that he would speak whatever God commands (v. 18). Somehow, it seems, the word of the Lord through the prophet would authenticate itself. Again in Jeremiah there is a negative definition of prophecy. The false prophets do not speak the word of the Lord because they have not stood in his council (Jer. 23:18-22). If there was any prophet who had stood in the council of the Lord and was sent by God, it was Jesus.

4. Jesus as the Obedient Hearer

Biblical theology helps us to appreciate a critical factor in the Christology of the New Testament: that Jesus comes as the one who fulfills all God's purposes for humanity and, in particular, for Israel. Adam and Eve show themselves to be disobedient to the word of God and rebellious in their rejection of it. However, in the wilderness outside of Eden God demonstrates his grace and mercy. Eventually a new son of God is chosen to receive this grace, but in this case it is an entire nation that enjoys the privilege. Yet Israel also shows itself to be disobedient to the word of the Lord. With the passage of time, and as the purposes of God unfold, the disobedient son of God comes under judgment, and the empire of David and Solomon declines and slides into oblivion. A small remnant of the faithful remain in exile, and the prophetic word declares that a day will come when a faithful remnant will be restored to the promised land and God's saving purposes will be worked out. The remnant will consist of people who listen to the word of God and obey. The word will be written on their hearts, and they will truly know God.[18] But where is this true son of God?

18. Jer. 31:31-34; Ezek. 36:24-28.

According to Matthew's account of Jesus' baptism (Matt. 3:1-17), John the Baptist is baptizing in connection with his call to repentance. He balks at the idea of baptizing Jesus but is told to do it, for "thus it is fitting for us to fulfill all righteousness." Then the Spirit descends on Jesus and a heavenly voice declares, "This is my beloved Son, with whom I am well pleased." Thus Jesus as Son of God is portrayed as the one who fulfills the filial righteousness demanded of Adam and Israel. Luke also deals with the temptation in a similar fashion as Matthew. Both record the first temptation as involving the challenge to Jesus' sonship and his reply, quoting Deuteronomy 8:3, which in full says:

> He humbled you by letting you hunger, then by feeding you with
> manna, with which neither you nor your ancestors were acquainted,
> in order to make you understand that one does not live by bread
> alone, but by every word that comes from the mouth of the LORD.

Thus, both Matthew and Luke begin their accounts of the adult ministry of Jesus by demonstrating that he is the true and obedient Adam, and the faithful Israel. He fulfills all righteousness by being the truly obedient human being. Here at last is a human that hears the word of God and obeys it perfectly. Jesus is thus the God who speaks the creating word at the beginning. He is the God who speaks now the new-creating word. He is himself the message of that word, and he is the faithful hearer of the word.

This latter point is important for the way we deal with the application of passages that concern the people of God. If, say, we are preaching on the Psalms and reference is made to the people of God, the fact that Jesus fulfills the role of the true people of God should affect our application. Our biblical-theological approach shows us that Jesus is both the true preacher and the true listener. In this way he justifies us as we struggle to preach faithfully, and he justifies the congregation as they struggle to listen faithfully.

The Word in the World

While he was still here in the flesh, Jesus began to transfer the task of preaching to his disciples. He sent them out to preach about the kingdom of God, that it has come near. So, for example, Luke 10:2 records the sending of the Seventy with the injunction, "The harvest is plentiful, but the laborers are few; therefore ask the Lord of the harvest to send out laborers into his harvest." When they return joyfully recounting the fact that demons have been subject to them he says, "I watched Satan fall from heaven like a flash of lightning" (Luke 10:18). Satan is defeated by Christ, but the victory is made effective by the ministry of preaching.

This particular direction in Jesus' ministry seems to become submerged under other developments, notably Jesus' determination to go to Jerusalem to meet his death. However, we shall see that in fact the suffering and death of Jesus is what makes the activity of proclaiming the kingdom effective and powerful. The death of Jesus comes as an unwelcome shock to the disciples. They do not seem to have grasped that the nearness of the kingdom of God is bound up with his death. Luke pointedly leaves it to the dying thief to uncover the reality, and even he has not got it quite right. He seems to recognize that Jesus is the king, but his humiliation in crucifixion surely cannot be a demonstration of his kingship. So he asks, "Jesus, remember me *when* you come in your kingly power" (Luke 23:42). Jesus' answer is "Today." The thief's inability to square the crucifixion with the kingdom is apparently shared by the two Emmaus-bound disciples of Jesus, and it earns them a strong rebuke:

> "Oh, how foolish you are, and how slow of heart to believe all that the prophets have declared! Was it not necessary that the Messiah should suffer these things and then enter into his glory?" (Luke 24:25-26)

The post-Pentecost activity of preaching the gospel is shown by Luke to continue the proclamation of the word once the incarnate Word leaves the scene. The resurrection has cast a new light on the crucifixion, and thus the disciples ask if the kingdom will now appear: "Lord, is this the time when you will restore the kingdom to Israel?" (Acts 1:6). Like the dying thief, they still expect the kingdom to appear as a political reality with Jerusalem and the temple at the center. The answer they get is that the kingdom will come in the world through the activity of preaching:

> "It is not for you to know the times or periods that the Father has set by his own authority. But you will receive power when the Holy Spirit has come upon you, and you will be my witnesses in Jerusalem, in all Judea and Samaria, and to the ends of the earth." (Acts 1:7-8)

They will be his witnesses, and if there is any doubt what that involves, it is dispelled when the Spirit comes on the day of Pentecost. The phenomenon of tongues signals a reversal of Babel and the fact that salvation comes through the preached and heard word of God. It is the word about Christ. And when the apostles are forbidden to preach, their answer is:

"Whether it is right in God's sight to listen to you rather than to God, you must judge; for we cannot keep from speaking about what we have seen and heard." (Acts 4:19-20)

So the apostolic task of preaching continues in the Early Church as the means of bringing about the reality of the kingdom. And thus it is to remain until the day when Jesus will return in great glory to consummate the kingdom. God goes on relating to his creation by his word. The preacher's task is a solemn one, for, "God decided through the foolishness of our proclamation to save those who believe."[19] The proclamation defies the logic of the godless mind-set, yet it is God's chosen way. The pattern that our brief biblical-theological survey has revealed is that of the proclaimed word of God as his chosen means of both creation and new creation. The Christological perspective involves the fact that, while God spoke directly to innocent and sinless humans in Eden, the pattern that emerges once sin enters is that of a humanly mediated word. The prophetic word prepares the way for the incarnate Word of God. After his ascension the ministry of preaching is the appointed means for the continuance of this saving principle. But since Christ is the creating word, proclamation that fulfills God's purpose is only ever the word about Christ. How does our preaching testify to Christ? That is a solemn and challenging question that we cannot avoid.

---

19. 1 Cor. 1:21. The foolishness refers primarily to the content of the proclamation, but this cannot be separated from the act of proclamation, which is meaningless without the content.

CHAPTER 5

Was Jesus a Biblical Theologian?

Jesus' View of Scripture

Asking if Jesus was a biblical theologian may appear to be somewhat fatu-
ous. I ask it in all seriousness because, if he was, then truly expository
preaching must be guided by biblical theology. In chapter 4 I have considered
Jesus as the focal point for a biblical theology of preaching. There is much
more that could be said about his actual reported words and the techniques
that, according to the Gospel authors, he employed as a preacher. In this
chapter I want to look specifically at the way Jesus is recorded as engaging
the text of the Old Testament and how he related it to himself. I will then look
at the way this impacted on the preaching of the apostles. One of the aims of
this chapter is to consider how the preaching and teaching of Jesus provide us
with principles of a theological method that can inform our preaching. It
seems eminently reasonable to suppose that Jesus, above all preachers,
should understand the function of biblical theology in preaching.

Much of the current interest in the New Testament's use of the Old Testament is directed to the first-century Judaic influences on Jesus and the early
Christians. This may indeed help us to understand some of the exegetical
methods employed in the use of Scripture, but, in my opinion, there is a danger in overlooking the distinctiveness of Jesus as the shaper of Christian
thought and understanding. According to Luke 24:45 it was, after all, the
risen Christ who opened his disciples' minds to understand the Scriptures,
not their study of contemporary Judaism. Let us by all means tap into the
wealth of background information to the New Testament found in the Dead
Sea Scrolls and rabbinic Judaism, but let us never forget that the testimony of
the New Testament is that the person and work of Jesus of Nazareth forced a
great gulf in biblical interpretation between Christians and Jews. The gospel

interprets Judaism as a historical and religious phenomenon, not the other way round.

The evangelical view of Scripture's authority has rightly appealed to the evidence of Jesus' attitude to Scripture.[1] Leon Morris provides a typical example when he states, "For the Christian the critical thing in this whole subject is the attitude of Jesus Christ. He is the norm for the Christian, and by definition the way he regarded Scripture is the Christian way."[2] Morris goes on to point out that there is something rather inconsistent in claiming to be a disciple of Jesus while at the same time asserting that he was "seriously astray in his view of revelation." James Packer summarizes the position thus:

> Jesus Christ, so far from rejecting this principle of biblical authority, accepted and built on it, endorsing it with the greatest emphasis and the full weight of His authority. And the authority to which He laid claim was absolute and unqualified.[3]

Packer points us to the many places where Jesus endorses the Old Testament as the authoritative word of God.[4] If he was mistaken here, can we have confidence in anything else that he claimed? The authority of Christ and the authority of Scripture stand or fall together. This fact of scriptural authority goes hand in hand with the question of Scripture's significance. An authoritative word must be rightly understood if it is to be obeyed and acted upon.

Jesus' View of Himself

1. The Fulfiller of Scripture

The preacher needs to be sensitive to the Christology of the New Testament. Its substructure lies in the Old Testament, while fuller expression is given to it both by Jesus and by the New Testament authors. This is not the place to try to give a comprehensive Christology, but we can at least mention a few of the salient points in the self-understanding of Jesus that demonstrate some of the principles of biblical theology.

---

1. James I. Packer, *Fundamentalism and the Word of God* (London: Inter-Varsity Fellowship, 1958); D. Martyn Lloyd-Jones, *Authority* (London: Inter-Varsity Fellowship, 1958); E. M. B. Green, *The Authority of Scripture* (London: Falcon, 1963).
2. Leon L. Morris, *I Believe in Revelation* (London: Hodder and Stoughton, 1976), p. 49.
3. Packer, *Fundamentalism and the Word of God,* p. 54.
4. For example, Matt. 5:17-18; 9:13; 12:3, 5; 19:4-5; 21:16, 42; Mark 12:24; John 10:35.

A key point in this is that Jesus did not see himself as coming to eradicate the old and to establish something totally new. The gospel event is not *de novo* but is seen as the completion and fulfillment of all God's saving acts and promises in the Old Testament. Jesus again and again speaks of his role as fulfilling Scripture.[5] We should note that while some of these passages are specific, there are real grounds for concluding that Jesus saw his role as fulfilling all of Scripture, not just the odd text here and there. The same conviction is clearly held by the Gospel writers and the apostles.[6] Thus, having said that the Scriptures testify to him and that Moses wrote of him, Jesus refers to his previous teaching, "that everything written about me in the law of Moses, the prophets, and the psalms must be fulfilled."[7]

2. The Son of Man

The most frequently used title of Jesus' self-understanding is Son of Man, and he alone referred to himself by this title.[8] It occurs some seventy times in the Synoptic Gospels. Is Jesus solely or even mainly dependent on Daniel 7 for his teaching about the Son of Man, or does he take this central figure in Daniel and fill it out with his own content? It should be noted that the NRSV translates the phrase in Daniel 7:14 as "one like a human being," and thus by this interpretation of the Aramaic phrase it obscures the link with Jesus' technical use of it. The vision of Daniel focuses on the way in which the godless power structures of human empires are destined to come to nought when all power and authority is restored to the saints of the Most High. This dynamic of the kingdom of God is the theme of the book of Daniel. George Eldon Ladd indicates three main areas or categories of Son of Man teaching in the Synoptic Gospels:[9]

---

5. Matt. 3:15; 5:17; 13:14; 26:54, 56; Mark 1:15; 14:49; Luke 4:21; 21:22, 24; 22:37; 24:44-47; John 13:18; 15:25; 17:12.

6. Matt. 1:22; 2:15, 17, 23; 4:14; 8:17; 12:17; 21:4; 27:9; John 12:38; 18:32; 19:24, 28, 36; Acts 1:16; 3:18; 13:27, 33.

7. John 5:39, 46-47; Luke 24:44.

8. Leonhard Goppelt, *Theology of the New Testament,* vol. 1, trans. J. Alsup (Grand Rapids: Eerdmans, 1981), pp. 178-99; Hans Conzelmann, *An Outline of the Theology of the New Testament,* trans. John Bowden (London: SCM, 1969), pp. 127-39; Morna Hooker, *The Son of Man in Mark* (London: SPCK, 1967).

9. George Eldon Ladd, *A Theology of the New Testament* (Grand Rapids: Eerdmans, 1974), pp. 145-58.

a. The Earthly Son of Man

Ladd suggests that in using the title Jesus was claiming, in his earthly ministry, to be the heavenly, preexistent, manlike being of Daniel:

> It was at the same time an unheard-of thing that the Son of Man should appear on earth as a man among men. How Jesus could be the earthly Son of Man in humility and lowliness and at the same time the heavenly, pre-existent Man was the essence of the messianic secret.[10]

b. The Suffering Son of Man

The Son of Man in Daniel cannot be said to achieve his mission through suffering. Yet Jesus made it a point in his use of the term that "the Son of Man must suffer many things, and be rejected by the elders and the chief priests and the scribes, and be killed, and after three days rise again" (Mark 8:31). Since the Son of Man in Daniel is the agent of the coming of the kingdom of God, the question of the relationship of this figure with the others involved in the kingdom in the Old Testament arises. Thus the king and the suffering servant come to mind. While this may have contradicted the contemporary Jewish expectations, it is quite consistent with the Old Testament. The note of suffering has already been injected into the history of David's rise and is developed in the Psalms, including Psalm 22 (a psalm of David). Ladd sees Jesus as having "consciously united in his person the two central concepts of the Jewish faith, *barnasha* (Son of Man) and *ebed yahweh* (the servant of the Lord)."[11] This represents a radical reinterpretation of the Daniel figure by uniting distinct strands that would not easily be related in Jewish thinking.

c. The Apocalyptic Son of Man

This takes in most of the passages that quote the Daniel passage, and those that speak of the coming of the Son of Man and of his rule in power. A common interpretation is to apply these sayings to the second coming or parousia. However, the reference to those contemporaries of Jesus who will not taste death before they see the Son of Man coming in his kingdom[12] suggests that we must also include the first coming. The ascension of Christ, which reflects the Daniel vision, perhaps gives us the clue (if we need one!) that both comings fulfill the expectation in ways that are the same and differ-

---

10. Ladd, *Theology,* p. 155.
11. Ladd, *Theology,* p. 156.
12. Matt. 16:28; Mark 9:1.

ent. The ascent of Jesus into the clouds is followed by the angelic message that Jesus will return in like manner to his departure (Acts 1:11).

We conclude from this that Jesus laid down firm biblical-theological principles in dealing with the Old Testament. He understood his relationship to the Old Testament as one of continuity and fulfillment. In taking a wholly unexpected path, from the point of view of Judaism, he laid claim to be the ultimate revelation that establishes for all time the correct way to interpret the Old Testament. He not only showed that contemporary Judaism was essentially on the wrong course but also demonstrated the radical point that the Old Testament simply cannot be understood apart from himself. We need to underline this principle as it will be important for the way we deal with the texts of the Old Testament in preaching. While it is true to a point that the Old Testament is needed to enable us to interpret the New, the overruling principle is that the gospel expounded in the New Testament is the definitive interpretation of all that the Old Testament was about.

Jesus' View of Salvation History

In the four Gospels there are over one hundred and twenty references to the kingdom. In the New Testament it is variously referred to as the kingdom, the kingdom of God, the kingdom of Christ, and the kingdom of heaven.[13] There is little doubt that this is a dynamic concept in that Jesus places it in the context of time and fulfillment. Mark informs us that Jesus began his ministry with the announcement, "The time is fulfilled, the kingdom of God is at hand" (Mark 1:14-15). Jesus is thus represented as understanding himself to be the bringer of the kingdom that fulfills the expectations of Israel in the Old Testament.

Theologians and biblical scholars have long argued the matter of the kingdom: does it refer to reign or realm, is it present or future, and what is the manner of its coming? The dichotomies are perhaps unhelpful as the evidence points to the kingdom being both reign and realm, both present and future. But, before that matter is settled, we should note that the subject of Jesus' preaching, and the subject he sent others to preach, is above all that the kingdom has come near.[14] The miracles and the parables of Jesus are but a part of the way in which the coming of the kingdom is expressed. Ultimately

---

13. See Graeme Goldsworthy, "The Kingdom of God," in *The New Dictionary of Biblical Theology,* ed. B. Rosner and T. D. Alexander (Leicester: IVP, forthcoming).

14. There are over one hundred references in the four Gospels to Jesus' teaching about the kingdom of God.

it is the royal Son of David's progress to Jerusalem to suffer, die, and to rise again that is at the heart of the coming of the kingdom.

It would be too much to say that Jesus is portrayed in the Gospels as setting out in any comprehensive way a biblical-theological salvation history. But he certainly sees himself acting within, and bringing to a climax, the whole process of salvation history. We see him accepting and presupposing the structures of the Old Testament in his words and deeds. The emphasis on his preaching of the kingdom only serves to highlight the fact that the notion of the kingdom of God is a central and ruling theme in the theology of the Old Testament. It matters not at all that the actual phrase "kingdom of God" is not used in the Old Testament. We are not conducting a word study but are primarily interested in the theological concepts that give coherence to the Bible. The kingdom is a key concept that gives this coherence.[15]

At this point I must say that I find the reticence of biblical theologians to accept that there can be a single central controlling theme in the Bible somewhat puzzling. This reticence is, I believe, largely born of the empiricist approach, which even some evangelicals have come to accept. As I stated earlier, the unity of the Bible is a matter of theological conviction and faith because of the testimony of Jesus and the nature of the gospel. The unity of the Bible is not based on the fact that it is an anthology of religious writings, but on the fact that it is the one word of God about salvation through Christ. Some biblical theologians have proposed a multiplex approach to the themes of biblical theology.[16] This is acceptable provided we also recognize that the diversity of the Bible exists within an overall unity. The unity is not simply a matter of an accepted canon of literature; it is also a matter of the coherent divine message of revelation. Reluctance to express the unity as well as the diversity in theology is perplexing.

I have proposed that the kingdom of God is a controlling theme because it allows a valid form of reductionist approach to the entire biblical message without that message becoming bland or distorted. To propose that God is the controlling theme is bland because "God" is a three-letter word without specific content. God is revealed through his saving work and words. The ontological trinity of systematic theology is not other than the God of the kingdom dynamic who reveals himself in his dealings with his people and, above all, in becoming one of them. The kingdom of God is never abstract

15. See Graeme Goldsworthy, *Gospel and Kingdom: A Christian Interpretation of the Old Testament* (Exeter: Paternoster, 1981); and *According to Plan: The Unfolding Revelation of God in the Bible* (Leicester: IVP, 1991).

16. Gerhard F. Hasel, "The Future of Old Testament Theology: Prospects and Trends," in *The Flowering of Old Testament Theology: A Reader in Twentieth-Century Old Testament Theology, 1930-1990,* ed. B. Ollenberger, E. Martens, and G. Hasel (Winona Lake, Ind.: Eisenbrauns, 1992), 373-83; and "Proposals for a Canonical Biblical Theology," *Andrews University Seminary Studies* 34.1 (1996): 23-33.

because it is both the rule and realm of God. It is never static because it is both present and future as the extension of the historic past. The kingdom of God is all-encompassing in the sense that, while there is a reality outside of the kingdom, all reality is understood in relationship to the kingdom. The kingdom of God is a reductionistic concept only in the sense that we can peel away the various time-related expressions that make up the progression within salvation history in order to expose the heart of reality as God, his people, and the created environment in which God relates to his people.

Jesus is portrayed in the Gospels as focusing on the kingdom of God, and not on some new concept that he then had to explain, but on a concept known to his hearers that he then clarified in terms of his own person and ministry. In this sense Jesus was a biblical theologian who recognized the salvation-historical structure of revelation and his definitive role in salvation history. Jesus didn't invent biblical theology. He showed himself to be the real subject of the biblical theology that had been developing ever since human beings first received revelation from God. He thus established biblical theology as the key to understanding the Scriptures, for he is the salvation-historical event that gives significance to all others. While the Old Testament is everywhere eloquent in describing the sovereignty of God in history to work out his purposes, Jesus declares that he is the goal of that sovereign working of God.

In the light of this it is nothing short of astonishing, in fact appalling, that evangelical biblical theology is so little appreciated by evangelical preachers. The front line of adult Christian education in churches ought to be a comprehensive course in biblical theology. This is not likely to happen while our theological seminaries do not make Biblical Theology a key required course in any diploma or degree curriculum. The idea that evangelical pastors can be sent to have ministerial oversight of congregations without first having a solid grounding in biblical theology is one of the scandals of our time. Show me a church without a good appreciation of the Old Testament and biblical theology and I'll show you a church with a weak understanding of the gospel.

The Apostles and the Postresurrection Appearances

The Gospel narratives portray the disciples of Jesus as, on the whole, fairly slow to learn — an irony given the meaning of the word "disciple" as "one who learns." There may be a number of reasons for this, but mainly it's because of the traditional Judaistic mind-set that they understandably possessed. The story of the disciples, and in particular the apostles, shows a transformation from one way of understanding God's revelation to another in which Jesus was at the center. One problem in the thinking of the disciples was undoubtedly their inability to grasp some key Old Testament concepts in relationship to the coming of the kingdom of God. The suffering of the Messiah is a case in point. Perhaps it was the predominance of a political model of the coming kingdom that created the difficulty. At the heart of this model was the idea of the Holy War that went back to the exodus from Egypt and the defeat of Pharaoh's armies at the hand of Yahweh.[17] The conquests of Israel in the promised land under Joshua and the judges led to the final subjugation of the enemies at the hand of David, the last great victory before the decline and destruction of the nation. After that, the Holy War and divine deliverance notion is reinforced in the account of Esther and the Maccabees, historic events occurring against the background of prophetic and apocalyptic portrayals of the victories of the people of God and the glorious restoration of the nation, its land, temple, and kingly rule.

In all this the Passover imagery of the slain lamb of God, the sufferings and rejection of the anointed David before his final vindication, and the suffering servant of the Lord seem to have been forgotten. The Jews of Jesus' time, including the disciples, were "slow of heart to believe all that the prophets had spoken," for the Christ indeed had to suffer before he entered his glory (Luke 24:25-26). So, whether it was Peter who rejected the notion of the suffering of Jesus, thus inviting the rebuke, "Get behind me, Satan" (Matt. 16:21-23); whether it was the dying thief who could not comprehend that crucifixion was indeed the way to Jesus' kingly rule (Luke 23:40-43); or whether it was the two disciples dejectedly making their way to Emmaus after the crucifixion (Luke 24:13-21) — all of these showed how hard it was to cope with the reality of the suffering Messiah.

Luke gives us the most comprehensive account, which helps us to understand in historical terms how the salvation history of the gospel was taken on board as the definitive understanding of the reality of redemption. The Emmaus road account reveals demoralized followers of Jesus ready to give it all away. They had hoped that this Jesus was the one to redeem Israel. And the women's account of him being seen alive again only served to confuse them further. Into this situation of folly, lack of belief, and despair, the risen Christ steps to put it all into perspective.

17. Yahweh the divine warrior is a theme that apparently stems from the Song of Moses in Exod. 15.

1. The New Hermeneutic (the Gospel)

The hermeneutic of the Old Testament, if we can speak of such a thing, was from one point of view fairly uncomplicated. Within the Old Testament we see a coherent sense of the history of God's dealings with his people. Although the process is quite a lengthy one, there is a cultural and linguistic stability that made the plain reading of older texts relatively simple. This only changed after the Babylonian exile and the consequent adoption of Aramaic as the spoken language of the Jews. Linguistic adaptations were again necessary when the world of the Jews was subjected to Hellenization and Greek became the commonly spoken language. Despite these linguistic changes, the ethos of the Jewish people remained one of continuity with the history of Israel and the prophetic faith of the fathers.

Outside of these linguistic matters the major issue was the theological interpretation of the history and experience of Israel and the Jews. The prophets were the proclaimers of this theological interpretation. What they had to say was sometimes misunderstood and frequently rejected, but the prophetic message remained the definitive interpretation of events and foreteller of the future purposes of God that should one day be worked out. The Israelites and the Jews had at times great difficulty in coming to terms with the prophetic message because it was so often one of indictment and divine judgment. When the word of prophecy ceased with the three postexilic prophets, there was a long period in which all kinds of uncertainties and erratic hermeneutics developed. At the heart of the more orthodox hermeneutics was the tradition of the Pharisees and the beginnings of rabbinic Judaism. From their point of view the apocalyptic sects such as the Qumran community would no doubt be regarded as more on the fringes. But then so would the apocalyptic sect led by Jesus of Nazareth.

Our concern is not how the Jewish contemporaries, the Pharisees and the Sadducees and others, regarded Jesus and his disciples, but how the Bible portrays both the continuity and the radical newness of the Christian hermeneutic. The Emmaus two are representative of a general inability to deal with the suffering Messiah as the bringer of the kingdom. Luke shows plainly that the encounter with the risen Christ makes the difference. Whatever transpired in the hermeneutical lecture that Jesus gave when he "interpreted to them the things about himself in the Scriptures" (Luke 24:27), it must have formed the basis for the later apostolic ministry. As Jesus speaks to the larger group of disciples and opens their minds to understand the Scriptures, it would appear that Luke intends us to understand the centrality of his suffering and resurrection for hermeneutics (Luke 24:45-47). This point cannot be emphasized enough for it signifies that the meaning of all the Scriptures is unlocked by the death and resurrection of Jesus. The practical issue for the preacher is whether we can afford to assume that people will understand this without being reminded of it. Can we truly and faithfully expound any text of Scripture apart from this heart of the gospel event? And, once again, if we believe that the link must be made, how do we avoid predictability and sameness in our application?

2. The Reorientation of the Disciples' Expectations and Worldview

Following the discourse of Jesus recorded in Luke 24, two events remained that would establish the nature of the Christian Church for all time until the return of Jesus. These are the ascension, a much neglected event in many people's thinking, and Pentecost. Both these events had been the subject of earlier discourses and should not have taken the disciples by surprise. For example, in the Last Supper discourse recorded in John 14–16 Jesus had told the disciples that he would go away and leave them, but he would not leave them bereft as orphans. Another Paraclete would come to them in the form of the Holy Spirit, and in this way he would be with them still.

Luke picks up the theme in Acts 1. The continuity of this postresurrection teaching with what had gone before is seen in that the kingdom of God is still the theme of Jesus' teaching (Acts 1:3-8). But the disciples' misunderstanding about the nature of the continuity is betrayed in their question, "Lord, is this the time when you will restore the kingdom to Israel?" It is as if they have adjusted to the notion of the suffering Messiah because they now perceive that death could not hold him. Yet they still hold on to the old notions about the coming of the kingdom.

Jesus' answer indicates that they misunderstand the nature of the moment that his death and resurrection has brought them to. He does not completely dismiss the old notions of the coming of the kingdom, but he reorients their thinking about the manner of the coming of the kingdom. The Holy Spirit will bring them power, and they will be his witnesses from Jerusalem to the very ends of the earth (Acts 1:8). This is how the kingdom of God comes: Jesus exercises his kingly power through the scepter of his preached gospel.

This kingdom strategy of gospel proclamation is reinforced by the fact of the ascension that takes place immediately after this last discourse. Luke appears to stress the connection of the ascension with the Son of Man theme as he recounts the departure of Jesus and the message of the angels. Jesus' being lifted into the cloud and the reference to his return in like manner point to the way the gospel structures the coming of the Son of Man. In Daniel 7 he comes on the clouds to God and receives the kingdom. This takes care of the ascension and the fact that some of Jesus' contemporaries would witness it.

Daniel then tells how this kingdom becomes the possession of the saints of the Most High. This takes care of the "like manner" return of Jesus and the fact that the second coming is also spoken of in Daniel 7 terms. Matthew's approach to this is of course in relating the "great commission" in which Jesus' last words, including the claim to all authority, are almost certainly a reference to the Son of Man in Daniel.

The ascension, then, functions in an important way to establish the implications of the gospel event for salvation history.[18] Essentially it has forced upon us a rereading of the significance of Old Testament eschatology. While in the Old Testament there is a growing intensity in the variegated prophetic view of the coming day of the Lord, it remains fixed on the perspective of one event in which God acts finally to consummate his purposes. The error of the disciples and the dying thief was to expect this consummation immediately. Whether or not the distinction exists in the Old Testament between a first coming and a second coming will probably remain a matter for argument. The indications of such a distinction are minimal if at all present in the Old Testament.[19] The most we can say is that the New Testament differentiation does not violate the prophetic view but rather fills it out. The ascension makes it plain that there is to be a return in like manner to the going. We will need to try to understand the relationship of the one to the other and to what lies in between.

The ascension, then, is the event that fixes in place some important perspectives on the nature of Christian existence between the going and the return of Christ. It establishes Jesus as the true and representative man for us in heaven. It shows that the kingdom comes through the ministry of the preached word in the church of God. It demonstrates the entry of history into the "last days" because all prophecy is fulfilled in the resurrection and ascension. Thus the church is an eschatological reality whose ministry to all nations is a sign that we have come to the end of history in a particular sense.

The Apostles and the Post-Pentecost Ministry

The giving of the Holy Spirit at Pentecost fulfills the promise of Jesus in Acts 1:8. The purpose of this gift has already been the subject of Jesus' discourse in John 14–16. A biblical-theological study of the role of the Holy Spirit leads us to conclude that he has always been present wherever the creative

18. See Thomas F. Torrance, *Space, Time and Resurrection* (Grand Rapids: Eerdmans, 1976).

19. See the discussion of prophecy in chapter 12.

and new-creative word of God is active. This relationship between God's word and his Spirit only serves to demonstrate that biblical and systematic theology complement each other. The biblical theologian that does not strive to be also a dogmatician will be less effective as a biblical theologian, and vice versa. This is because dogmatics involves the attempt to get behind the specifics of biblical theology to the underlying principles that govern these specifics. When the Christian Church was driven by the biblical specifics to formulate the doctrine of the Trinity it recognized that the God who acted in the specific words and events is a consistent God who always acts in character. One implication of the Trinity is the distinction between the Word and the Spirit, but not their separation.

In Luke's record of the events of Pentecost we are struck by his emphasis on the preaching of the gospel so that the signs and wonders of the apostles serve the proclamation of the saving event. Another striking feature is the way Peter, in Acts 2:16-21, appeals to Scripture to explain the phenomenon and has no qualms about using a passage that describes not only prophesying and visions, but also the apocalyptic signs of the end such as the darkened sun and bloodlike moon. He regards this coming of the Spirit as an end-time event.

1. The Centrality of the Resurrection

Evangelical thinking has tended to stress, rightly, the substitutionary atoning death of Jesus. Sometimes this is at the expense of the importance of the resurrection. While we become agitated when radical theologians attack the notion of the bodily resurrection of Jesus, the significance of this resurrection is not always appreciated or emphasized. We should never take away from the importance of the death of Christ, but the centrality of the resurrection in the apostolic faith is as important. In Peter's Pentecost sermon he refers clearly to the death of Jesus, yet there is really no theological interpretation of it other than it didn't happen by accident but according to God's plan (Acts 2:23). By contrast with this brief reference, Peter treats the resurrection far more expansively and theologically (Acts 2:24-36). First, the resurrection demonstrates the impossibility of death to hold him, a fact reflected in Psalm 16. Second, the resurrection is the fulfillment of the Davidic covenant, in which God promises the throne of the kingdom to one of David's descendants. Third, the resurrection demonstrates the status of Jesus as the one who merits the giving of the Spirit to his people. Fourth, it shows that God has made him both Lord and Christ.

The apostolic preaching seems to be more concerned with focusing on the theological significance of the resurrection, although, I say again, this does not take away from the importance of the death of Jesus, which is presupposed by the resurrection. We note also the sense of biblical theology in the apostolic message. Thus, Peter and John, in the portico of Solomon after the healing of the lame man, link the ministry of Jesus with the God of the patriarchs (Acts 3:11-26). His death is as foretold in the prophets and demands repentance of the hearers. When he returns, the universal restoration announced by the prophets will come in a way that consummates the covenant with Abraham.

Stephen's apology before the council is a masterly piece of biblical theology (Acts 7:2-51). The logic is simple. First, God called Abraham to move out of Mesopotamia. Second, the patriarchal history led to the situation in which Moses was prepared for his ministry. Then God used Moses to bring the people out of Egypt. Third, though Israel's history climaxed in the building of Solomon's temple, the time has now come for Israel to move on from these old images, for God does not dwell in a temple made with hands. Stephen's final word before he is stoned is to report his vision of the Son of Man standing at the right hand of God. Once again the vision of Daniel is seen as fulfilled in the resurrection and ascension of Christ.

When we come to Paul's first recorded sermon, in the synagogue in Antioch of Pisidia, we are again treated to a biblical-theological exposition. He begins with a reference to the Exodus and proceeds with an outline of salvation history that includes the wilderness sojourn, the possession of Canaan, the rule of the judges leading to the kingship of Saul, and then the reign of David. Paul then moves from David to David's offspring, Jesus. The death of Jesus fulfills prophecy. The climax of this sermon is the significant claim that the promises of God are fulfilled in the resurrection. Exegetically it would probably be unsafe to claim on the basis of this one text that Paul means that all prophecy is fulfilled in the resurrection. But the evidence mounts for such a comprehensive meaning, and it is not inconsistent with this passage. Furthermore, it fits the New Testament view of the resurrection to say that this is Paul's meaning. At this point I want simply to anticipate the discussion in chapter 7 in which I will maintain that the distinction between the first and second coming is not so much in what happens but in the manner of its happening. In asserting that Paul implies that all prophecy is fulfilled in the resurrection as the climax of the first coming, I am not therefore taking away from the connection between prophecy and the second coming. Once again it is biblical theology that helps us to sort out this matter.

The theological assessment of the resurrection is given apostolic expression in Paul's letter to the Romans. The summary of the gospel in Romans 1:1-4 links it to prophecy and salvation history in the Old Testament. The resurrection is the declaration of Jesus' sonship, which, as we have seen, is a recognition of his true humanity. Thus the later statement in Romans

4:24-25 shows that the resurrection of Jesus effects our righteous standing with God or our justification. The resurrection was the Father's "Amen" to the finished work of Christ. The bodily resurrection is a necessity if our complete humanity, including our bodies, is to be included in the saving work of Christ.[20] We are justified by the resurrection because Jesus, our representative before the Father, is thereby justified in the demonstration of his acceptance with the Father.

2. The Relationship of the Gospel to Christian Living

One of the dynamics of preaching involves the selection of a limited amount of text that can be reasonably dealt with in the short time available for any one sermon. Preachers with a taste for expository preaching will often have recourse to series of sermons in which the longer text is divided up into manageable portions. Preaching through a New Testament epistle is frequently done on this basis, even if not every single part of the text is engaged. The individual parts become separated into the distinct sermons, and the separation is magnified by the fact that a whole week elapses between each one of them. The potential danger of this method is for the isolation of texts about Christian living from those texts that explicitly expound the nature of the gospel. Thus, in preaching from Ephesians, for example, the bulk of the ethical matters arise in the last three chapters of the book while the first three chapters have dealt mainly with the theological issues that underpin Christian living. The logic is obvious when the epistle is read as a whole, but can be obscured by a lengthy process of fragmentation.

One of the gains of biblical theology in preaching is that it helps us to appreciate the inner structure of the apostolic testimony and its relationship to Christian living. In Pauline theological terms we are concerned with the relationship of sanctification to justification. In broader biblical-theological terms we are concerned with the relationship of law to grace.[21] If eternal life is not the reward for meritorious living but the gift of grace, then all ethical imperatives are given as implications of the gospel and should be clearly seen as such. The alternative is to preach law and to leave the impression that the essence of Christianity is what we do rather than what God has done. Legalism easily creeps in even when we think we have avoided it. The preacher may well understand the relationship of law and grace, but the structure of the sermon program may undermine it in the thinking of many in the congregation.

20. See Graeme Goldsworthy, "'With Flesh and Bones': A Biblical Theology of the Bodily Resurrection of Christ," *Reformed Theological Review* 57.3 (1998): 121-35.
21. See David G. Peterson, *Possessed by God: A New Testament Theology of Sanctification and Holiness* (Leicester: Apollos, 1995).

A fundamental biblical-theological fact of the law-grace relationship is that the giving of the law to Moses on Sinai came after the mighty act of redemption in the Exodus. The Song of Moses in Exodus 15 celebrates the victory of God over the enemy, which was a demonstration of God's steadfast love or covenant faithfulness. The redeemed people of God are sustained in the desert by manna, quails, and water as a divine provision (Exod. 16–17). Then, when they reach Sinai, God reminds them, "how I bore you on eagles' wings and brought you to myself" (Exod. 19:3-4). The giving of the law is prefaced by the statement that Yahweh is their God who has already saved them.[22]

The Implications for Preaching

1. Whom Is the Bible Primarily About?

One of the implications of Jesus' attitude to the Scriptures is that it should sensitize us to the fact that the Bible is primarily about God and his saving acts in Jesus Christ. The human element is of course important, but it needs to be kept in perspective. Human beings are created by God, who defines our being and our destiny. God sovereignly controls all that comes to pass in human history. The definition of our humanity begins with the key statement of Genesis 1:26-28 that we are created in the image of God. This simple fact alone, that human self-understanding must be in terms of God and his revealed purposes, ought to be determinative for how we treat the Bible. In the long process of salvation beginning once Adam and Eve were ejected from Eden, humans' self-understanding has been consistently based on their relationship to the true and living God. One way of expressing it — all people can be categorized as either covenant keepers or covenant breakers. That is simply a way of saying that God and our relationship to him is the determinative characteristic in the Bible. To preach about us, our problems, and our way to a better life, and to do so without recourse to the significance of the gospel, is to radically distort the understanding of humanity and the meaning of Scripture.

That the Bible is first and foremost about God as he reveals himself in Jesus Christ means that the preacher must be absolutely scrupulous in mak-

---

22. Exod. 20:1-2. Studies that have suggested that the law is deliberately structured on the pattern of ancient suzerainty treaties bear out the notion that the law was never a means of becoming acceptable to God but was the consequence of being acceptable to him. See, for example, William J. Dumbrell, *Covenant and Creation: An Old Testament Covenantal Theology* (Exeter: Paternoster, 1984), pp. 94-99. See also the discussion in chapter 11 below.

ing this clear. The relationship of the biblical imperatives, the things we are commanded or exhorted to be and do, to the biblical indicatives, the things that are already fact, is crucial. We will need to consider these things further when we deal with the various genres, but for the moment let us recognize that preaching needs to keep drawing attention to the biblical perspective on the relationship of God and his people.

2. How Is It Relevant to Us?

Preaching must be relevant, I'm sure we would all agree. But what does "relevant" mean? Who determines what is relevant and on what basis? How often do we hear the statement that a proposition or particular message is not relevant to certain people? Yet the Christian preacher or convention speaker is bound from time to time to receive comments about his or her talk as to how "helpful" or "relevant" people found it. The Christian speaker needs encouragement, and nothing can be more demoralizing than to have no one comment one way or the other about a talk delivered after hours of preparation. However, standing at the door after church is not really a good time to probe people about why the sermon was helpful or in what way they were blessed.

Relevance is relative. It is relative to how we perceive a situation. Often it is based on as simple a thing as enjoyment. A sermon was deemed relevant because the preacher stimulated and even entertained us. Maybe it seemed relevant because it confirmed our already formed ideas or prejudices. The preacher needs to beware. A lot of congratulations and noise about relevance and how the Lord blessed us through the sermon or talk can be very seductive. Relevance can easily be assessed on purely pragmatic grounds. Perhaps this only underlines the need for opportunities to discuss a sermon in a more informal context of, say, small groups. As a preacher I have often wished I had more opportunity to probe people's responses.

There is an important gospel-based principle that applies here. Since it is the gospel that, by revelation, shows us the real nature of our human problem as well as God's answer to it, relevance has to be assessed by the gospel. There is a practical problem in this. We know that, depending on the audience, we have to use various means to arrest the hearers' attention. A congregation of maturer Christians, sitting expectantly with Bibles open on their laps, will be easier to motivate than a group of uncommitted people who live in a culture of instant gratification. The further away from a gospel-oriented mind-set people are, the harder it will be to motivate them to listen to the exposition of God's word. Thus, we frequently begin by "scratching where it itches." We start with a commonly felt need or problem, which may be anything from low self-esteem to animal rights or global warming. There is nothing wrong with such an approach, and, indeed, it may be necessary in some situations. But unless the felt problem is then redefined by the gospel, we are in danger of reducing the Christian message to a pragmatic one of helping us feel better or make the world a better place to live in.

The gospel not only defines the problem and God's response to it, it should also define the Christian buzz words that we use to assess sermons and talks. One might be tempted to say that two thousand people at a convention can't be wrong when there is almost total approval of the speaker's addresses. At the risk of sounding a little cynical, I would have to say that it is entirely possible for them to be wrong. So much depends on what people have been taught to expect. It is not only possible but highly probable, unless we are constantly vigilant in this matter, that human nature will take over. In short, what is relevant is defined by the gospel; what is helpful is defined by the gospel. The first question we all need to ask is not, "Was it relevant?"; "Did I find it helpful?"; or "Were we blessed?"; but "How did the study (the sermon) testify to Christ and his gospel as the power of God for salvation?"

CHAPTER 6

What Kind of Unity Does the Bible Have?

Continuity and Discontinuity as a Gospel Principle

As a student, my own introduction to biblical theology included books such as John Bright's *The Kingdom of God,*[1] and the classic *Biblical Theology* of Geerhardus Vos.[2] It was somewhat of a surprise to me to learn that there was a whole range of books that were classified as biblical theologies but that dealt with only one or the other of the two Testaments. In what sense can a theology of the Old Testament be a biblical theology? Up to a point its method can be that of biblical theology. But, if what we have said about the Bible and the nature of biblical theology is valid, then, by definition, a theology of either the Old or the New Testament is not really a biblical theology. The separation of the Testaments may at times simply be driven by the need to specialize and by the division of labor in theological faculties. I also suspect that there is a more serious reason behind the separation of the Testaments: hermeneutics. Once again there is a need for preachers and teachers of the Bible to recognize both the reasons and the effects of emphasizing the distinction between the Testaments rather than the unity of the Bible. A continual emphasis on distinction leads to separation.

The relationship between the two Testaments is not an academic question. We assume some kind of relationship every time we read the Bible and seek to apply it. We are supported in this view, for as we read the New Testament we soon discover that certain assumptions are constantly being made by the various biblical authors concerning the relationship of what they write

---

1. John Bright, *The Kingdom of God* (New York: Abingdon, 1955).
2. Geerhardus Vos, *Biblical Theology: Old and New Testaments* (Grand Rapids: Eerdmans, 1948).

about and the Old Testament. Almost every book in the New Testament makes direct quotations or allusions to the Old Testament. The assumption is constantly made that the reader will have an appreciation of this relationship and will understand the connections being alluded to. We may think that the question really only relates to our use of the Old Testament, but this is not the case. Preachers frequently make assumptions about where the contemporary Christian stands in relation to the sayings of Jesus. Thus, if Jesus said something to his immediate hearers, he must also be saying it to us. Yet we understand that some adjustments need to be made to his statements about future events that are fulfilled in the history recorded in the Gospels or Acts. For us they are no longer in the future. How do events like the death and resurrection of Jesus affect the application of what goes before them? We need also to grasp something of the hermeneutical implications of the ascension and Pentecost for everything that precedes them.

Since biblical theology is concerned with understanding the dynamics of progressive revelation, it brings us to consider how the various parts of the Bible relate to the whole. At the heart of this whole is the gospel event that we perceive as the basis for understanding. One aspect of this is that the gospel forces upon us a way of understanding one of the basic philosophical questions of all time: the relationship of the one to the many. How does the individual relate to the group, and, ultimately, what is the relationship of God to creation and to the individual?[3] Specifically, we are concerned here to understand how we can have one Bible with a unified message yet two Testaments — and, for that matter, sixty-six books.[4] The problem with this question is that there seems to be a natural tendency in human thinking to solve such issues in terms of one or the other, that is, by stressing *either* unity *or* distinction in relationships. Yet the Christian gospel has pointed us in a different direction: that of *both* unity *and* diversity (or distinction). We must examine how this comes about.

One principal issue facing the disciples of Jesus was the apparent conflict between his obvious humanity and his claims to divinity. For the gospel to be the gospel, Jesus has to be acknowledged as both true God and true man. The issue is that of how Jesus could be both God and man since these two natures seem incompatible. History shows us the various solutions that were given to this conundrum. First, there was the Jewish or Ebionite solution, namely, Jesus was not God at all, but only a man. This is a classic "either-or" solution. Logic demands that he be either one or the other; he can't

---

3. The historical and philosophical issue is discussed, from a Christian point of view, in Rousas J. Rushdoony, *The One and the Many: Studies in the Philosophy of Order and Ultimacy* (Fairfax, Va.: Thoburn Press, 1978).

4. An important contribution to this discussion is made by David L. Baker, *Two Testaments, One Bible,* rev. ed. (Leicester: Apollos, 1991).

be both. This is the error that is echoed in every attempt, ancient and modern, to reduce Jesus to the good teacher and leader of an ethical movement. The second solution was the Greek or Gnostic solution, which concluded that it was demeaning to Jesus to give him material or human existence and maintained that he was purely divine spirit.[5] Between these two extremes of humanity (with no divinity) and divinity (with no humanity) there was a whole range of part-human, part-divine views. These worked on the assumption that to the extent that Jesus was divine, something of his humanity had to be diminished. The common feature of all these aberrations of Christian orthodoxy is the failure to see both full deity and full humanity as existing together in the one person, Jesus of Nazareth.

It was obviously important for Christians to sort out this issue because it involves the way we perceive reality. A formal expression of the orthodox solution was established at the council of Chalcedon in 451.[6] By that time the related issue of the nature of God as Father, Son, and Holy Spirit had been the subject of much debate. The two issues boil down to this: the way God is in himself, is reflected in the way he has created all things, and is reflected in the way he relates to the creation. Furthermore, the relationship of the divine and human natures of Christ was seen to reflect the way God relates to us as humans. Chalcedon's strength was that it did not solve the problem of how the one person could be at the same time both fully God and fully human. Instead of solving the mystery the council preserved it. By so doing it gave us a way of dealing with the matter so that we could avoid distorting the reality. It recognizes a mystery in the incarnation: we simply can't explain how one person can be both God and man. This mystery in turn reflects the mystery in God, namely, of how one God can be three distinct realities or persons. In the perspective of Chalcedon both the doctrine of the incarnation and the doctrine of the Trinity involve us in a "both-and" situation.

Christian orthodoxy, then, has adopted the Chalcedon definition, which says that the relationship of the divine to the human nature of Christ is one of unity without fusion, and distinction without separation. The heresies that the Early Church fought were seen as challenges to the very nature of the gospel and the integrity of the Christian faith. In each case they represented a perspective that rejected this "both-and" perspective that the gospel requires of us.[7] For the gospel to be the gospel, for the Bible to be the Bible, and for real-

5. That Jesus only seemed to be human, while being purely spirit, was a position given the name docetism from the Greek verb *dokein* "to seem."

6. See John H. Leith, ed., *Creeds of the Churches: A Reader in Christian Doctrine from the Bible to the Present,* rev. ed. (Richmond: John Knox, 1973), pp. 34-36. A similar perspective to Chalcedon is found in the so-called Creed of St. Athanasius, which presents the unity-distinction aspects of the Trinity and the incarnation.

7. A discussion of the disastrous consequences of these ancient heresies in the modern church is found in C. FitzSimons Allison, *The Cruelty of Heresy* (London: SPCK, 1994).

ity to be what it is, Jesus has to be both true God and true human, and God must be both one and three.

These dogmatic formulations of the Trinity and incarnation help us to see that the data of biblical theology are pointing us to certain key aspects of reality. First, God is in his being unity and distinction. We say the Trinity is ontological (a matter of essential being), not merely economic or modal (a matter of activity). A popular form of modalism says that when God is creating we call him Father, when he is among us to save us we call him Son, and when he dwells in his people we call him Spirit. But they are all the same; it is just that God, as it were, wears three different hats and plays three distinct roles. This is clearly erroneous. The three persons (an inadequate term but it serves the purpose) relate in such a way that expresses both the oneness of God and his plurality in his being. Unity means that God is one. Distinction means that God is three. No fusion means that distinction must be maintained and the three persons are not interchangeable. No separation means that in making the distinctions we never lose sight of the oneness of God.

The ontological nature of the Trinity can be expressed by saying that if God had never created anything, and thus there never was a human race that needed to be saved and that could be indwelt, God would still be Father, Son, and Holy Spirit from eternity to eternity. This ontological aspect of God is reflected in the created order and above all in the way God relates to it. The incarnation in Jesus involves the same kind of unity and distinction and reveals the perfect relationship between God and humanity. All relationships that exist are structured on this basis. Everything has some point of unity with everything else, but there will always be some kind of distinction to be preserved. The exact nature of the unity and the distinctions between any aspects of reality depends on how God made them to relate. We can see this principle at work all around us and in the various relationships described for us in the Bible. It stands in contrast to the worldviews of some non-Christian philosophies that move either to fragmentation and lack of unity, as we see in postmodernism, or to the monistic oneness of all things, as in Buddhism or Hinduism. Only the doctrine of the Trinity, an implication of God's self-revelation in Jesus Christ, can give us the handle on the nature of reality that enables us to understand it truly. The Christian doctrine of the Trinity, which maintains the distinction between God and the creation, is totally opposed to the fusion of these realities as found in pantheism or panentheism.[8]

8. In pantheism the universe and God are the same thing; God is everything and everything is God. This is total fusion. In panentheism, while the universe is God, God is more than the universe. The fusion is not as serious as in pantheism, but the distinction between God and the creation is still seriously blurred.

The Basis for Unity: One Word of God

Biblical theology reinforces the understanding of the unity of the Bible, as we have seen in chapter 2. Once again I would stress that our acceptance of the unity of the Bible is not an empirical matter based on an examination of the apparent coherence of the texts. It is primarily a theological conviction based on what God reveals of himself in the gospel. That God is one and there is one mediator between God and man is a principle applied by the apostle Paul. It has, as I have already stated, ramifications for our understanding of the unity of the Bible. The God of the gospel is one God who has acted in one way to bring salvation to all the nations of the world. How this oneness is found in the Bible is a matter for our continuing investigation. It will be as important for us to understand what it does not mean as it is for us to designate what it does mean. In other words, we cannot engage the subject of the unity of the Bible without at the same time being involved in the question of its manifest distinctions.

The principle of unity-distinction is relevant to our understanding of the Bible and the kind of unity that exists within it. The ancient heresies about God and Jesus are transferable to other realities, including the Bible. An Ebionite view of Jesus soon translates into an Ebionite view of the Bible (a purely human book). This, of course, was what happened during the Enlightenment when God was left out of the assessment of the Bible and the historical-critical method proceeded on the basis that the Bible must be treated like any other book. The extreme result of this perspective is to reduce the Bible to documents testifying to the religious ideas of the authors. The unity of the Bible is seriously undermined, while its value as revelation is cast into doubt or plainly rejected.

Furthermore, a docetic view of Jesus will also translate into a docetic view of the Bible. If Jesus only seemed to be human while being purely divine, the Bible as the word of Christ comes to be seen in the same light. The apparent humanity of the Bible, evident through its human language and its historical narrative about people, is not the reality we seek at all. Behind or beneath these externals lies a hidden divine spiritual meaning that bears little or no relationship to the historical externals. The allegorical interpretation of the Alexandrine fathers shows the influence of Hellenistic Gnosticism, which simply could not accept that material reality could be good. It was the Gnostic Marcion who drove a wedge between the two Testaments on the grounds that the Old Testament story portrayed a wholly different and inferior God from the God of the New Testament.

The matter of the nature of the unity of the Bible is quite a complex one. Yet it is one the preacher has to grapple with constantly. Biblical theology is a discipline based upon the recognition of both the unity and the distinctions in the Bible. While the major point of distinction is seen to be the two Testaments, we need to recognize distinctions within as well as between them. In all this we do well to remember the lesson of Chalcedon that distinction viewed without unity becomes separation, and unity viewed without distinction becomes fusion. Both situations are aberrant and mark a departure from the gospel perspective of unity *and* distinction. We must turn now to consider this principle in its specific application to the Bible as a whole.

1. Literary Variety

The evangelical preacher makes certain assumptions about the nature of the Bible. Having arrived at an evangelical position concerning the inspiration and authority of the Bible, we naturally do not feel bound to rethink this every time we sit down to prepare a new sermon. We will, from time to time, find it necessary to reconsider our understanding of various aspects of Scripture, and that is what I hope this book will assist us to do. The literary dimensions of the Bible have come under more careful scrutiny with the new literary criticism. Some key hermeneutical questions have been raised about the relative importance of the author, the text itself, and the reader. While postmodernism has presented us with some challenges by moving attention away from the author, and even from the text, to the reader, we need to recognize that this is a theological matter relating to our understanding of God and revelation. Postmodernism is a challenge to the gospel because it grows out of the philosophy of the death of God.[9] It is a form of literary atheism that cannot accept that the author's intention is recoverable. The death of the author means of course the death of both the divine and the human authors. This is totally at variance with historic Christian theism.

Evangelical interpretation recognizes that behind the variety of literary expression in the Bible lie both the divine intention and the human expression of it within a particular historical context. The literary unity of the Bible, if it can be said to exist at all, is not a linguistic or a stylistic one, nor based on any other literary characteristic. In fact, the literary diversity in the Bible is one of its most notable characteristics. We recognize the unity of the collection to be based both on the content of the various literary constructions and on the coherence of the content, not on the kind of literature that is present. Thus, a collection of books written over a period of perhaps fifteen hundred years, in Hebrew, Aramaic, and Greek, and containing a wide range of genres, is accepted by the community of the faithful to be the one word of the one God.

9. See Kevin Vanhoozer, *Is There a Meaning in This Text?* (Grand Rapids: Zondervan, 1998).

Historically as well as linguistically, the Hebrew-Aramaic corpus that we call the Old Testament has a distinct existence. The evidence indicates that it was already accepted as an authoritative collection or canon by the time the events recorded in the New Testament were happening. The Hellenization of the region meant that Greek was the language of the earliest Christian writings that make up the New Testament. The literary characteristics are clearly historically based, but this does not confine us to a cultural relativism in biblical interpretation. It does mean that the preacher needs to engage in a careful exegesis that includes consideration of the historical context out of which the various literary corpora have arisen.

2. Historical Progression

Biblical theology is a historical and descriptive discipline insofar as it sets out to understand how the theology of the Bible was expressed. Once the historical framework is recognized, the task is to try to understand how the biblical writers present the account as one that reveals God's purposes and acts. The unity of the biblical history lies in the selective way in which the story is pursued in certain directions and not by other possible routes. There is a continuation to the story line that resists turning into blind alleys. Thus we follow Seth, not Cain; Shem, not Ham; Abraham, not Lot; Israel, not Edom; David, not Saul; Judah, not Samaria; Jerusalem, not Babylon. Finally, the most significant selection is that of Jesus as the Messiah over against the current Jewish rejection of him. The New Testament sees the real historical continuity of the nation of Israel as the people of God being found in Jesus Christ. This assessment of history is profoundly theological and not empirical. Thus, we note that the relationship of the literary, historical, and theological dimensions again illustrates unity and distinction.

At the practical level the expository preacher must work to make the historical framework of biblical revelation part of the exposition that informs the listener. This historical dimension needs to be constantly referred to if we are to avoid docetic interpretations that engage in wild allegory, on the one hand, or bland moralizings that ignore the real theological issue of the text, on the other hand. It is a challenge to the preacher to create this historical context without lapsing into long preambles to the main part of the sermon. Furthermore, it is not only the historical narratives that need this contextualizing. The texts without any overt historical reference provide an even greater challenge since we must step outside the immediate text to find the connections and to make the historical relationships.

Probably one of the most useful things we can do in this matter is to help a congregation to engage biblical history without fear. This can be accomplished by using a simple diagram that can be printed in a sermon outline or projected as a visual aid (see chapter 8).[10] A simple time line representing the movement from creation to new creation can be used with a minimum of detail in order to show the relative position in history of the major persons and events.

One issue that has challenged the evangelical position on biblical history is that of the historical nature of the biblical documents. Just to take one simple example: evangelicals are divided over the exact historical intention of the creation narrative in Genesis 1. It would be very hard to preach on this passage without referring to the different views and without committing oneself to one or the other of them. Does Genesis 1 present a strictly historical picture committing us to believe in creation in six days of twenty-four hours, or is it a schematized account that is more accommodating to various secular and scientific theories? Some would argue that the unique literary genre used here cannot be treated as if it were a piece of modern history writing. Others would say that the same applies to all the historical texts and that we need to allow the biblical historians to write according to the conventions of their day.[11]

This example of the creation narrative illustrates something of the interaction of the literary, historical, and theological dimensions. The preacher will have to grapple with this interaction constantly in order to deal fairly with the text. But there is one area where an evangelical position must clearly stand out against the secular canons of historical criticism. We must allow that God, the Lord of history, not only directs the outcome of events but can, and has, spoken in various ways of events of the future. The writing of biblical histories that are driven by secular canons of historiography results in works that are skeptical of the past and totally unbelieving of the future. Because there are no extrabiblical records of the primitive history in the Bible, and obviously none for the future, the historical-critical method cannot accept that primitive history as having any historical validity. The early stories of Genesis are thus confined to the status of myth or referred to as sagas. The connection between the myths or sagas and what really happened is either left open or denied.[12]

---

10. I have provided a simple diagram that can be used to great effect in teaching, and which is also found in Graeme Goldsworthy, *According to Plan: The Unfolding Revelation of God in the Bible* (Leicester: IVP, 1991), p. 102, and *Gospel and Kingdom: A Christian Interpretation of the Old Testament* (Exeter: Paternoster, 1981), p. 32.

11. See V. Philips Long, *The Art of Biblical History,* Foundations of Contemporary Interpretation 5 (Grand Rapids: Zondervan, 1994).

12. John Bright, *A History of Israel,* 2nd ed. (Philadelphia: Westminster, 1972), p. 91, is less skeptical than many and is prepared to accept the probability of the historical nature of the Abraham accounts. He goes so far as to say, "We can assert with full confidence that Abraham, Isaac, and Jacob were actual historical individuals." Martin Noth used a similar approach to historical verification but was more skeptical than Bright. He concluded that there was nothing to be known of Israel before the formation of the twelve-clan league in Canaan. See John Bright, *Early Israel in Recent History Writing* (London: SCM, 1956).

The evangelical expositor cannot avoid the problem of history but should nevertheless be aware of the presuppositions that drive both the evangelical and nonevangelical positions. While we recognize the need to guard against imposing twentieth-century canons of historiography on the Bible, there are in practice few places where a biblical historicism will get us into trouble. If we take the gospel as our point of reference, it is clear, the Jesus Seminar and other quests for the historical Jesus notwithstanding, that essential to the gospel is its historical nature. The four Gospels may not share a modern view on the best way to present historical records, but they will not lead us astray.

The essential character of the biblical history has been compromised by a range of critical and theological positions.[13] Thus, as we have seen above, the Gnostics and allegorists tended to play down the significance of the historical events recorded in the Old Testament. This was consistent with a growing tendency in the Early Church to dehistoricize the gospel. The challenges of Gnosticism and allegorism merged with those of medieval Catholicism in which allegory remained the dominant hermeneutic. In Catholicism grace is redefined and the heart of the gospel is removed from the objective and historic acts of God in Christ. Grace now operates as a spiritual influence in the heart of the believer, and justification is made the consequence of sanctification.

While the Reformation rejected allegorism and sacramentalism by restoring the center of grace to the objective gospel in history, the historical nature of the gospel was again to come under attack. The Enlightenment and the historical-critical method changed the whole presuppositional basis for assessing history, which included biblical history. It was simply assumed that God was not, or could not be, involved in either the events of history or the recording of history. The universe is a closed system of cause and effect, and thus all historical events are similar. The zenith of this method was reached with Ernst Troeltsch at the end of the nineteenth century. His rules for historical criticism included assumptions that ruled out the possibility of divine intervention and unique unrepeatable events such as the resurrection. Miracle was by definition unhistorical and inadmissible.

The last great challenge to biblical history before the advent of post-modernism was existential theology. Biblical theologians who brought this philosophical perspective to bear to varying degrees drove a wedge between the events that happened and the events as recounted in the text. Unlike the older historical critics, they were not so interested in trying to recover the real events behind the text. The issue of the historicity of the account was secondary to the question of how the story aided self-understanding. For Rudolf

---

13. See Graeme Goldsworthy, "The Gospel and the End of History," in Explorations 13, ed. R. J. Gibson (Carlisle: Paternoster, forthcoming).

Bultmann, "the meaning of history lies always in the present, and when the present is conceived as the eschatological present by Christian faith the meaning in history is realized."[14] Helmut Thielicke penetrates to the heart of the issue of history:

> Bultmann, then, is not interested in whether NT facts like Christmas, Easter, or Pentecost are real facts or whether they are myths or perhaps commentaries on facts in mythological form, like the Easter stories. The thought-content of historical events and also that of myth can equally affect the understanding of my existence.[15]

Elsewhere I have expressed my concern that these anti-historical forces are often to be found in evangelical preaching.[16] Thus, "Jesus in my heart" theology not only distorts the Trinitarian perspective of the New Testament, it comes very close to the internalized gospel of medieval Catholicism. The doctrine of the new birth is often thought of as an evangelical distinctive, but when "you must be born again" is made to be the gospel, the real objective and historical nature of the biblical gospel is compromised. Another subjectivistic expression in some popular evangelicalism involves a preoccupation with feeling and experience. The latter is usually undefined and equated with an ability to look and feel happy. This phenomenon will be found frequently in self-styled evangelical churches where serious reading, study, and exposition of the Bible is minimal. The "feel good" religion is closer to the liberal religion of Friedrich Schleiermacher than to the evangelicalism of the Reformers. Finally, the evangelical concern for decision, as important as it is to call people to decision, can become decision for decision's sake. This is very much like the existential preaching of Bultmann in that it tends to ignore the importance of the objective historical facts of the gospel as the grounds and object of our decision.

3. Progressive Revelation

At the heart of our concern in biblical theology is the progressive revelation that provides us with the data for theology. Evangelical biblical theology accepts that Jesus and the apostles got it right and that the Scriptures give us a

---

14. Rudolf Bultmann, *History and Eschatology: The Presence of Eternity* (Edinburgh: Edinburgh University Press, 1957), pp. 154-55. Quoted in Hendrikus Berkhof, *Christ the Meaning of History* (Grand Rapids: Baker, 1979), p. 31.

15. Helmut Thielicke, *The Evangelical Faith,* vol. 1, *Prolegomena* (Grand Rapids: Eerdmans, 1974), p. 58.

16. Goldsworthy, "The Gospel and the End of History."

true and faithful account of this revelation. Within the overall unity of God's revelation of his one great universal plan of salvation there is a progressive unfolding of this plan that involves us in the distinctions or diversity of the Bible. We are concerned here not only with how the Old Testament relates to the New Testament, but how the parts of each Testament relate to the whole.

The idea of progressive revelation is that God began to reveal his purposes of salvation very early in the Bible — some would say in Genesis 3 while Adam and Eve were still in the garden. In the wisdom of God this revelation was meshed with events of history that were clearly not chance happenings but under the control of the Lord of history. By this means a historically based revelation of salvation and its goal is given. From one point of view the revelation is not complete until the great consummation, the final stage when the people of God see God face to face and are revealed with Christ in glory.[17] But that is not the only perspective, for the New Testament itself structures biblical revelation according to certain key events and persons. We have already touched on the significance of the ascension of Jesus for such a structuring of the period between the first coming of Jesus and his return. For the moment let us note the implication of progressive revelation for preaching. At its simplest it means that not all texts stand in the same relationship to the contemporary believer as others. We recognize this as soon as we make some adjustments in the way we perceive the law of Moses applied to Israel in the wilderness and the way we understand it speaking to us today as Christians.

The unity of the biblical revelation, then, does not mean uniformity of application. Yet progressive revelation does not mean that there are parts of the Bible that are irrelevant to us. The task we have is to understand the nature of the diversity within the unity so that we can fairly treat and apply texts from anywhere in the Bible. If we are not prepared to do that, we will create a canon within the canon. The bottom line in all this is that all texts somehow testify to Jesus.

In seeking to understand the structure of progressive revelation, a number of polarities have been observed and variously propounded as the essence of the relationship between the two Testaments.[18] These include salvation history and eschatological consummation, type and antitype, promise and fulfillment, literal sense and fuller sense, old covenant and new covenant, law and gospel, and Israel and the church. Each of these polarities has its contribution to make to our overall understanding of the structure of revelation, and the fact that we can engage so many different perspectives only serves to

---

17. 1 Cor. 13:12; Col. 3:4.

18. See Graeme Goldsworthy, "The Relationship of the Old Testament and the New Testament," in *The New Dictionary of Biblical Theology,* ed. B. Rosner and T. D. Alexander (Leicester: IVP, forthcoming), and Baker, *Two Testaments, One Bible.*

show the complexity of the matter. But that complexity does not in any way remove the possibility of viewing revelation in a comprehensive way, and it is not destructive of the basic unity of the message.

These various polarities, as I have called them, represent the opposite ends of a process in which there is an essential unity underlying the diversity. We thus focus on the dynamic nature of revelation. Simply put it means that, in the process of progressive revelation, Abraham knew more than Noah, Moses knew more than Abraham, David knew more than Moses, Ezekiel knew more than David, and Paul knew more than all of them. The other aspect of this progressiveness is that the pattern we observe and that is confirmed in the New Testament is not a simple, gradual progression, like light gradually increasing at the dawning of the day. There are discernible stages or epochs that structure revelation. This is an aspect that has long been recognized by biblical theologians, though there are considerable differences in opinion as to what the major epochs are.

As early as 1770 Carl Friedrich Bahrdt proposed a "biblical system of dogmatics" in the Old Testament containing four periods: (1) from the fall to the flood, (2) from the flood to Moses, (3) from Moses to the Babylonian exile, and (4) from the exile to Herod the Great.[19] Some more recent examples of the standard works of biblical theology are:

Geerhardus Vos:[20]
1. The Mosaic epoch, which includes,
    a. Noah.
    b. From Noah to the great patriarchs.
    c. The patriarchal period.
    d. The period of Moses.
2. The prophetic epoch.
3. The New Testament (which Vos never completed).

Edmund Clowney:[21]
1. Creation to the fall.
2. Antediluvian period.
3. From the flood to the call of Abraham.
4. From Abraham to Moses.
5. From Moses to Christ (when God deals with the theocracy).
6. The coming of Christ and the latter days.

---

19. Hans-Joachim Kraus, *Die Biblische Theologie: Ihre Geschichte und Problematik* (Neukirchen-Vluyn: Neukirchener Verlag, 1970), pp. 26-30.

20. Vos, *Biblical Theology: Old and New Testaments.*

21. Edmund Clowney, *Preaching and Biblical Theology* (London: Tyndale Press; Grand Rapids: Eerdmans, 1961).

Willem VanGemeren (who identifies twelve periods of redemptive history):[22]

1. Creation in harmony.
2. Creation in alienation.
3. Election and promise.
4. A holy nation.
5. A nation like other nations.
6. A royal nation.
7. A divided nation.
8. A restored nation.
9. Jesus and the kingdom.
10. The apostolic era.
11. Kingdom and church.
12. The new Jerusalem.

The question is whether or not these analyses actually penetrate to the essential structure of revelation. No one can deny that these writers have focused on key persons or events in salvation history to mark off the epochs. The designated epochs (and note the differences of approach) suggest the diversity or progression in revelation, but do they really underline also the unity? One is reminded of the approach of earlier Dispensationalism, which divided, quite literally, salvation history into seven completely distinct periods that have little unity with each other. This was set out in the *Scofield Reference Bible* and the works of J. N. Darby. More recently it has been revived in the works of Hal Lindsey, including especially his *The Late Great Planet Earth.*[23] This system designates the dispensations of:

1. Innocence (Eden).
2. Conscience (Pre-flood).
3. Human government (Noah to Babel).
4. Promise (Abraham to Egypt).
5. Law (Moses to John the Baptist).
6. Grace (Church Age).
7. Kingdom (Millennium).

Dispensationalism, along with some other forms of premillennialism, is a system of biblical theology that is flawed because it does not draw its interpretative presuppositions from the Bible. For example, it stresses that all

---

22. Willem VanGemeren, *The Progress of Redemption* (Grand Rapids: Zondervan, 1988).

23. Hal Lindsey with C. C. Carlson, *The Late Great Planet Earth* (Grand Rapids: Zondervan, 1970).

prophecy is fulfilled in a literal sense. This is not according to the evidence of the New Testament, which interprets prophecy in the light of Christ. All analyses of an epochal structure of salvation history are in a sense "dispensational." We must try to find the structure that is really there and describe it in such a way that it will open up the essential pattern of the whole Bible in its unity as well as diversity.

Preaching Progressive Revelation

Depending on the particular text we are expounding at the time, our preaching should reflect the progressive nature of revelation. Preaching from the Old Testament demands of us some appreciation of how the text relates to Christian existence. A sermon should not simply assume the connections if we want people to learn how to read and apply the whole Bible themselves. Our preaching ought to demonstrate, and from time to time explicitly describe, the structure of the Bible and the connections it requires us to make between the ancient text and the contemporary Christian. In dealing with the New Testament the preacher should be aware of the presuppositions of the text that link it with salvation history back into the Old Testament. While the preacher needs to understand these links in order to get the best out of the text, it may not be desirable to give a long discourse on the background every time we preach. However, we do need to be constantly putting the New Testament text into its wider context, including its Old Testament background. Furthermore, it would be hard to preach systematically on any New Testament book without very quickly coming upon some direct reference or allusion to the Old Testament. Since the Old Testament is the presupposition of the New, understanding what the New Testament is saying can only be sharpened by making clear the real links that are there. Some of the ways this can be done include the polarities mentioned above. Here I will comment on three of them.

1. Type-Antitype

Typology has been a somewhat controversial subject, possibly because of strange excesses proposed by certain exponents of the method. But it is clearly a method based in the Scriptures themselves, and it cannot be ignored. Rightly understood it opens up the structure of revelation in a way that does not leave the connections to chance or imaginative thinking. Typology takes its name from the Greek word τύπος *(typos),* which can mean an impression or stamp, but is most frequently used in the New Testament in the sense of an example or pattern to follow. It needs to be said that the New Testament use of the word is not really determinative of typology as a structural principle. Typology may take its name from this word, but it is used to describe something far wider than the word usage might suggest.

The essence of typology is the recognition that within Scripture itself certain events, people, and institutions in biblical history bear a particular relationship to later events, people, or institutions. The relationship is such that the earlier foreshadows the later, and the later fills out or completes the earlier. It is a way of saying "this is that," that is, that a later significant event is what an earlier one points to (Acts 2:16). Peter's statement on the day of Pentecost affirms that the phenomenon being witnessed is that of which the prophet Joel spoke. Typology goes beyond this fulfillment of prophetic word and recognizes that even historic events can correspond to some antitype or fulfillment.

Typology is sometimes written off as just a variant form of allegory that is thus uncontrolled and invalid. This is a common confusion, and one to be studiously avoided. There are some similarities in that allegory (the method of the Alexandrine fathers) and typology (the method of the Antiochene fathers) both recognize some kind of correspondences. The difference, however, is vital. On the one hand, allegory was a method that saw the old events and images as largely unimportant in themselves. They may have some significance, but the real task was to get behind them to the deeper spiritual meaning. This deeper meaning was often quite unrelated to the original historical meaning. There was no real historical or theological connection between the text and its spiritual meaning. The connection was often made on the most superficial grounds and tended toward a kind of free association of ideas.

Typology, on the other hand, recognizes that the original historical meaning of the text is theologically related to the later expression that fills it out and usually completes it. The validity of this approach depends upon the right understanding of how progressive revelation is structured. The unity-distinction principle is important in determining what is the essential unity of revelation that allows us to apply ancient texts to ourselves. Typology helps us to deal with questions of how God actually "saved" people before the one and only saving event of Jesus Christ was revealed. While allegory sees mainly a superficial conceptual relationship between Old Testament events and the Christian gospel, typology sees the type as part of the theological process of revelation that leads to the antitype or fulfillment in the gospel. The type is a shadow of the reality to be revealed in the antitype, but it is not mere shadow. It is theologically bound up with the antitype in a unity that means that those who related to the type are similarly related to the antitype.

Jesus said, "Abraham rejoiced to see my day; he saw it and was glad" (John 8:56). In other words, the promises to Abraham were a type of Christ, and the fact that Abraham embraced these promises can be spoken of as if Abraham actually saw Christ and embraced him by faith. Allegory, like typology, sought to answer the question of the meaning of Old Testament texts for the Christian. Allegory, unlike typology, could not answer the questions about how the people of the Old Testament related to salvation in Christ. To typology we must return in chapter 8.

2. Promise-Fulfillment

The polarity of promise and fulfillment is a specific aspect of the wider structure of typology. It needs to be said that the New Testament view of fulfillment is not always confined to the answer of Old Testament revelations of things to come. For example, in Matthew 2:15 there is a reference to the return of Joseph and Mary with the infant Jesus from Egypt, an event to fulfill the prophetic word, "Out of Egypt I have called my son," taken from Hosea 11:1. In fact the Hosea passage was not predicting anything but was recalling the historic event of the exodus from Egypt under Moses. A similar comment could be made about the use in Matthew 2:18 of Jeremiah 31:15, which is again a historical reference rather than a prediction. All that needs to be said at this point is that these references help us to see the wider principle of typology at work.

Mostly, however, we see the promise-fulfillment aspect as the claim in the New Testament that promises and prophetic predictions made in the Old Testament have been fulfilled. As is often pointed out, such fulfillment is not necessarily confined to one event. Promises, prophecies of judgment, and prophecies of restoration usually find some partial fulfillment in the Old Testament, and this is another pointer to the structure of revelation. When we come to the so-called latter prophets, or writing prophets, we can discern two levels of prophetic judgment and restoration. First, there is a more immediate fulfillment in the history of the nation, such as the destruction of Jerusalem by the Babylonians and the decree of Cyrus to set the captives free. Second, there is the longer view that sees judgment as a catastrophe of cosmic proportions and restoration as a whole new creation of the heavens and the earth.

The most important aspect of the promise-fulfillment perspective is the claim of Jesus and the apostles that all is fulfilled in Christ. Again I would stress that the nature of the fulfillment is not self-evident. Those Jews in Jesus' day who thought they knew how promise and prophecy would be fulfilled were not able to perceive in Jesus the fulfillment of these things. Either we allow Jesus to dictate the terms of fulfillment or we have to conclude that he was mistaken. The New Testament shows that it was certainly not self-evident to contemporary Jews that Jesus fulfilled the expectations of Israel. We might ask why this is. The answer lies in the fact that Jesus is God's final and fullest word on the matter. That is, he is not simply fulfillment; he is also further and final revelation. While the Old Testament helps us to understand what the New Testament is all about, it is above all the New Testament understanding of Jesus that makes the Old Testament meaningful to us. Paul reminds us that readers of the Old Testament who do not see it in terms of Christ have a veil over their minds, and it is this that makes the difference between a consistently Christian view of the Old Testament and all other attempts to understand it (2 Cor. 3:14-16). It is a very significant statement for our preaching of the Old Testament that only in Christ is this veil set aside.

3. Salvation History-Eschatological Goal

The biblical perspective on salvation history is one that sees God moving world events inexorably toward a goal in which all things are restored to the proper order. Eschatology, or the study of the last things, is usually confined to the last chapter of textbooks on systematic theology. This sounds logical: last things, last chapter. There is another logic: a *theo-logic,* which recognizes that eschatology is chapter 1.[24] Some of the old Reformed theologies that began with the eternal decrees of God were on the right track in that they recognized the priority of the plan and purpose of God. Beginning with eschatology reminds us that all events take their meaning from the events that happened in Christ, and in what is yet to happen as God consummates his plan at the return of Christ. Thus, Paul reminds us in Colossians 1:16 that all things were created in, through, and for Christ. Salvation was not an afterthought brought on by the unforeseen catastrophe of the fall. God's original plan in creation was that it should find its meaning and fulfillment in Christ and his gospel. This Christocentric perspective is vital to understanding the Bible, and the preacher should constantly remind the congregation of it.

Salvation history is the process of eschatology being worked out in the history of our world. Salvation history and eschatology are at the heart of the biblical message and provide for us the way to an understanding of the meaning of our existence. It is grossly irresponsible for a preacher to

---

24. Peter F. Jensen, *At the Heart of the Universe* (Leicester: IVP, 1994; Wheaton: Crossway, 1997), provides an outline of Christian doctrine that places eschatology and the return of Jesus in chapter 1.

moralize on isolated texts and to convey the notion that the real issue is finding self-esteem, happiness, health, self-fulfillment, or any other desirable quality in life, as if these were valuable in themselves. All these good qualities need to be put in perspective through the gospel and its framework of salvation history.

CHAPTER 7

How Does the Gospel Function in the Bible?

What Is the Gospel?

Almost everyone uses the word "gospel" in both a religious and a secular way. In the religious world it is used often without any real consensus as to what is meant by the term. Even when the word "gospel" is proposed as a biblically based term, there are some significant differences among, say, a Christadelphian, an evangelical, and a liberal view of gospel. Among evangelicals there are also differences in the way the word is used. It is a matter for some concern that some books and study courses on evangelism seem to assume that every Christian is absolutely clear about what the gospel is, and that what is needed most is help in the techniques of explaining the gospel to unbelievers. Experience suggests that this assumption is poorly based and that there is a great deal of confusion among believers about what the gospel is.[1] Preachers may have a theoretical gospel and an operative gospel. Theoretically we will get into a theological mode and produce, as far as possible, a biblically based notion focusing on the person and work of Christ. But, in pastoral practice it is easy to be pragmatic. Our operative gospel will be the thing that preoccupies us as the focus of our preaching and teaching. It may be a particular hobbyhorse or a denominational distinctive. Baptism, a particular view of the second coming, social action, creationism, spiritual gifts, and the like are all easily raised to the status of gospel by becoming the main focus of our preaching. This is especially deplorable when these spurious gospels are made the basis of our acceptance of other Christians.

Sooner of later someone will assure us that the whole Bible is the gospel,

---

1. See Graeme Goldsworthy, "The Gospel," in *The New Dictionary of Biblical Theology,* ed. B. Rosner and T. D. Alexander (Leicester: IVP, forthcoming).

a commendable emphasis on the unity of the Bible but a rather impracticable view when it comes to the application. If the whole Bible is the gospel, which part do we give priority to when doing evangelism? The Bible itself gives us the needed information that the gospel is a message with a definable content, and that it is what is to be believed if we are to be saved. There is enough biblical evidence to justify our understanding of the gospel as the event, or the proclaimed message of that event, which is set forth by God as the object of our faith and trust if we are to be saved. Of course the proclamation of the event involves more than simply recounting what happened. The significance of the event is paramount. The difference is between saying "a man named Jesus was executed on a cross by the Romans" and proclaiming "Christ died for our sins." Even if we want to use the word in a less restricted sense, we will sooner or later face the need to make certain distinctions in our thinking and preaching. The question, "what is the gospel?" must be addressed.

According to Mark 1:14-15, Jesus began his ministry preaching the gospel of God, a message summed up as "The time is fulfilled, and the kingdom of God has come near." The response demanded by this gospel is "Repent, and believe the gospel." It hardly needs to be said that this indicates a distinction between the gospel and the appropriate response to it. If we take the imperative to repent and believe as part of the gospel we end up with faith in faith. The distinction between the message and the demand to believe it is vital. It means that preaching the gospel must involve more than simply calling on people to make a decision. The content of this gospel message that Jesus preached consists of two main elements, that of certain expectations that are now fulfilled,[2] and the approach of the kingdom of God. Both elements are saturated with the salvation history of the Old Testament message. It is a message about God's activities, the prophetic pronouncements concerning where these activities are leading, and the announcement that Jesus is the one who brings these expectations to reality.

This perspective in Mark is similar to Paul's outline introduction to the gospel in Romans 1:1-4. Here he defines the gospel as the message about God and by God: it is God's gospel. It is the gospel that has been given prior expression in the Old Testament prophetic word. It is the gospel that concerns the Son, who is identifiable historically in terms of his human lineage from David. This lineage has deep theological implications because it links him to the historic pattern of kingship among God's people, and to the prophetic expectations concerning the coming glorious rule of God through a Davidic king. Finally, Paul identifies the resurrection as the climax of the

---

2. The NIV is unhelpful in translating πεπλήρωται ὁ καιρός as "the time has come." The notion of fulfillment in the verb is much stronger in that it implies something about the past in relation to the time that has now arrived.

whole gospel event. The resurrection shows him to be the son of God and is the event that, in Romans 4:25, is designated as the means of our justification. It is clear from the way Paul expands on this outline in the rest of the Epistle to the Romans that the resurrection of Jesus presupposes the atoning death on the cross. The death of Jesus is also to be seen as presupposing his life. The resurrection shows him to be the son of God, a title that almost certainly indicates the true humanity of Jesus. That he is raised bodily from death is a testimony to the perfectly obedient human life lived on our behalf. This is the basis of the Adam-Christ comparison in Romans 5:19:

> For just as by one man's disobedience the many were made sinners,
> so by the one man's obedience the many will be made righteous.

The bodily resurrection is the justification of Jesus as the human son of God and is thus the basis of the justification of all who believe in him.

There is no need to labor this point. The gospel is the message about Jesus in his life, death, and resurrection. It is the distinct work of God the Son who, by his incarnation, becomes for us son of God, a role attested to by his resurrection. But perhaps we need to remind ourselves from time to time that there are truths related to this gospel message that are not themselves the gospel but that without which the gospel would not be the gospel. The unity-distinction perspective that we receive from the incarnation and the Trinity reminds us that the persons of the Trinity, though one God, are not interchangeable. The Father was not incarnate in the womb of Mary, and the Holy Spirit was not crucified. Thus, when Paul indicates that his gospel concerns the Son, we recognize that there is a real sense in which it is the distinct work of the Son, and not that of the Father or the Holy Spirit.

The point of this distinction is certainly not to deny that all three persons of the Trinity are involved in the gospel, but only to indicate that their manner of involvement is distinct for each. The Father sends the Son, not the other way round. The Holy Spirit brings about the conception in the womb of Mary. Only the Son is born of Mary, lives, dies, and rises again. Most people understand that, but confusion often arises when distinctive ministries of the Father or the Spirit are seen to be the gospel or are allowed to take the place of the gospel. Preaching predestination, or creation, or the new birth, or the baptism of the Spirit is not preaching the gospel. All these things are related to the gospel and are necessary for the working of the gospel, but they are not the essential message to be believed for salvation. Furthermore, unlike the gospel message, they do not directly address the matter of our justification and assurance of salvation. Only the message that another true and obedient human being has come on our behalf, that he has lived for us the kind of life we should live but can't, that he has paid fully the penalty we deserve for the life we do live but shouldn't — only this message can give assurance that we have peace with God through our Lord Jesus Christ.

The Gospel Is the Hermeneutical Key

By referring to the gospel as the hermeneutical key I mean that proper interpretation of any part of the Bible requires us to relate it to the person and work of Jesus. This was recognized in Article III of the Chicago Statement on Biblical Hermeneutics, which says, "We affirm that the Person and work of Jesus Christ are the central focus of the entire Bible."[3] We have already considered some of the ramifications of Jesus' postresurrection claims that all the Scriptures are about him. This is another way of saying that Jesus is the sole mediator of the truth of God. This mediatorial role has great significance for how we understand the Bible.

> For there is one God; there is also one mediator between God and humankind, Christ Jesus, himself human who gave himself a ransom for all. (1 Tim. 2:5-6)

The Jesus who mediates the word of God to us is the Jesus who is defined in terms of his historic saving act. The meaning of the Bible, in that case, is tied to the saving work of Jesus. Another perspective on this truth is seen in Paul's summary confession in Romans 1:16:

> For I am not ashamed of the gospel; it is the power of God for salvation to everyone who has faith.

Once we recognize that a part of the business of being saved is coming to a right understanding of what God says to us in his word, we are driven to the conclusion that the gospel is the power of God for hermeneutical salvation. Salvation must include being saved from sinful interpretations of the Bible, but like every other dimension of our sanctification we have to work at it. Furthermore, it will not be perfected until Christ returns. One other passage we could apply here is Paul's word to Timothy:

> From childhood you have known the sacred writings which are able to instruct you for salvation through faith in Christ Jesus. All Scrip-

---

3. Earl D. Radmacher and Robert D. Preus, eds., *Hermeneutics, Inerrancy, and the Bible* (Grand Rapids: Zondervan, 1984), p. 882.

ture is inspired by God and is useful for teaching, for reproof, for correction, and for training in righteousness, so that everyone who belongs to God may be proficient, equipped for every good work. (2 Tim. 3:15-17)[4]

Paul here expresses the important hermeneutical principle that the Old Testament instructs us for salvation, but only in relation to Jesus Christ. The function of the gospel as the means of interpreting aright the Old Testament is inescapable unless we believe that there is something other than salvation involved as the main subject of God's word to us.

Christ-centered interpretation was a feature of the Reformation, which marked a radical departure from medieval Catholicism. By the time of the Reformation the Roman Catholic theologians had mostly adopted the thinking of Thomas Aquinas (1226-74) who underplayed the effects of sin on human thinking and understanding. He proposed a system in which knowledge of God, true but not saving knowledge, was achievable by human senses and reason without either the special revelation in the Bible or the ministry of the Holy Spirit.[5] This revelation in nature was completed by special saving revelation, that is, by grace.[6] The Reformers rejected this idea of "nature plus grace" in favor of "grace alone." Grace for the Reformers was redefined in more biblical terms than Aquinas's ecclesiastical and sacramental concept. "Grace alone" means not only that we are saved by God's gracious gift in Christ alone, but that the right knowledge of God through his word is a part of this salvation. To understand the Bible correctly requires faith in Christ along with the Spirit's enlightenment. Christ is revealed as the meaning of the Scriptures so that no part can be rightly understood without reference to him.

---

4. The "sacred writings" (ἱερὰ γράμματα) of v. 15 and "all Scripture" (πᾶσα γραφή) in v. 16 refer to the Old Testament.

5. This application of Aristotelian empiricist philosophy shows a remarkable similarity to the starting point of liberal Christianity. This similarity of Catholicism and neo-Protestantism is carefully analyzed in Jacques de Senarclens, *Heirs of the Reformation* (London: SCM, 1963).

6. It should be noted that Thomas's idea of grace was very different from that of the Reformers. Catholicism had largely attached grace to the sacramental ministrations of the church, which tended to remove the gospel from the historic deeds of Christ and to make it primarily a present event that happens in the soul of the believer. The saving revelation of grace would thus be tied more to an ecclesiastical interpretation rather than to the self-interpreting text of Scripture.

The Gospel Is the Biblical-Theological Center

Closely related to the fact that the gospel is the hermeneutical key is the recognition of the gospel as the theological center of the whole Bible. Biblical theology uncovers this in no uncertain way. It does this by showing us the specific details in the process that leads through the whole progressive revelation and comes to focus on Christ as the fulfiller.[7] The theology of the Bible is about God as creator and redeemer of the world. Biblical theology looks at the way this subject matter is unfolded throughout the process of salvation history. Perhaps one of the most important aspects of this process for the preacher is the way it shows the unity of the Scriptures so that every part is linked in some way to the person and work of Christ.

I have underlined this unity of revelation by proposing the kingdom of God as the comprehensive unifying feature in the biblical message. Reality in biblical terms consists of two main elements, God and the created order. We can say this because the Bible gives no grounds for proposing the existence of anything beyond these.[8] What is created is further differentiated in the Bible so that the human race, the only part created in the image of God, is given a distinct status above that of the rest of creation. The pattern that emerges in all parts of the Bible is that the revelation of God's plan involves three focal points:

1. God as Lord;
2. his people living before him as his willing and loving subjects;
3. and the created environment within which God relates to his people.

This reductionist[9] view of reality is consistent with all parts of the Bible. There is always an expression of God relating to his people in some defined place. The schema of God-people-place presupposes certain also clearly defined relationships that are initially identified in the creation narratives. The upsetting of these relationships by human rebellion is answered through a process by which humankind is to be restored perfectly through redemption.

This process by which the restoration is effected, the "mechanics" of salvation, is what biblical theology seeks to understand, for that is the way we learn to relate ancient texts to contemporary Christian existence. In proposing

---

7. See Graeme Goldsworthy, *Gospel and Kingdom: A Christian Interpretation of the Old Testament* (Exeter: Paternoster, 1981), and *According to Plan: The Unfolding Revelation of God in the Bible* (Leicester: IVP, 1991).

8. We must assume, then, that if anything were to exist other than God and the created universe, it is not necessary for us to know about it, and it does not in any way affect biblical truth.

9. By reductionist here I mean that we can discern the essential and basic ingredients of reality in these terms.

this analytical approach I fully recognize the need to constantly check the broad plan with the details of Scripture. In doing so we need to remember that checking the whole by the parts must go hand in hand with checking the parts by the whole. Above all we need to understand that our basic starting point is the gospel. Let us, then, take the God-people-place schema and observe how it is employed in the unfolding revelation of the Bible. In this we must include the element of relationship that is at the base of the notion of the kingdom of God, namely, that the essence of the kingdom is God's people in God's place under God's rule.[10] Sin means that the rule of God is repudiated, and the resulting judgment threatens the complete undoing of the whole fabric. God will remain sovereign but the life in fellowship with God enjoyed by humans is lost. Only the loving plan of redemption can deal with the problem.

In the unfolding revelation of the kingdom we can observe the following manifestations of the basic kingdom notion in sequence:

In the Garden of Eden

God, his people, and the place all exist in the perfect relationships intended by God.

Outside the Garden of Eden

The relationships established by God at creation are dislocated and confused because of sin. They are not totally disrupted, and the world goes on while under sentence of death.

In redemptive history

God calls one family of people, and their successors, to be the context within which he reveals his plan and purposes for the redemption of people out of every nation. The relationships of the kingdom of God are put in place but never fully realized by sinful people.

In prophetic eschatology

The pattern of redemption, and the promised kingdom of God that failed to eventuate in Israel's history, constitute the pattern of a future glorious salvation and kingdom promised by the prophets.

In Jesus Christ

Where Adam failed, and where Israel failed, Jesus comes as the last Adam and the true Israel to carry out God's purposes perfectly. Believers from all periods of history are credited with his perfection and righteousness as a gift.

10. See Goldsworthy, *Gospel and Kingdom,* chapter 5.

In the consummation

> The perfection that is in Jesus, and that believers possess by faith, is only fully formed in believers and the world when Christ returns in glory.

We can say this in another way:

1. The pattern of the kingdom is established in the Garden of Eden.
2. This pattern is broken when sin enters in.
3. The pattern is reestablished in salvation history in Israel but never fully realized.
4. The same pattern shapes the prophetic view of the future kingdom.
5. The pattern of the kingdom is perfectly established in Jesus in a representative way.
6. The pattern of the kingdom begins to be formed in the people of God through the gospel.
7. The pattern of the kingdom is consummated at Christ's return.

The "mechanics" of salvation, then, consist in this: that what is lost with the fall God foreshadows in the history of redemption in Israel. Then the solid reality comes, namely, Jesus, who bears in himself the fullness of the kingdom in that he is God, man, and created order, all existing in perfect relationship.

The Gospel Structures History and Eschatology

The way the gospel structures history is by structuring salvation history. We should, perhaps, clarify the relationship of salvation history to the general history of the world. First, we note that we use the word "history" to designate what actually happens in the affairs of human beings. This could be extended to include "natural history" or what happens in the universe whether or not human beings are involved. From the biblical point of view, history happens because of God and his purposes. History, therefore, can be thought of not only as what has happened, but also as what is going to happen. Salvation history refers to that aspect of universal history in which God is specifically active both to reveal and to effect the salvation of his people. It relates to general history in that God has revealed that salvation history has universal implications: God is working to redeem a great multitude from every nation, tribe, and language group (Rev. 7:9). From a biblical point of view, all world history is bound up with salvation history.

There is only one history, but we are justified in distinguishing salvation history for the reasons given.

How, then, does the gospel structure salvation history? Some might suggest that it is the other way around and that salvation history structures the gospel. That is true in the same way the Old Testament structures the gospel. The truth is that they are interdependent, but the gospel is God's ultimate plan that all other aspects of history must serve. For the preacher the immediate concern is to understand how the gospel relates to the structures of history. History serves the gospel. World history, written from God's point of view and without the debilitating effects of human sinfulness and human ignorance, is ultimately the history of the gospel.[11] Eschatology, the study of the last things, focuses on the fact that all events serve the end or goal that God has determined. Eschatology begins in the eternal purposes of God according to which "he chose us in Christ before the foundation of the world to be holy and blameless before him in love" (Eph. 1:4). Because history is the story that God controls and that will inevitably reach the end he has determined, it is structured by salvation history and eschatology.

One of the striking features of the New Testament treatment of the gospel is the emphasis given to certain key areas of salvation history in the Old Testament. For example, a much neglected passage is the genealogy of Jesus with which Matthew begins his Gospel. He summarizes its structure as taking us from Abraham to David, from David to the exile, and from the exile to Christ (Matt. 1:17). In chapter 6, I have referred to some of the different ways that biblical theologians have understood the structure of salvation history. The question we need to ask is, What structure does the gospel give? Some approaches seem to start with an investigation of the Old Testament in order to understand which events are most significant and why. But, why does Matthew order things with an emphasis on Abraham, David, the exile, and Christ? When we come to Peter's first gospel sermon we find his focus is mainly from David to Christ. Paul's sermon at Antioch alludes first to Abraham, moves through salvation history to David, and then jumps from David to Christ (Acts 13:17-23). In addition, both Peter and Paul give special place to the resurrection. Paul's summary of the gospel in Romans 1:1-4 reinforces this understanding. We gain from these passages a basic structure in the proclamation of the gospel. There is a starting point with Abraham involving the history of his descendants, climaxing with David. Then we move to the descendant of David in whom it all comes to fruition, namely, Jesus of Nazareth. Bearing in mind that the coming of Jesus Christ is not an accident, and that salvation history serves

---

11. I use the word "history" here to refer to the recording of history, which should be distinguished from history as the events that actually happen.

the gospel, we can propose that the gospel is determinative of the Old Testament events that make up salvation history.

Abraham, David, and Jesus Christ stand then as keys to the structure of the biblical revelation that culminates in the gospel event. We might note here that Stephen's apology in Acts 7 makes one significant addition to this structure in that Solomon is mentioned as the one who actually carries out David's intention to build a temple (Acts 7:47). We recognize Solomon as the son of David in whom the promises to David begin to be worked out. But the real point to all this is that the structure of biblical revelation is clearly a gospel one. In the concrete terms of salvation history, this gospel structure is discernible within the parameters that these key New Testament passages indicate. In other words, revelation deals with an entity bound by the historical parameters of Abraham to David (and Solomon). That entity directs us then to Christ, yet in order to do so it has to project our view through a thousand years of history. The New Testament informs us how this can be; it is through the medium of prophecy. Thus Paul's gospel is the gospel promised beforehand through the prophets (Rom. 1:2). Once again we come to the understanding of the gospel as the event that fulfills the expectations of the Old Testament. The nature of the gospel event, the actual details of the person and work of Jesus, is comprehensive of all these expectations.

While the gospel event can be summed up in terms of the history of Jesus of Nazareth, the New Testament exposition of its significance enables us to discern distinct aspects of what God is doing. As we saw in chapter 6, Jesus is proclaimed to be the one who fulfills all God's purposes for Israel as the people of God. He is God's chosen one; God's human covenant partner. The multiplicity of Old Testament images applied to him show that the role of fulfiller is very specific. All the saving roles of the Old Testament are summed up in him. Christology is the understanding of what it means for Jesus to be the Christ. In traditional Reformational thinking Christology designated the offices of Christ that enabled him to be the Savior of the world. Specifically this involved understanding Jesus as the one who not only fulfilled the Old Testament offices but gave them their real meaning. Jesus is first the prophet *par excellence.* The words of revelation through the Old Testament prophets not only point to him but actually depend upon him for their ultimate meaning and validity. Thus, while the words of a prophet often had a more immediate fulfillment in Israel's history, the whole reason for prophetic utterance was to foreshadow the fulfillment in Christ. This has tremendous implications for the way we preach from the prophets. Furthermore, Jesus himself is the fullest prophetic word. Whereas God once spoke through the prophets, in these last days he has spoken through his Son (Heb. 1:1-2). Jesus is *the* prophet who renders all other prophets meaningful. He is also the word spoken and, as the true Israelite, he is the listening child of God.

In similar fashion Jesus fulfills the role of priest, for he alone is the true high priest who enters into the presence of God on our behalf (Heb. 9:24-28). Yet he fulfills also the roles of the sacrificial offering and of the temple as the place of sacrifice where God and man are reconciled. He fulfills the role of the king, being the true successor to King David, the one greater than Solomon who is known as God's son.[12] As the true Israelite he is also the perfectly obedient subject. To the traditional reckoning of prophet, priest, and king, we can justifiably add the office of wise man. Jesus is not only the revealer of the wisdom of God, he is also the truly wise man. As such he imparts wisdom and instructs us in the way we gain wisdom and learn to deal with life in this world.

The Gospel and the End of the World

Salvation history has as its goal the final working out of redemption and the coming of the kingdom of God in all its fullness. The gospel is thus directed to the end. The idea of the end of the world evokes all kinds of images of universal catastrophe, apocalyptic destruction, and the cessation of life as we know it on this planet. There is good biblical reason for this, but the Bible also presents a view of the end of the world that is somewhat more nuanced than the popular idea. The first postresurrection Christian sermon ever preached was prefaced by a reference to the apocalyptic prophecy of Joel being fulfilled at that moment. The Pentecost phenomenon of tongues fulfills Joel's words about the last days when God will pour out his Spirit on all flesh (Acts 2:17). Peter goes on to quote the rest of the oracle as if it were also fulfilled at Pentecost:

> And I will show portents in the heaven above and signs of the earth below, blood, and fire, and smoky mist. The sun shall be turned to darkness and the moon to blood before the coming of the Lord's great and glorious day. (Acts 2:19-20)

Thus, despite the clear recognition that Jesus' resurrection and ascension meant that the kingdom now is coming through the preaching of the gospel in the world, and despite the message that the ascension would be matched by a similar return of Christ, the apostles seemed to find no difficulty in proclaiming the end as having already come. John declares that it is the last hour and many antichrists have come (1 John 2:18). Jude understands

---

12. He thus fulfills the promise of 2 Sam. 7:14.

that last-time predictions are already being fulfilled (Jude 18). Paul describes his contemporaries as those upon whom the ends of the ages have come (1 Cor. 10:11). Hebrews tells us that "in these last days, God has spoken to us by his son" (Heb. 1:2). It also describes Jesus as having "appeared once for all at the end of the age to remove sin by the sacrifice of himself" (Heb. 9:26).

In addition, New Testament writers also see an end in the future. The contemporary situation does not exhaust the reality of the end, and Christians must understand that there is a future end also. This is described as the time when the last trumpet will sound and the dead shall be raised (1 Cor. 15:52). The prophets spoke of scoffers in the last days, and these, says Peter, have now come. However, the subject of their scoffing, Christ's return, is yet future (2 Pet. 3:2-7). The present heavens and earth will be consumed on that day of judgment.

We are forced by these considerations to admit that the old argument about whether eschatology was realized (present) or future is resolved by the gospel in terms of *both* the present *and* the future. In fact, the evidence we have just cited indicates that the end is past and future in the sense that the historic gospel event is the coming of the end. Furthermore, the New Testament characterizes Christian existence as being life lived at the end of the ages. Thus, the gospel event is the end, Christian existence is at the end, and the end will come at Christ's return. How can this be? Most Christians are familiar with the suggestion that the question, "Are you saved?" should be answered with the affirmation "I have been saved; I am being saved; and I will be saved." This is only another way of saying "I have reached the end; I am reaching the end; I will reach the end." This simple response embraces the heart of the New Testament perspective of the gospel and eschatology. This "now and not yet" perspective recognizes a distinction between the first and second comings of Christ as well as a very close connection between them. What then is the distinction, and what is the unity?

1. The Gospel as the Work of Christ FOR Us

The gospel is the past historic event in which Jesus did for us what we could not do for ourselves. To do this work of redemption he, as God incarnate, actually reaches the goal, the *telos,* the *eschaton,* in himself. He is that end, for in him God and humankind and the whole created order are perfectly related. Jesus is the kingdom of God as it invades this alien world of rebellion against the kingdom. In Jesus the end of the world has come on our behalf, for us. This reaching of the end can only be for us if there is some bridge provided between the kingdom and rebellious sinners, some way of propitiation of the righteous anger of God. Jesus, conceivably, could have come and lived as the true human covenant partner of God without reference to sinners. The end result would be one, and only one, human being in heaven for eternity — Jesus. Such a "gospel" would not be for us, but only for Jesus. However, the gospel is the event for us. The incarnation was necessary only for the sake of those Jesus came to serve.[13]

It is important to remember here the testimony of Jesus about the fulfillment of prophecy. I want to assert categorically that ALL prophecy was fulfilled in the gospel event at the first coming of Jesus. There was only one coming projected in prophecy, yet somehow we must understand the New Testament perspective of two comings as consonant with this. There is a tendency to try to differentiate Old Testament prophecies of the end into two groups, those applying to the first coming and those applying to the second coming.[14] It would be tempting to take the prophecies that speak in ultimate terms, for example, the new heavens and earth in Isaiah 65:17, as referring only to the second coming. This is a mistake. A more biblical perspective is one that recognizes that the distinction between the first and second coming is not in what happens but in how it happens. Nothing will happen at the return of Christ that has not already happened in him at his first coming. All the expectations of the Old Testament have come to fulfillment IN HIM. And this has happened FOR US.

2. The Fruit of the Gospel as the Work of Christ IN Us

If something has been done for us there needs to be some point of contact so that it actually benefits us. The preaching of the gospel is the preaching of the message that the kingdom has come in Christ. The Holy Spirit applies that message to the elect so that they embrace the gospel by faith and are baptized into Christ. Faith, in other words, involves us in a union with Christ so that what belongs to him as the one faithful and accepted human being is attributed or imputed to the believer. This union, or unity, that we are given with Christ is spoken of in the Bible as our being *in* Christ and as having been *with*

---

13. Mark 10:45; Phil. 2:6-8.

14. Anthony A. Hoekema, *The Bible and the Future* (Grand Rapids: Eerdmans, 1978), p. 1, says, "The Old Testament abounds with prophecies concerning future blessings for Israel. In the New Testament many, yet not all, of these prophecies are fulfilled in the person of Christ. It becomes obvious, therefore, that some prophecies will find fulfillment only in the Second Coming." This, in my view, is not accurate, and Hoekema himself recognizes a close connection between the two comings. He asserts that the eschatological event predicted in the Old Testament has happened, that what was seen as one event in the Old Testament now involves two stages, and that the present fulfillment is a pledge of the future (pp. 21-22). However, it is important to understand that the process involving two stages does not mean that some prophecies have no reference to the first coming.

Christ in the saving events. We have been crucified with Christ (Gal. 2:19-20). We have died with him (Col. 3:3). We have been buried with him, having been united with him in his death (Rom. 6:4-5). We have been made alive together with Christ, raised up with him, and made to sit with him in heavenly places (Eph. 2:5-6).

The reason for understanding this involvement, by faith, in the historic events of our redemption in Christ is so that we may be conformed more and more to his image. In other words, the end that has already come in Christ is now coming among the people of God. The gospel is conforming us to the image of Christ. Sanctification is the end as it grows IN US now, not as a legalistic fulfilling of law, but as the fruit of faith in Christ the fulfiller. The Old Testament prophecies and promises of God are being fulfilled in us; the end is a present, growing reality among the people of God. Because we have died, we are called upon to put to death that which is earthly within us (Col. 3:5). We must consider ourselves to be dead to sin and alive to God (Rom. 6:11-13).

3. The Consummation of the Gospel as the Work of Christ WITH Us

At the return of Christ, everything that has already happened in Christ for us, and that has been the growing reality among the people of God in this age of the Spirit, will be consummated universally. There is no residue of prophecy waiting to happen. As all prophecy has been fulfilled in Christ, so all prophecy will be fulfilled in this consummating fashion at his return. In Christ the end of the world, of the old age, has come. Yet we live in the overlap of the ages. There is an ongoing tension between what we have now in Christ, and what will be the reality in ourselves at his return. The prospect of what we will be is also set out as a motive to be in ourselves what we already are in Christ.[15] It is important for preaching that we have a clear understanding of the New Testament perspective on the reaching of the end:

– the end has come FOR us;
– the end is coming IN us;
– the end will come WITH us.[16]

---

15. Col. 3:4; 1 John 3:2-3.
16. I have expounded this perspective at greater length in *According to Plan* and in *The Gospel in Revelation* (Exeter: Paternoster, 1984). A fuller treatment of this view of eschatology is to be found in Adrio König, *The Eclipse of Christ in Eschatology* (Grand Rapids: Eerdmans, 1989).

The Gospel in Preaching

Since the aim of this book is to understand the place of the gospel in expository preaching, I will only foreshadow here some of the aspects to be treated in part 2. Up to this point I have stressed that, while there is much in the Bible that is strictly speaking not the gospel, there is nothing in the Bible that can be truly understood apart from the gospel. This being the case, it needs to be said that the frequently made distinction between gospel preaching and teaching needs to be carefully qualified. All preaching, to be true to the biblical perspective, must in some sense be gospel preaching. But there are still some distinctions that need to be made.

1. The Gospel in Evangelism

My concern about evangelism is that sometimes there is a greater emphasis on the need for some kind of response than on the clear exposition of the gospel. Telling people they need to come to Jesus, that they must be born again, that they should commit their lives to Christ, and so on, is not preaching the gospel. It is, at best, telling them what they ought to do or, in the case of the new birth, what has happened when they have received the gospel. It is a remarkable thing in Acts 2 that Peter's sermon contained no appeal. The appeal came from the congregation: "What should we do?" It was the power and clarity of the gospel message that impressed them with the need to do something about it.

The evangelistic sermon, as we see in Acts, will therefore contain elements other than the gospel. Telling people the need for the gospel, both their felt need and the real need, is plainly important, but it is not itself the gospel. When we have explained what God has done for us in Christ — the gospel — then we may go on to explain the benefits of receiving the gospel and the perils of ignoring it. However, telling people that they can choose either heaven or hell is not telling them the gospel. Telling them, as Peter did, that repentance and faith go hand in hand with the gift of the Holy Spirit is important, but it is not the gospel. Whenever people's sense of assurance of salvation is expressed in the first person, something is amiss. When the question "How do you know God will accept you?" is answered by "I have Jesus in my heart," "I asked Jesus into my life," "The Holy Spirit is in me," and so on, the real gospel basis for assurance needs to be reviewed. We rejoice when the answer comes in the third person: "God gave his only Son to die on the cross for me," "Jesus died, rose, and is in heaven for me." When the focus is on the finished and perfect work of Christ, rather than on the yet unfinished work of the Spirit in me, the grounds for assurance are in place.

2. The Gospel in Discipleship and Spiritual Growth

To say that we need the gospel both to get started and to continue in the Christian life can be deceptive though it is absolutely true. The problem is when the gospel is viewed only as how we start the Christian life, for then the only way to continue is law. Yet the perspective consistently set out in the New Testament is that we need the gospel to grow. It has been wisely said that sanctification is justification in action. Another view on this is that those renowned men and women of faith that we all look up to usually have a greater sense of their unworthiness and of the greatness of God's grace. The greater our sense of being forgiven and justified sinners, the greater will be the likelihood that others will see in us the character of Christ. It is difficult to see why Christians, almost universally, recognize the benefits of regularly celebrating the Lord's Supper, which is a visible proclamation of the gospel, if the gospel were not the means of growth.

3. The Gospel in Ethical Issues

Finally, a word about the place of the gospel in ethical issues. Again we anticipate a later discussion. At the risk of sounding simplistic, I want to suggest that there is only one question to be asked in settling ethical issues. I do not thereby suggest in any way that giving the answer is always easy, but it does help to have the right question to begin with. When the New Testament writers were faced with ethical issues in the various churches to which they wrote, it would have been relatively easy to appeal to the Ten Commandments. This they do not do. Let us state this fact as a rule of thumb: the New Testament basis for ethical decisions is no longer Moses on Sinai but Christ on Calvary. This is not to drive a wedge between the two, however, for they are related. Christ on Calvary embraces and completes the principles that lie behind the law of Moses. We will consider this again in chapter 11. Meanwhile, in dealing with ethical issues, indeed all matters of decision making (ethical or otherwise), the question we should ask ourselves is, "What course of action or behavior is consistent with the gospel?"

I conclude by stating again the principle that expository, biblical, preaching is always an exposition of the gospel and its implications. While we don't always focus on the heart of the gospel, no text will yield its true significance unless it is understood in its organic relationship to the gospel.

CHAPTER 8

What Is the Structure of Biblical Revelation?

Applying the Gospel Structure

It is tempting for biblical theologians to think that the historical structure of progressive revelation is best observed by a simple chronological approach. This method involves starting with the earliest events, creation and fall, and proceeding along the biblical time line, picking up the information in the relevant texts as we go. There is, however, a fundamental error in this methodology that ignores the function of the final word of God in Jesus Christ in interpreting the nature of all that has led up to it. It might be argued that a chronological methodology was all the biblical characters and authors themselves had, and it should therefore be good enough for us. This ignores the fact that the gospel event was not anticipated in the form it took. The prophetic revelation was undoubtedly revealing the gospel events that should therefore have been recognizable on the basis of the Old Testament. Hence the rebuke Jesus gave to the disciples on the road to Emmaus. As we have already seen, however, the fulfillment of the prophetic expectations involved further revelation. It was not empirically demonstrable that Jesus was the fulfiller of the prophetic expectations. It was his self-authenticating word that proclaimed him as the fulfillment. The manner of the coming of the kingdom, which the Jews and disciples expected, required radical modification in the light of the person and work of Jesus.

The consequence of this for us is simply that we need to start with the definitive word of fulfillment in the gospel and allow this to show us what the real structure and significance of the Old Testament revelation is. This has been my argument in chapters 6 and 7. Now, with the preeminence of the gospel established we are in a position to consider the overall structure of biblical revelation and its application to biblical interpretation in preaching.

The History in Salvation History

Not all events in history have the same significance. Even in the writing of secular history certain events will be seen to have greater significance than others, and to have had a greater impact on the course of world history than others. In the biblical account of salvation history not all the events that are noted in the texts are of the same importance. It is clear that, above all, the advent of Jesus of Nazareth is a unique event; it is the only recorded occasion in which God became a man and walked among us. We also recognize the uniquely important nature of this event in that it is the only event in history in which the salvation of humankind is effected. A feature of biblical salvation history is that the importance of events is determined by the purposes of God and not by the empirical evidence of the impact on humankind. Israel was reminded of its comparative insignificance in world history from one point of view, and its central significance from another point of view:

> It was not because you were more numerous than any other people that the Lord set his heart on you — for you were the fewest of all peoples. It was because the Lord loved you and kept the oath that he swore to your ancestors, that the Lord has brought you out with a mighty hand, and redeemed you from the house of slavery, from the hand of Pharaoh king of Egypt. (Deut. 7:7-8)

The political or military clout of the nation was not the point. The real significance of a nation was its place in the saving purposes of God. From the perspective of the biblical writers the great movements in world history are only reportable insofar as they impinge upon the elect nation at the center of God's saving purposes. No book of the Bible digresses to give a historical account of the early Romans, Greeks, or Chinese.

History within salvation history, then, is highly selective. Furthermore, even the history of the elect nation contains events of greater and lesser importance. The importance of the event is always a matter of its theological interpretation and significance. According to the evidence we have already considered, the theological significance is bound up with the relationship of events to the one plan of God for salvation that comes to its climax in the person of Jesus Christ. Understanding biblical history is a matter of understanding how the individual events stand in relation to this overall divine plan. Salvation history is theological history. Salvation history is the history of the gospel. We have noted in chapter 7 that the gospel focuses on certain events that give us the essential framework to work out salvation history. We need now to try to apply this gospel-based framework to the more detailed biblical history.

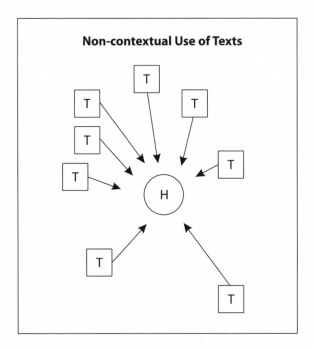

Diagram 1: Intuitive direct application of individual and unrelated texts (T) to hearer (H) while ignoring the salvation history structure of revelation.

Abraham, David (and Solomon), then Jesus Christ — these are the key reference points in salvation history. How, then, does the rest of biblical history relate to these great figures? Let us note first of all an important implication of this question for the evangelical preacher. Expository preaching can only proceed if it places the text into the salvation-historical context so that its inter-textual relationships can be seen. Without a sense of this unifying structure in salvation history the Bible becomes fragmented and the road from text to hearer is a matter of the preacher's intuition, preference, or prejudice (see diagram 1).

Even when there is some understanding that different parts of the Bible stand in different historical relationship to the contemporary hearer, it can be so much in the background that it has little effect on the application. The sermon application remains a matter of intuition or preference. We see this when the real theological significance of the events, particularly Old Testament events, is ignored in favor of a concentration on character studies. The structure of revelation and the unity of Scripture as a book about Christ demands that the preacher search out the real relationship of the text to the per-

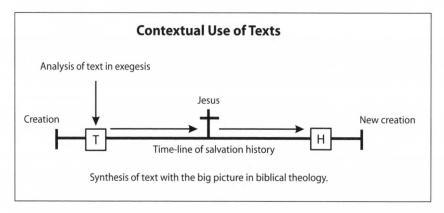

Diagram 2: Placing the text in its salvation history context. The text (T) is first linked theologically to Christ as the focal point of all Scripture, then the connection is made with the believer or hearer (H).

son and work of Christ. Since we know from the New Testament what the relationship of the hearer is to Christ, we can move according to the unified structure of the Bible from the text, via the gospel, to the hearer. Diagram 2 illustrates how we might move from an Old Testament text (T) to the contemporary hearer (H). The hearer exists somewhere between the first and second comings of Christ and, in that sense, within salvation history.

Our next concern is the placement of the details of biblical history within the salvation history structure that has its high points in Abraham, David, and Christ. One of the features of any history writing is the process of selection according to the interests of the historian. A history of any nation can be written from any number of different perspectives so that, within the same time span, one will be a political history, another a military history, yet another an economic history, and so on. The selection process in biblical history is based on the theology of redemption and the coming of the kingdom of God. The biblical authors thus partake in the ongoing process of doing biblical theology. One major difference between biblical theology done by the biblical authors and that done subsequently is that the former is part of the process of inspired revelation.

This is not the place to give any kind of detailed treatment of biblical history. I would, however, stress again that we need to distinguish clearly between the biblical testimony to history, both past and future, and the attempts of modern critical historians to reconstruct what happened in the past using secular historical method. The issue for the evangelical interpreter is to try to understand how writers of biblical history actually wrote their history and the rules they employed. I include at this point the very useful diagram of bibli-

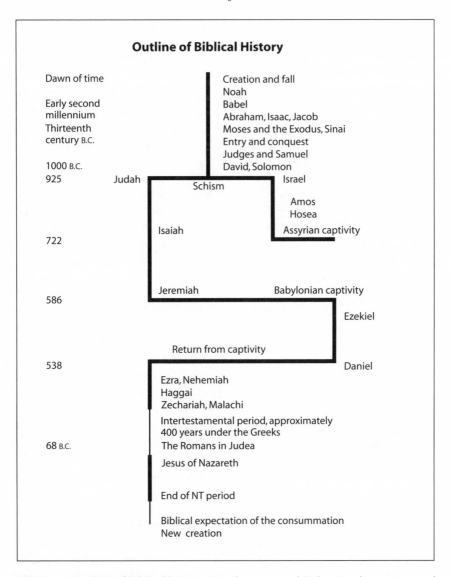

Outline of Biblical History

Dawn of time		Creation and fall
		Noah
Early second millennium		Babel
		Abraham, Isaac, Jacob
Thirteenth century B.C.		Moses and the Exodus, Sinai
		Entry and conquest
		Judges and Samuel
1000 B.C.		David, Solomon
925	Judah	Israel
	Schism	
		Amos
		Hosea
	Isaiah	Assyrian captivity
722		
586	Jeremiah	Babylonian captivity
		Ezekiel
	Return from captivity	
538		Daniel
	Ezra, Nehemiah	
	Haggai	
	Zechariah, Malachi	
	Intertestamental period, approximately 400 years under the Greeks	
68 B.C.	The Romans in Judea	
	Jesus of Nazareth	
	End of NT period	
	Biblical expectation of the consummation New creation	

Diagram 3: Outline of biblical history (not drawn to scale) showing key events and persons in salvation history.

cal history that has served us well over the years.[1] Its value lies in its simplicity in visually representing the whole of biblical history.

1. See Graeme Goldsworthy, *Gospel and Kingdom: A Christian Interpretation of the Old Testament* (Exeter: Paternoster, 1981), and *According to Plan: The Unfolding Revelation of God in the Bible* (Leicester: IVP, 1991).

When we examine the New Testament treatment of this history, we find that some aspects are simply assumed, and we are left to try to understand their relationship to the major persons and events. The New Testament concentrates on certain parts of the Old Testament, as we have seen, but this does not relieve us of the task of seeking to understand the function of the less prominent parts. It is not difficult to discern the way that Genesis 1–11 serves as the preparation for the birth of the elect nation, the story of which begins with Abraham in Genesis 12. While there are a number of problematic aspects in this prologue to salvation history, its essential meaning and purpose is not difficult to grasp.[2] It is also important that we don't simply reduce these parts to some kind of mythical backdrop. The modern historian's prejudice against biblical history results in nonbiblical presuppositions being applied to the textual evidence. The evangelical position accepts that God, the Lord of history, knows exactly what happened and how he wants it to be recorded by the inspired biblical authors. The humanity of the biblical word demands that we try to understand ancient methods of historiography. Ultimately it is the authority of the gospel that must determine how we view these things. For example, it is clear from the use of the Adam-Christ analogy in Romans 5 and 1 Corinthians 15 that Adam must be regarded as referring to a real human being who, as progenitor of the human race, rebelled against his Creator.

The process of selectivity is important to observe. Creation involves certain specified relationships into which the fall, sin, or human rebellion brings confusion, dislocation, and the wrath of God. The promise of redemption starts with a broad focus on all humankind in Genesis 3:15. Then the process of selection, or election, is seen to operate as the focus is on a single line from Adam, that of Seth, leading to Noah, then on the single line of Shem leading to Abraham. World history is reflected in the tables of the nations in Genesis 10 and the Babel narrative in Genesis 11. Out of this world of rebellious humanity God calls one man to be the father of the one elect nation. From this point onward the story is of the descendants of Abraham through Isaac and Jacob. From them arises a comparatively insignificant nation that later and fleetingly becomes great. From a down-trodden rabble of slaves in Egypt the saving hand of God brings them to be an ordered nation in the wilderness, and from there to possess the land of Canaan. Despite much ambiguity in this nation's attitude to its Savior-God, it is led to be a great nation under its greatest king, David. The capstone to this greatness is provided by Solomon the temple-builder. This greatness is short-lived, however, as apostasy emerges as the governing principle in this favored nation's life.

We might ask why, as our investigations have shown, the New Testament tends to move from David straight to Jesus Christ. A period of one

---

2. Goldsworthy, *Gospel and Kingdom,* chapter 6.

thousand years intervenes, yet the New Testament gives little space to the historical events during this time. Matthew notes the exile as kind of historical mid-point but not much more. Furthermore, the Old Testament itself ignores the last four hundred years of this intervening period. Yet Matthew's lead reminds us that a considerable amount of the Old Testament literature deals with the post-Davidic period. It contains a large slice of the historical books and all of the prophetic books. The history takes us through the decline of the Israelite kingdom to its destruction; through the period of exile in Babylon; then into the fortunes of the postexilic Jews both in the dispersion and in the reordered Jewish state in Palestine.

The pattern that emerges is this:

1. Creation, fall, and primeval history (Genesis 1–11) are the preamble and theological presupposition of the main aspects of salvation history.
2. The history of Abraham's descendants is described in a way that, despite the many failings of the elect, shows predominantly the saving grace of God. The discernible elements of redemptive history from Abraham to David and Solomon are these:
   a. God's election of the nation.
   b. The covenant promises to Abraham: descendants who will possess a land, live as God's people, and be the means of a blessing to all nations.
   c. The captivity in Egypt, which appears to negate the covenant promises.
   d. The redemption from captivity to become the liberated people of God.
   e. The Sinai covenant as the structure for life as the people of God.
   f. Entry into and possession of the promised land.
   g. God's rule of the people expressed through the kingship of David.
   h. The temple as the focus of God's dwelling among his people.
3. After Solomon builds the temple things go drastically wrong through increasing apostasy.
4. Thereafter, despite a couple of attempts at reform, the history of Israel and Judah moves inexorably to destruction and exile.
5. After the exile a very pale reflection of the former glory is restored in the second commonwealth of Israel. Before the Greek invasion in the fourth century the Old Testament comes to an end.

Thus, if we include the first part of Solomon's reign as the rounding off of David's, we can easily see why the New Testament stresses the structure of Abraham to David and thence to Christ. The salvation-historical process

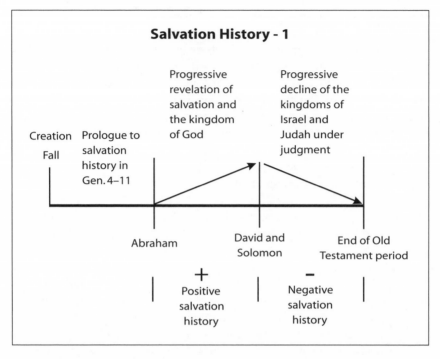

Diagram 4: Salvation history in the Old Testament. The period from Abraham to David (and Solomon) shown as definitive for the structure of redemption and the coming kingdom of God.

from Abraham to David is not difficult to trace. The move from David to Christ must be understood on other than purely historical evidence. It is in fact the prophets and their message about the future kingdom that become the focus. Thus far, then, we might represent the first part of the salvation-historical structure of the Old Testament, as diagram 4 suggests, as a period in which the revelation of salvation and the kingdom of God is given in the context of biblical history up to and including the first part of Solomon's reign. While the period from Abraham to David can be characterized as a positive salvation history revealing the nature of redemption and the kingdom of God, the period after Solomon's apostasy is negative as far as these are concerned. It is a period that reinforces the covenant sanctions of judgment. In order to keep the diagram as simple as possible I have not tried to represent the return from exile. This would need to be dealt with in preaching as a partial recapitulation of the kingdom pattern. The books of Ezra and Nehemiah belong here as tangible, if very temporary, expressions of restoration prophecy being fulfilled. However, this part of Israel's history demonstrates that the return from exile is only a pale shadow of the reality of God's kingdom yet to come.

Prophecy and the Recapitulation of Salvation History

The history of the actual fortunes of the people of God in the kingdoms of Israel and Judah could be said to lead nowhere once the rot sets in. The question could well be asked whether there was any substance to the promises made to Abraham and reiterated in various ways to the nation of Israel. All seems to be evaporating, although the reason is quite obviously one that can be laid at the door of this ungrateful and rebellious people. Nevertheless, the pattern already established is that God intends to bring in his kingdom and will not be thwarted by human sin. The reality of grace is that somehow the goal will be achieved in a manner consistent with the righteousness of God. How then do we follow the New Testament lead that takes us from King David across the unpromising centuries of apostasy and exile to the Messiah himself? The answer, also indicated in the New Testament, is in the word of the prophets.

Prophecy in the Old Testament can be said to begin with Moses, though there is a sense in which any humanly mediated word from God can be called prophecy. However, Moses is seen to be the definitive prophet who mediates the word of God to the people of God in the context of salvation history. Moses is given more than one role in that he mediates the redemptive miracle in the plagues and exodus from Egypt, and he exercises covenant rule over the people of God. This link between the word and redemption is significant because biblically there is no ground for the modern view that revelation is the event while the word is regarded as only human reflection on the event. The biblical pattern is that God says what he will do and why, then he does it, and later he repeats the word about what he has done.

Moses' prophetic word, then, sets up the interpretative basis for the salvation history that ensues. Only a word from God can truly interpret the meaning of the events from the Exodus to the kingship and beyond. Even in the presence of signs and wonders it is impossible to say empirically that the exodus from Egypt is a redemptive event worked by God in keeping with his covenant promises. Thus, the prophetic word interprets history and designates what aspects of empirical world history can be understood as part of salvation history.

3. Martin Noth, *The Deuteronomistic History,* trans. from the 2nd German ed. of 1957 (Sheffield: JSOT, 1981), proposed the view that the Former Prophets (Joshua, Judges, Samuel, Kings) consist of a single work shaped by the conditional theology of Deuteronomy. This theory has been slightly modified by subsequent scholars but retains general acceptance. The major strength of the theory is in showing the theological shaping of the history writing in these books.

The next feature of prophecy is choice: human beings are given two ways to live. One way, the way of life, is the way of covenant obedience. The other leads to death because it is a denial of the claims of the Lord of the covenant of life. This conditional nature of blessing, which characterizes the book of Deuteronomy, is seen to operate in the subsequent history of Israel.[3] This theological assessment in the historical texts, along with the prominence given to the prophetic office exercised by Samuel and others, lies behind the designation of the historical books (Joshua, Judges, Samuel, and Kings) in the Hebrew canon as the Former Prophets. These prophetic books trace the rise and the fall of the kingdom of Israel and thus focus on both redemptive grace and judgment.

After the death of Solomon, as the kingdom splits and declines, there is one last burst of prophetic activity from the old style of prophets. The ministries of Elijah and Elisha focus essentially on the old covenant structures as recoverable. But eventually the apostasy is so great that even that possibility seems increasingly remote. It is at this point that the new breed of prophets, the so-called writing prophets, emerge with a new emphasis. Various kinds of indictments are leveled at the people: ritual, ethical, and social. What they have in common is that they represent one form or another of covenant breaking. With the indictments comes the word of judgment, which consists of two main perspectives: a more immediate national consequence and, particularly in the later prophets, a far-reaching and universal consequence for the whole creation.

The good news is of course that all these Latter Prophets, on top of their word of judgment, have a word of comfort and restoration. There are some key aspects of this that the preacher cannot afford to ignore. First, there is the message of the day of the Lord on which God will act finally and definitively to bring in his kingdom. This is a day of salvation for the people of God, but also a day of judgment for all those who resist the coming of the kingdom. Salvation and judgment are inseparably bound together in the biblical understanding of God's activity. We see it in Noah's flood, in the Exodus, in the prophecies of final salvation and, ultimately, in the crucifixion of Christ. The day of the Lord is seen in the Old Testament prophets as one single coming of the Lord to bring in his kingdom. I have already broached the subject of the modification of this perspective in the New Testament.[4]

---

4. See Graeme Goldsworthy, *The Gospel in Revelation* (Exeter: Paternoster, 1984); published in the U.S.A. as *The Lamb and the Lion* (Nashville: Nelson, 1985), in which I have proposed the thesis that the book of Revelation incorporates the Old Testament perspective of a single coming of the end by its use of the literary idiom of apocalyptic. It then provides the gospel modification of this view of the end in the material, mainly hymnic, that surrounds the apocalyptic visions. The same approach can, I believe, be taken to other parts of the New Testament such as the "little apocalypses" in the Synoptic Gospels.

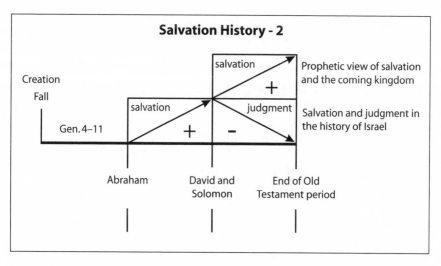

Diagram 5: The prophetic view of the coming salvation and kingdom of God as a recapitulation of what has happened in the past history of Israel in presenting the pattern of salvation and the kingdom.

Second, and for our purposes most significantly, the prophetic words of restoration conform to the already established pattern of salvation history in the past. The whole redemptive program that has been put in train in Israel's history, especially from Abraham to David, is the pattern for what God will do when he acts to save his people and bring in his kingdom. The prophetic eschatology, then, functions to confirm the structure of the salvation history that has already happened. In doing this it also confirms the completeness of this structure as that which establishes the nature of God's saving work and also the characteristics of the kingdom of God. Thus, the prophets predict, or promise, a new nation consisting of a faithful remnant of the old apostate nation. They speak of a new exodus from exile and captivity, and a new coming into the promised land. There will be a new covenant written on the hearts of people and not on stone. There will be a new Jerusalem, a new temple, and a new Davidic king who will perfectly mediate God's rule. This new kingdom will be the place to which all nations come to find reconciliation with God. Salvation will have universal and cosmic implications and will result in the creation of a new heaven and a new earth.

The pattern that now emerges can be simply represented. What was revealed in the salvation history embracing the history of Israel from Abraham to David, and which fell into decline and decay, is the pattern of an even more glorious salvation and kingdom yet to come. The prophets simply recapitulate the "gospel" pattern of salvation history and project it as the pattern of the coming glorious and everlasting reality. The two triangular areas in diagram 5 that contain the plus (+) sign represent the dimensions of salvation and the resulting kingdom of God. The difference between them is not in the "shape" but in the level. That is, what is revealed in Israel's history is not in itself the reality of the kingdom to which it points. It never could be, because the redemptive event in the exodus from Egypt cannot remove the real cause of the alienation of people from God. In like manner the sacrificial system instituted at Sinai is illustrative of the reality, but "it is impossible for the blood of bulls and goats to take away sins" (Heb. 10:4). The prophetic view of salvation and the kingdom is that of the true goal being reached. Even though they couch their message in the terminology of Israel's past history, the prophets portray the future not as another shadow of things to come, but as the solid reality.

That this prophetic message is described as the gospel when we get to passages like Romans 1:2 indicates an important point about the Old Testament revelation. While it is not itself the solid reality upon which all salvation is based, its unity with this saving event is such that it serves as the means of salvation for its contemporaries. How else could Abraham represent the reality of heaven (Luke 16:22), and how else could Moses and Elijah appear with Jesus on the mount of transfiguration? The saints of the Old Testament were saved by believing the promises of God. How else could Abraham exemplify justification by faith?[5] It is thus quite acceptable to say that the Old Testament saints were saved through faith in Christ, for he is the ultimate substance of all the promises of God in which these people trusted (2 Cor. 1:20).

Fulfillment Completing the Picture

This brings us to the matter of the fulfillment of the Old Testament patterns and expectations. The reason Matthew and Paul can leap from David to Jesus is that the sum total of prophetic expectation is the coming of the glorious kingdom foreshadowed in David's kingdom. The fulfillment is seen to be through the literal descendant of David who comes to save and then to reign over the kingdom.

There is always the danger that these neat little diagrams will distort the very complex reality that they are intended to represent. However, they are meant only to illustrate some of the major dimensions that give us the overall structure of biblical revelation. We must constantly test their validity against

5. Rom. 4:1-25; Gal. 3:6-29.

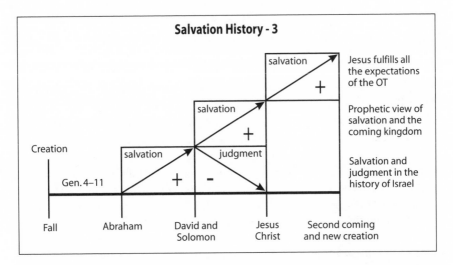

Diagram 6: Jesus Christ is declared to be the fulfiller of all the expectations of the Old Testament. He is the solid reality of which the history and prophetic expressions are the foreshadowing.

the actual text of Scripture and, if necessary, adjust our understanding of the shape of revelation. Some conceptualization is necessary if we are to preach the Old Testament as Christian Scripture.

The Nature of Typology

On the basis of the foregoing I want now to propose a biblical approach to the subject of typology. Typology, as I have already indicated, involves the principle that people, events, and institutions in the Old Testament correspond to, and foreshadow, other people, events, or institutions that come later.[6] It is unfortunate that some approaches to typology have aroused a good deal of suspicion toward it as a principle of interpretation. Often this has been a result of

6. As David L. Baker says in *Two Testaments, One Bible,* rev. ed. (Leicester: Apollos, 1991), p. 179, "Since the nineteen-fifties many biblical scholars have used the term 'typology' to express one aspect of the 'salvation history' approach to the relationship between the Testaments."

7. See Goldsworthy, *Gospel and Kingdom,* pp. 110-11, where I refer to a printed radio Bible talk on Nehemiah rebuilding the gates of Jerusalem. The logic in dealing with rebuilding the sheep gate was a progression from sheep to shepherd to the Good Shepherd. Similarly, the horse gate went from horses to soldiers to putting on the whole armor of God! A number of gates, including the dung gate, were not taken up in this sermon.

a mistaken zeal to find Christ in all the Scriptures by using what amounts to free association of ideas. Thus, some kind of conceptual approach is used to move from an Old Testament person or event, or even object, through to some Christian significance purely on some, often quite peripheral, similarity of concept.[7] When this spurious approach was applied to the directions for building the tabernacle, every detail prescribed by God was seen to speak somehow of Christ. The wood of the ark represented his humanity, while the gold overlay represented his divinity, and a very Nestorian Christology was the result.[8] The pomegranates adorning the priestly robes were taken as speaking of the fruits of the Spirit, while the circular hole in the robe for the priest to get his head through was said to represent Christ's eternal existence. The problem with such an approach is that it does not inquire into the real relationship between the texts in question and the fulfillment in Christ.

The suspicion aroused by such wild typology, which is really allegory, has tended to dampen the enthusiasm of many responsible exegetes and preachers. However, there has been among respected biblical scholars a revival of interest in and concern for understanding typology as a legitimate principle in biblical interpretation.[9] Many of the studies on typology begin with a consideration of the word "type" and its usage in the New Testament. This is not unimportant since the word is used to indicate a line of connection between the Old Testament events and the Christian existence of those being addressed.[10] It is also used in other ways, however, that are not so germane to this discussion of the relationships within the structure of revelation.

Rather than being concerned with the usage of the particular word group for "type," we are more concerned here with how the New Testament authors made the connection between their contemporary situation and what had gone before in the Old Testament. We should therefore not be content with a study of word usage and instead attempt to get behind the relevant use of these words for the principle being applied. Why does Paul refer in 1 Corinthians 10:6 to the historical events in the wilderness as types *(typoi)* for his contemporaries, and why in Romans 5:14 is Adam a type *(typos)* of Christ?

---

8. Nestorian Christology reputedly attributed not only two natures but two distinct persons to Jesus.

9. Gerhard von Rad, "Typological Interpretation of the Old Testament," in *Essays on Old Testament Hermeneutics*, ed. Claus Westermann (Richmond: John Knox, 1964), pp. 17-39; G. W. H. Lampe and K. J. Woollcombe, *Essays on Typology* (London: SCM, 1957); Francis Foulkes, *The Acts of God: A Study of the Basis of Typology in the Old Testament* (London: Tyndale Press, 1958); Leonhard Goppelt, *Typos* (Grand Rapids: Eerdmans, 1982).

10. In 1 Cor. 10:6 Paul says, Ταῦτα δὲ τύποι ἡμῶν ἐγενήθησαν, and in v. 11, ταῦτα δὲ τυπικῶς συνέβαινεν ἐκείνοις. Here *typos* and *typikos* express the organic relationship between what happened in the past and the present situation. In Rom. 5:14, Ἀδὰμ ὅς ἐστιν τύπος τοῦ μέλλοντος signifies that Adam is a type or foreshadowing of Christ, the one who is to come.

What is Paul's hermeneutic of the Old Testament? If we can nail that down, we should be in a position to apply the principle whether or not the New Testament identifies a specific piece of typology. In their anxiety to avoid the kinds of typological excesses that often amount to an exercise in uncontrolled allegory, some scholars have proscribed the use of typology to the point where it is reduced to something with very restricted usefulness in interpretation. David Baker rightly comments that "in the Bible the typical approach is so unsystematic that it does not even have a fixed terminology."[11] He is correct in identifying two characteristics of typology, namely, that it deals not with words but historical events, and that it identifies real correspondences between historical events.[12] John Currid[13] identifies four principal characteristics of a type. First, it must be grounded in history; both type and antitype must be actual historical events, persons, or institutions. Second, there must be both a historical and theological correspondence between type and antitype. Third, there must be an intensification of the antitype from the type. Fourth, some evidence that the type is ordained by God to foreshadow the antitype must be present.

What Currid describes is the technical use of the term "typology" in the New Testament. He goes on to lament the absence of typology in preaching today, which he regards as due mainly to ignorance regarding typology and a lack of appreciation of its importance. I can only express a hearty concurrence with these sentiments. I would go further, however, and suggest that typology is neglected because the word in the New Testament is tied to only a few actual examples of typology and extends to other meanings not central to the derived hermeneutical concerns.[14] I want to suggest that behind the technical uses that fit Currid's criteria there is a principle that is far-reaching in its application. We may refer to this as macro-typology because it indicates that we are not dealing merely with scattered examples but with a broad pattern. If Paul could legitimately make the typological connection he does, is this not evidence of his understanding of the overall structure of revelation that I have been at pains in this chapter to understand? If I am right, the typological correspondence is not simply between persons, events, and institutions, but between whole epochs of revelation. These correspondences are represented in diagrams 4, 5, and 6 above. I don't want to labor this point, but it needs to be empha-

11. Baker, *Two Testaments, One Bible*, p. 191.

12. Baker, *Two Testaments, One Bible*, p. 195.

13. John Currid, "Recognition and Use of Typology in Preaching," *Reformed Theological Review* 53.3 (1994): 121.

14. Baker, *Two Testaments, One Bible*, p. 186, lists the occurrences of the words of the *typos* word group in the Greek Bible: *typos* occurs seventeen times, including twice in the OT. Usages include "images," "nail prints," "pattern," "example," as well as the correspondence of persons or events. The adverb *typikos* occurs once. *Antitypos* and *hypotyposis* each occur twice.

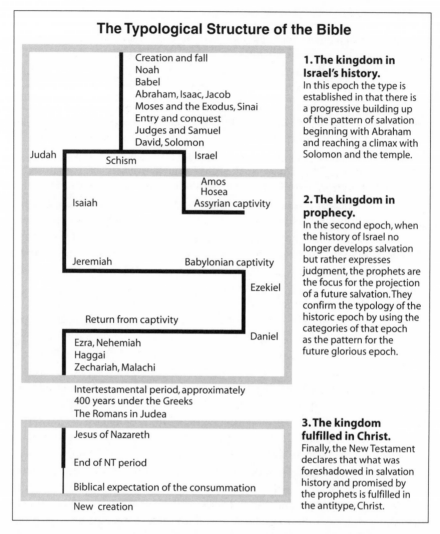

The Typological Structure of the Bible

Creation and fall
Noah
Babel
Abraham, Isaac, Jacob
Moses and the Exodus, Sinai
Entry and conquest
Judges and Samuel
David, Solomon

Judah   Schism   Israel

1. The kingdom in Israel's history.
In this epoch the type is established in that there is a progressive building up of the pattern of salvation beginning with Abraham and reaching a climax with Solomon and the temple.

Isaiah   Amos
Hosea
Assyrian captivity

2. The kingdom in prophecy.
In the second epoch, when the history of Israel no longer develops salvation but rather expresses judgment, the prophets are the focus for the projection of a future salvation. They confirm the typology of the historic epoch by using the categories of that epoch as the pattern for the future glorious epoch.

Jeremiah   Babylonian captivity

Ezekiel

Return from captivity

Ezra, Nehemiah   Daniel
Haggai
Zechariah, Malachi

Intertestamental period, approximately 400 years under the Greeks
The Romans in Judea

Jesus of Nazareth

End of NT period

Biblical expectation of the consummation

New creation

3. The kingdom fulfilled in Christ.
Finally, the New Testament declares that what was foreshadowed in salvation history and promised by the prophets is fulfilled in the antitype, Christ.

Diagram 7: Macro-typology. The entire epoch of salvation history from Abraham to David and Solomon, is confirmed in prophetic eschatology, and fulfilled in Christ. All aspects of Old Testament salvation history bear a typological relationship to Christ.

sized that the epoch of Israel's history from Abraham to David is, as a whole, a type of the fulfillment it finds in Christ. Between that historic epoch (type) and Christ (antitype) comes the whole prophetic recapitulation that confirms this typological structure. We have here the structural basis for the preacher's application of Old Testament texts, from anywhere in the Old Testament, to the contemporary Christian. I repeat, however, the antitype is not first and foremost the Christian, but Christ. We can merge diagram 3 with the essential structure of diagrams 4, 5, and 6 to show how this typological structure lies with salvation history.

Applying Macro-Typology to Preaching

The implications of this analysis for preaching are far-reaching. It underlines the central thesis of this book: all texts in the whole Bible bear a discernible relationship to Christ and are primarily intended as a testimony to Christ. Lest a skeptic should ask how texts about sin and the devil testify to Christ, I would respond by saying that such texts are an important testimony to the victory and the salvation Christ has won for us, and to the fact that he was made to become sin for us (2 Cor. 5:21). It is important to recognize the implication of this analysis as reinforcing for us the biblical witness that the whole Bible testifies to Christ. I shall examine some of the practical aspects of this analysis in the second part of the book. For the moment let us summarize some of the implications for preaching of the macro-typological approach to the structure of biblical revelation.

Perhaps one of the most contentious aspects of the central thesis of this book is the assertion that the application of the meaning of any text must proceed theologically via the application it has to Christ. This is a principle that stands firmly on the fact that the whole of Scripture testifies to Christ. It seeks to take Paul seriously in his intention "to know nothing among you but Christ and him crucified." The Bible is the word of God by virtue of its relationship to Christ and not by virtue of its spiritual application to our lives. I will not reiterate the argument of earlier chapters further, but any attempt to relate a text directly to us or our contemporary hearers without inquiring into its primary relationship to Christ is fraught with danger. The only thing that controls the matter of the relationship of the text to us is its prior relationship to Christ.

Thus, we may propose a general approach to the interpretation of the central thrust of any text when we wish to engage in truly expository preaching.

1. The exegesis of the text seeks to understand how it functions in its own context of salvation history and biblical revelation. Macro-typology is concerned with the overall correspondence of the epochs described above. Thus the historical details, the characters, or the institutions that

figure in the text need to be examined for their theological function in the epoch to which they belong.

2. If the text occurs in one of the historical documents of the Old Testament, including those dealing with the decline of the kingdom, by relating its theological significance to the prophetic eschatology we can confirm the theological pathway that leads to the fulfillment in Christ.

3. The corresponding theological function in the person and work of Christ, as the antitype, is identified as the point of contact with our contemporary situation.

4. The implications of this aspect of New Testament Christology for Christian existence are then deduced on the basis of what the New Testament teaches about our relationship to Christ.

CHAPTER 9

Can I Preach a Christian Sermon without Mentioning Jesus?

All Themes Lead to Christ

In the introduction I posed the problem of how we can show the Christian significance of Old Testament texts without becoming predictable and repetitive. It would not appear that Paul's determination to know nothing among his hearers but Christ and him crucified led him into the trap of predictability. Of course, if by predictability we mean that people will come to expect every sermon to expound something of the glories of Christ, then let us by all means be predictable! Since there are inexhaustible riches in Christ, and the implication of these for our Christian existence are endless, I doubt very much that there is any need for a preacher to be boring and repetitive.

Why do I keep on emphasizing that we need to proceed with an eye to Christology? Is it possible to preach a Christian sermon without mentioning Jesus? I want to avoid simplistic answers here. Perhaps I can put it another way: Why would you even want to try to preach a Christian sermon without mentioning Jesus? Is there anywhere else we can look in order to see God? To see true humanity? To see the meaning of anything in creation? Let us unpack, as the saying goes, what is meant by that. Earlier in chapter 7 I spoke of using a reductionist approach to the structure of the Bible, by which I mean a process of abstraction, so that behind the specific details of any text we can see the enduring dimensions of reality as the Bible portrays it. It is rather like an X-ray picture of reality. No one imagines that an X-ray of some person's head is the same as a photograph that shows all the external features. Yet the X-ray is valuable for understanding the structures that underlie the externals. So too with the biblical picture of reality. We can attempt to understand the "skeleton" behind all the details. This is what I mean by being reductionist.

The dimensions that are in the Bible are first distinguishable as: *God and creation.* Within the creation, however, a further vital distinction is made between humanity, which is created in God's image, and the rest of the creation. Human beings are given dominion over the creation while at the same time they are subject to the sovereign God. Sin is the human rejection of this order and involves our rebellion against the sovereign rule of God. Salvation is God's plan to restore all of reality to right relationships. God ruling his people who, in turn, rule over creation is the essence of the kingdom of God. There is no part of the Bible that does not portray this kingdom situation as it was or will be, or which does not project this plan of God into the context of present human fallenness. Every text may be said to deal with reality as the Bible presents it under this basic structure: *God and creation,* where *creation equals humankind plus the world.*

Now, if we stop and reflect on the significance of our Christian existence in biblical terms, we note that the proper relationships are being restored in us and among us through the gospel. The only way we can possibly know what our lives should conform to is to see first what the reality is in Christ. Of course, it is not simply a matter of taking a look to see how things work in Christ, though there is very definitely that cognitive aspect. More significantly, it is a matter of our own union with Christ by faith in him. Our union with Christ means that what belongs to him as the true human covenant partner of the Father is attributed to us as his joint heirs.

This view of reality — God plus God's people plus the created order — translates into Christology. If we would see God, he is most clearly revealed in Jesus Christ. If we would see what God intends for our humanity, it is most clearly revealed in Jesus Christ. If we would see what God intends for the created order, we discover that it is bound up with our humanity and, therefore, revealed in Christ. While the temptation in preaching will be strong to proceed directly from, say, the godly Israelite to the contemporary believer, this method will inevitably produce distortions in the way we understand the text. There is no direct application apart from the mediation of Christ. That is the theological principle that I have wanted to emphasize in this study. While, no doubt, the direct approach will produce nice thoughts and, to a limited extent, even edifying ones, we simply cannot afford to ignore the words of Jesus that the Scriptures testify to him. I say again, if this be the case, then the Scriptures only testify to us insofar as we are in him. Of course this means that the Scriptures also make clear what it means for us to be outside of Christ. However, even that negative aspect can only be understood in the light of God's answer to the problem. As Cornelius Van Til maintains, since God has made us as covenant beings

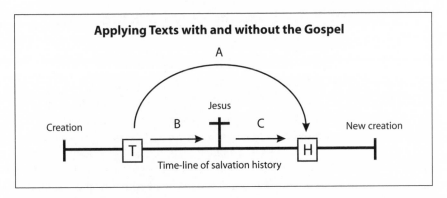

Diagram 8: The invalid method of proceeding from text (T) to hearer (H) directly or intuitively (A) avoids the structure of revelation. The valid procedure is to trace the biblical path (B) from text to Christ and to link this with the biblical path (C) from Christ to hearer.

dependent upon him, there are only two types of people, covenant-keepers and covenant-breakers.[1] We may rephrase this as people in Christ and people outside of Christ; there is no third category.

In diagram 8, we see illustrated the two ways of relating the Bible to our hearers. One ignores the Christological implications of the salvation-history structure of biblical revelation. This, in effect, is a denial of the unique role of Christ as the one mediator between God and humankind. It ignores the fact that Christ is the interpreter of Scripture and, indeed, of all reality. If he is the living Word of God, the truth, and the one for whom all things were made, no fact in this universe can be truly understood for its ultimate significance apart from him. This must include our understanding of the Bible. The correct approach proceeds through the biblical structures that inevitably lead us to Christ before they lead to the hearer.

It needs to be said here that places in the New Testament where the Old Testament is applied to the hearer do not contradict this principle because the connection through Christ does not have to be indicated in every instance once the principle is established in the wider text. Thus, Paul will expound the gospel at the beginning of an epistle and, on that basis, go on to exhort his readers to Christian living without necessarily going over old ground in each instance.

---

1. For example, Cornelius Van Til, *The Reformed Pastor and Modern Thought* (N.p.: Presbyterian and Reformed, 1974).

Exhortations without the Gospel Are Legalistic

Preaching in the right manner involves a certain amount of exhortation as a part of the application of the Bible to the lives of the hearers. If for no other reason exhortation is important because the Bible contains so much of it. Preachers must, of course, work out their own styles of exhortation that they deem to be appropriate to the occasion and the particular congregation. A former colleague of mine used to express the conviction that often congregations seem to have an almost masochistic approach to preaching. If the preacher really told them what a hopeless bunch they were and what they need to do about it, or if he really laid down the law about how they needed to improve their spiritual lives and performance, they would come away feeling really good. Battered and bruised, but good! Now this may be a bit of an exaggeration, but I suspect there has been many a holiness convention when this is exactly what happened.

Why do we like to be given this kind of treatment? We may not enjoy being taken to task, but somehow we feel that, when we have been so treated, we have benefited all round. Things are looking up. There's a chance if we all pull together that we can get this church back on track. I now know exactly what I need to do in order to be living the victorious Christian life. And so on. I suggest that we love this kind of treatment because we are legalists at heart. We would love to be able to say that we have fulfilled all kinds of conditions, be they tarrying, surrendering fully, or getting rid of every known sin, so that God might truly bless us. It is a constant temptation to want to take our spiritual pulse and to apply the sanctificational barometer. This is not necessarily the same as the worthwhile discipline of self-examination. Self-examination is a way of uncovering and coming to terms with the very problem under review. True self-examination is a means of going back to the source of our salvation because it reminds us of the constant need of grace.

The preacher can aid and abet this legalistic tendency that is at the heart of the sin within us all. All we have to do is emphasize our humanity: our obedience, our faithfulness, our surrender to God, and so on. The trouble is that these things are all valid biblical truths, but if we get them out of perspective and ignore their relationship to the gospel of grace, they replace grace with law. If we constantly tell people what they should do in order to get their lives in order, we place a terrible legalistic burden on them. Of course we should obey God; of course we should love him with all our heart, mind, soul, and strength. The Bible tells us so. But if we ever give the impression that it is possible to do this on our own, not only do we make the gospel irrelevant, but we suggest that the law is in fact a lot weaker in its demands than it really is. Legalism demeans the law by reducing its standards to the level of our competence. There is a hopelessly misleading adage that one hears from time to time, and from people who ought to know better, that God does not require of us anything that we cannot give. This implies either that God requires less than perfection, or that perfection is less than perfect because we can achieve it. In fact the law of God was not framed according to the sinful human ability to keep it, but as an expression of the perfect character of God.

In practical terms, if we as preachers lay down the marks of the spiritual Christian, or the mature church, or the godly parent, or the obedient child, or the caring pastor, or the responsible elder, or the wise church leader, and if we do this in a way that implies that conformity is simply a matter of understanding and being obedient, then we are being legalists and we risk undoing the very thing we want to build up. We may achieve the outward semblance of conformity to the biblical pattern, but we do it at the expense of the gospel of grace that alone can produce the reality of these desirable goals. To say what we should be or do and not link it with a clear exposition of what God has done about our failure to be or do perfectly as he wills is to reject the grace of God and to lead people to lust after self-help and self-improvement in a way that, to call a spade a spade, is godless.

What Is Expository Preaching?

A cursory glance at the available literature will enable us to ascertain that the term "expository preaching" is fairly elastic. Most of us who aspire to employ the method believe that it is synonymous with truly biblical preaching, yet pinning down a working definition of it is not so easy. Harold Bryson[2] maintains that the usage of the word "expository" is fairly diverse: people mean different things by it. An anonymous thirteenth-century tract on preaching designates three main kinds of preaching, and this classification has been used in modern discussions of the subject.[3] So, it is said, the topical sermon uses a series of biblical passages to support a theme. A textual sermon takes a verse or short passage as a jumping-off point to a subject that may or may not be the focus of that text. "By contrast, expository preaching focuses predominantly on the text(s) under consideration along with its (their) context(s)."[4] While recognizing the dangers of trying to define such a dynamic concept as expository preaching, Haddon Robinson nevertheless proposes the following definition:

2. Harold T. Bryson, *Expository Preaching* (Nashville: Broadman, 1995), pp. 12-13.
3. Bryson, *Expository Preaching,* p. 12.
4. Richard L. Mayhue, "Rediscovering Expository Preaching," in *Rediscovering Expository Preaching,* ed. John MacArthur, Jr. (Dallas: Word, 1992), p. 9.

> Expository preaching is the communication of a biblical concept, de-
> rived from and transmitted through a historical, grammatical, and lit-
> erary study of a passage in its context, which the Holy Spirit first ap-
> plies to the personality and experience of the preacher, then through
> him to his hearers.[5]

There are some problems with this definition as it stands, but that only serves to show the difficulty we have in trying to get something down to a succinct general principle. Perhaps, without laboring the point of definition, we can propose that expository preaching is essentially the practice of explaining the meaning of a passage of Scripture. Bringing the Holy Spirit's role into the definition, as Robinson does, tends to a definition by results, as important as results are.[6] The expository sermon should, I believe, be defined in terms of the preacher's method and approach irrespective of its results. Any proclama-tion of the word requires the Holy Spirit to make it effective, and this is not distinct to expository preaching unless we maintain that all biblical preach-ing is expository.[7] Sidney Greidanus proposes the following definition:

> Expository preaching is "Bible-centered preaching." That is, it is
> handling the text "in such a way that its real and essential meaning as
> it existed in the mind of the particular Biblical writer and as it exists
> in the light of the over-all context of Scripture is made plain and ap-
> plied to the present-day needs of the hearers."[8]

Both Robinson and Greidanus agree that expository preaching is a matter of exposing the meaning of the biblical passage as it stands in its own context and in the wider context of the unity of Scripture. The wider context is essen-tial to the matter of application. Even those who take the invalid direct appli-cation approach (see diagram 8 above) can only do so because, unwittingly, they have assumed the structures demanding the valid approach. That is, they

---

5. Haddon W. Robinson, *Expository Preaching* (Leicester: IVP, 1986), p. 20. It is inter-esting that the British edition of this book has changed the American title, which is *Biblical Preaching* (Grand Rapids: Baker, 1980). It must be assumed that the terms were understood to be synonymous.

6. I am reminded of James I. Packer's important criticism of a definition of evangelism because it was tied to results, something that is not in our control: James I. Packer, *Evangelism and the Sovereignty of God* (London, Downers Grove: IVP, 1961, 1991), pp. 37-41.

7. This position, that all true preaching is expository preaching, is taken by Donald Miller (*The Way to Biblical Preaching* [Nashville: Abingdon, 1957]) and James Daane (*Preaching with Confidence* [Grand Rapids: Eerdmans, 1980]). Both these works are quoted in this connection in Sidney Greidanus, *The Modern Preacher and the Ancient Text* (Grand Rapids: Eerdmans, 1988), p. 11.

8. Greidanus, *The Modern Preacher,* p. 11, quoting from Merrill Unger, *Principles of Expository Preaching* (Grand Rapids: Zondervan, 1955), p. 33.

have assumed that there is an organic connection between the text and the believer that is more significant than being merely illustrative.

The long and the short of it is that this kind of expository preaching is a matter of responding to the Bible as it really is (see chapter 2). Textual and topical preaching, to use the terms suggested, are invalid if they abuse the nature of Scripture. If, for example, a text is simply a springboard to launch out into a discourse that has the flimsiest of relationships to what that text is about, it is clearly an abuse. However, it is possible, permissible, and at times extremely desirable to preach on a single verse, or even to focus on a single word. I would qualify this by saying that the verse, or word, must be dealt with according to the meaning it has in its own context. A word study that proceeds under the mistaken idea that meaning is inherent to a word is bound to lead astray. Meaning comes from the particular usage of the word in its context, and it needs that context to determine the meaning. The most basic meaningful communication unit is the sentence, and if we focus on a word or a phrase, it must be in the context of a meaningful unit. Thus, the smaller the textual unit, the stronger must be our qualification regarding its meaning in its context.

The essence of any approach to preaching that seeks to be truly biblical is the determination of the preacher to sit under the authority of the word of God. To do this we must come with one main agenda: to allow the Bible to dictate to us the nature of proclamation and the shape and content of our message. This does not ignore the fact, to be considered later, that different aims and circumstances may dictate the strategy we apply, but no strategy of preaching can afford to ignore the way God has spoken, the content of Scripture, and the forms that the scriptural message has taken under the inspiration of the Holy Spirit. The way to expository preaching is therefore the way of biblical theology pursued with an eye for the literary vehicle, and the historical context of the theological content.

Some scholars have suggested that the term "expository" be dropped in favor of "biblical" preaching. If we allow the basic etymological definition, that expository means to expose the meaning of the text, we must then proceed to ask how the meaning of the text is thus exposed. It is in this that the question of what we designate the style of sermon becomes rather academic. Most would agree, though some preachers seem to be slow to learn, that an expository sermon is not merely an exegetical exercise. The nature of the sermon is to apply the word of God to the wills of the hearers with a view to moving them to want to conform to that word. Exegesis is an important aspect of the preparation of any sermon, but exegesis is not the sermon. Exegesis seeks to understand what the text means in its own immediate context. A sermon must move from the meaning of the text to the legitimate application of that meaning to our contemporary context in the light of the gospel. This involves hermeneutics, and at the heart of hermeneutics is biblical theology. I would suggest that, once the basic exegetical matters of linguistics and literary form have been dealt with, the hermeneutical procedure demanded by the evangelical understanding of the Bible is the relating of the theological meaning of the text to the gospel. The key question of interpretation is, "How does this text testify to Christ?" The evangelical preacher needs to resist the modern hijacking of hermeneutics by purely literary and linguistic interests that ignore the ultimate purpose of God's word, which is to proclaim Christ to a lost world.

The Strategies of Different Teaching Contexts

There are different contexts within which the Bible will be expounded. They don't all involve formal sermonizing, but that in itself raises the question again about the essence of preaching. However, let us take a practical view of some typical expository (i.e., exposing the meaning of the biblical text) situations, which are formally very different. The one is the Sunday morning sermon in the context of a church service that, according to the denominational or local traditions, will be more or less formal. The second is an ongoing study of a biblical book undertaken by a small home-group belonging to the local church. The context is informal, the leadership is low-key, and the leadership of the group is shared by its members. The third is a family situation involving a parent or parents and some older children, say between twelve and sixteen years old, who are quite able to read the Bible and discuss it. We return to our original question: "Can I preach this sermon, lead this study, discuss the meaning of the daily Bible reading, without mentioning Jesus?"

The simple answer, based on the principles discussed thus far, is a resounding "NO!" No Bible passage yields its true significance without reference to Jesus Christ in his gospel. That is so basic that I sometimes wonder why we even need to raise the question. However, the strategy we use may differ from situation to situation. My concern here is to consider how flexible we can be in the strategy of Sunday preaching. I have been critical of the approach that sees the need to strike devotional paydirt at every turn. The desire for the happy thought, the immediate word from the Lord for the day, that every brief foray into the text must yield can easily lead to a distortion of the meaning of the text and substitute wishful thinking or romantic notions for reality.

Let us consider the family group at home first. The congregation here is fixed and constant, allowing for occasional absences of one or another family member and occasional interruptions to the family routine. The sense of continuity can be maintained when all the members are present and when all comprehend the lessons. We may conceive of a teaching unit that extends over many days, each day building on and revising the previous ones until the picture is complete. For example, the story of the exodus from Egypt may involve the progressive reading of Exodus 1–15 over two or three weeks, even longer. There may be pauses to pick up some of the background historical material, or to link these events with the story of Abraham's descendants and how they find themselves in Egypt. Recapitulating the Abrahamic promises or the Joseph narratives would be a useful exercise. Eventually, the whole event is read. Now, it is likely that in a Christian family of this kind and age distribution some one during this time would have raised the question of the relationship of these events to the gospel. However, assuming the question hasn't come up during the course of these studies, in a more formal way the question can still be asked at the end. The lesson of the Exodus is, certainly from an evangelical understanding of the Scriptures, a testimony to the nature of the gospel. There may be many other details to be picked up along the way: the qualities of the principal characters, something of the significance of the signs and wonders, attributes of God, and so on. Yet all these really only serve the main significance of the passage in the context of salvation history. They serve the gospel and, rightly understood, they increase our appreciation of what it means to know that Christ our Passover Lamb is sacrificed for us.

We can say a similar thing about the strategy of the small group. It will probably consist entirely of adults or of members of a senior youth group. Its continuity will inevitably be more at risk than the family group, but it will exist. Thus there will be a more relaxed feeling about the completeness of any one session. If time is lacking, there is always next week to take up the discussion again. There are some groups in which the members may be more mature and better read as Christians. In such cases again it is unlikely that members will allow the studies to go on for long before someone raises the question of the Christian application. Thus, in the family, or in the small group, or any other situation of fairly unstructured study of the Bible, and in which there is a high expectation of consistent, continuous attendance, the answer to our question may be modified. There may indeed be sessions of studying an Old Testament passage in which there is no mention made of Jesus, but in the end it would be a strangely defective study if the passage were discussed with only a few general moralizing remarks about Christian living as the outcome.

Let us come now to the sermon. There are at least two considerations here that lead me to suggest that every sermon, to be biblical, must include Jesus. The first is practical. Sermons preached in church are delivered inevitably to a more floating congregation. There will be the staunch regulars who can be depended on to be there every Sunday except when they are sick or away on holidays. There will be those who consider "regular" attendance to mean once a month. There will be those whose attachment to church-going is fairly loose, who will go when the weather is good and if they feel like it. Then there are those who have no real attachment to any church or particular congregation, and who are brought as a one-time venture by friends, or who just turn up. As a colleague of mine puts it, those who just happen to be there once ought to at least have the opportunity to hear what we are really on about. Thus, suppose we happen to have been preaching through an epistle and on that Sunday have arrived at the ethical exhortations. We happily expound on these and ignore the wider context of the gospel. In so doing, we confirm the visitors' worst misconceptions about Christianity: being a Christian, they now know, is indeed a matter of trying to live a good life. That consideration alone is sufficient, in my opinion, to make us think hard about the Christ-centeredness of our sermons.

The second consideration is the formal one of the actual nature of preaching. I have expressed myself on this matter in chapter 4. It needs only to be said that the nature of preaching, as we have looked at its biblical foundations, can only be truly defined in terms of the setting forth of the way of salvation. We have seen that the gospel event upon which our salvation is grounded must be carefully delineated in terms of the life, death, and resurrection of Jesus Christ. But the salvation that these events achieve is the whole process by which sinners under the judgment and wrath of God are reconciled, restored, justified, sanctified, and finally glorified. Salvation must be seen as the whole process culminating in the consummation of the kingdom. It is vital that we make clear that all of these fruits of the gospel are just that: fruits of the gospel, and not the fruits of self-effort or moral determination or whatever.

Any sermon, then, that aims to apply the biblical text to the congregation and does so without making it crystal clear that it is in Christ alone and through Christ alone that the application is realized, is not a Christian sermon. It is at best an exercise in wishful and pietistic thinking. It is at worst demonic in its Christ-denying legalism.

Types of Sermonizing

It should be clear by now that I favor the view that expository preaching means biblical preaching and that biblical preaching involves a great deal more than the exegesis of a biblical passage. Even if the sermon is well crafted so that the exegetical groundwork is not exposed but nevertheless provides a solid foundation for the accurate exposition of the passage, there is still the purpose of the sermon to apply the truth of God's word to the hearer. This application can only be achieved in terms of the gospel. Thus, a biblical passage explicated and then applied to the hearers does not constitute a biblical sermon if the application is made without reference to the person and work of Christ. Like Paul, the preacher must determine to know nothing among the congregation but Christ and him crucified.

In view of what I have been saying about biblical preaching, I would suggest that different types of sermonizing amount to different foci and different approaches to the biblical text. The intention of the sermons may vary according to the congregation's needs, but one tradition definitely needs to be qualified. This is the practice of some churches to have a "teaching" sermon in the morning service, and a "gospel" sermon in the evening. Such a distinction is fraught with danger, for it suggests that the gospel is only what gets us started as a Christian and is confined to evangelistic preaching, while the gospel is unnecessary for teaching Christians. This is clearly false. The distinction must therefore be made in terms of intention: conversion of unbelievers on the one hand, and edification of believers on the other. Both need the gospel, but the focus or emphasis will be different.

Expository preaching that is guarded from abuse by biblical theology is thus able to be turned in many directions. Topical sermons that address current ethical or social issues may need to rove further afield than the confines of one single passage, but the application of biblical theology will prevent texts from being used willy-nilly as spurious proof texts. Topical sermons might also focus on some doctrinal issue, but every sermon should be doctrinal in the sense that it exposes the biblical truths of the passage. Linking these truths with systematic theology is only one aspect of edifying a congregation. I suspect that there are no hard and fast rules in this matter other than to allow the biblical text itself to govern the way we present its content.

Letting the Old Testament Speak

Sooner or later the question arises as to whether the Old Testament can speak in and of itself to the Christian without a Christological interpretation. Related to this is the matter of how far we should allow the Old Testament passage to speak to its own situation before we look to its Christological fulfillment. These two questions are related but not the same. The second, on face value, is asking about the exegesis of the passage in its own context, and there is no doubt that we have to explore as fully as possible what the author was wanting to say to his contemporaries. This is basic to a sound understanding of the Bible: we need to understand what was being said, what the meaning of the passage is, before we can go on to consider its significance for the contemporary Christian. Once we have done a responsible job at the level of exegesis, however, there is still the matter of what we then do with the message. This is where the first of the above questions comes in.

It has been suggested that to answer this question in the negative and to require the fulfillment in Christ of all Old Testament passages is to deliver ourselves into a trap whereby we are left preaching the same message from all passages: "Ten thousand, thousand, are their texts, but all their sermons one!" This quip may indeed reflect a bad experience at the hands of a lazy preacher who has not bothered to explore the multifaceted revelation in the Bible. It may also reflect a very narrow idea of who and what Jesus is. It is easy to talk in pious tones about Jesus and the Lord while at the same time having very little notion of the richness of the biblical revelation concerning him. The idea that by preaching Christ in every sermon we thereby preach the same sermon is so appalling that one wonders how anyone could ever fall into such torpor. Far from taking the rich variety of the Old Testament and squeezing it through a narrow mold of superficial Jesus piety, preaching Christ from every part of the Bible should mean expanding this great variety into the endless riches of Christ the fulfiller. If we are not going to proclaim some aspect of the riches of Christ in every sermon, we shouldn't be in the pulpit.

In order to approach the questions posed above, I would like to add another. If we do not seek the Christological significance of the Old Testament passage on the grounds that it can speak directly to us in and of itself, what kind of application are we suggesting? I maintain that no Christian preacher ever lets the Old Testament speak purely in and of itself. The Christian preacher who operates on this theory of direct application of Old Testament texts is presumably not imagining for one moment that there is no distinction between his hearers and the original audience or readers. Even a modern Jewish preacher would have to make some adjustments when applying a text to his hearers. Christian preachers know that their hearers are not ancient Israelites, or Jews, or, in most cases, even modern Jews. Thus, the assumption is made that when God is spoken of it is the God of Jesus and the apostles. When this God addresses us as his people, we haven't suddenly become followers of Judaism. We remain Christians.

Can a Christian relate to God in any other way than through faith in Jesus Christ? We have noted that the New Testament could not allow such a proposition, for God is one and there is one mediator between God and man, the man Christ Jesus. What thus in fact happens when Christian preachers apply the Old Testament to their Christian hearers without mentioning Jesus is that the connection is made by implication and assumption. The preacher is assuming that the people are responding not as ancient Israelites but as modern Christians. Unless these people have two religions, two different notions of God, and two different ways of relating to him — one that they bring out for Old Testament passages, and the other for the New Testament — then they must be responding as Christians. The question is whether the preacher's application and the hearers' response is truly Christian and appropriate to the message. Why leave it to chance? To do so is pastorally irresponsible and homiletically sloppy.

Preparing a Sermon

The preparation of a sermon is essentially governed by the nature of the task: expounding the truth of God's word. The preacher is neither giving a lecture on an issue of public concern, nor engaging in an exercise in oratorical skills, nor entertaining, nor imparting some religious convictions or opinions. The preacher is exercising a sacred ministry of proclaiming the word of God. Since the task is God-given and involves the communication of an authoritative word, the preacher must also submit to the rule of this word. Prayerful diligence in preparation should mark the evangelical expository preacher. When we lose the sense of awe at the gravity and solemn nature of proclaiming God's word, it is certainly time to take stock and to seek to recover it. Such will only happen as we submit ourselves to the rule of God in our lives. Thus, in preparing a sermon we should pray that the Spirit of God will be active to reveal to us the riches of that word. Yet the Spirit's ministry is not an automatic and mystical thing. He works through our minds and our efforts to responsibly explain the biblical text.

Beyond the preacher's personal submission to the authority of God's word, the nature of the Bible demands at least three aspects in the preparation of a sermon: exegesis, hermeneutics, and homiletics. These are not strictly consecutive because they constantly interact. Exegesis is the formal analysis of the passage in which we seek to uncover what the author was saying. It involves us in a close reading of the text, a concern for its literary characteristics including linguistics and genre, and a general concern for its immediate historical and theological context.

Hermeneutics is often the neglected dimension in books on preaching, and, if it is mentioned, often little by way of concrete help is given on how to interpret a passage. The goal of interpretation, or hermeneutics, is nothing more nor less than to uncover the links between the ancient text and the contemporary hearer (or reader) of the Bible. I have emphasized in this study that these links are not intuitive, nor are they a matter of some mystical direct communication of the Spirit. They come from the nature of the Bible as a book about Christ. Biblical theology is the discipline of seeking to understand the structure of biblical revelation, which enables us to make the correct connections between any text and the contemporary hearer. Biblical theology shows that the essence of hermeneutics lies in the fact that every part of the Bible leads us to Christ, and thus to the believer who is in Christ. A neglect of biblical theology means putting ourselves and our hearers in danger of losing the way so that an unbiblical application is substituted for the biblical one. Biblical theology is, I submit, a matter of giving free rein to the great Protestant principle that was enunciated at the Reformation: Scripture interprets itself.

The third aspect of sermon preparation is the homiletic application. Biblical theology shows us the theological link between what the text meant in its own context and what it means in relation to the gospel. The preacher's pastoral role is to make the links to the specific needs of the congregation. Obviously the preacher cannot address the individual need of every person in the congregation, even if these needs were known, but he can instruct people so that they learn to make the specific application themselves. More importantly, the homiletic task involves the distinct role of proclamation of the word of the sovereign Lord. The biblical message must be conveyed as God's word to us all in the here and now; a word that carries supreme authority and that we ignore to our spiritual peril. Here it is pertinent to mention a point made by James Packer: the preacher is part of the message.[9] While the preacher has a task of addressing others, the word of God comes to all alike, both preacher and congregation.

The Preacher's Christian Education Program

It would be pastorally irresponsible for any preacher with oversight of a congregation to imagine that the sermon can ever be a sufficient diet for the healthy life and growth of the individual and the congregation as a whole. It in no way diminishes the importance of the sermon and the ministry of preaching to say that we all need more exposure to biblical truth than can be provided for in forty to fifty sermons a year. That is why personal Bible study and small-group study are so important. Yet so often these are left to chance and, where they do exist, there is often no pastoral leadership. The entire

---

9. James I. Packer, "The Preacher as Theologian," in *When God's Voice Is Heard: Essays on Preaching Presented to Dick Lucas,* ed. C. Green and D. Jackman (Leicester: IVP, 1995), p. 88.

ministerial needs of the congregation need to be examined, and some kind of plan for adult Christian education is vital as a means of supplementing the preaching ministry and aiding its application to the life of the church.

There are a number of biblical principles that apply to Christian education and cannot be ignored. To begin with, we understand that service and ministry are the same thing. More and more churches have come to recognize that the professional, paid, full-time ministry, however we understand ordination, functions mainly in the capacity of leadership and oversight. It is recognized that ministry is the role of every believer. The recovery of the emphasis on the recognition of spiritual gifts was simply the return to an understanding that "ministry" was not restricted to the ordained leader's activities, but that every member is a minister with the potential for an identifiable ministerial role. Christian education is the equipping of people to exercise these ministerial roles. It can be done haphazardly or it can be done with an eye to the reason for its existence and with a concern for doing it effectively.

A manifesto, or creed, for a local church program of adult Christian education might look something like this:

> *We believe:*
> That every believer in Jesus Christ is part of the body of Christ.
> That God calls us to express this fact through fellowship with a local congregation.
> That God gives to every believer spiritual gifts for the benefit of the body.
> That God calls every believer to serve by using gifts and talents.
> That believers need to be equipped for such service through teaching and training.

We cannot begin to expand on such a set of principles without first acknowledging again the centrality of the gospel. The life and ministry of the local church needs to be self-consciously gospel-centered if it is to maintain any kind of effectiveness for the kingdom of God. When thinking of a Christian education strategy we recognize at least four main areas that are implicated by the gospel:

1. Reconciliation to God through the gospel means a new attitude to God's word and thus to the study of the Bible. Nothing can substitute for knowledge of what the Bible contains.
2. From our study of the Bible we gain an understanding of what God is like, the way God works in the world, and how God relates to us and to the world. This means that the main outcome of our study of the Bible

is the formation of theology, which is a worldview based on God and his self-revelation.

3. The practical application of theology to the believer's individual existence and corporate life in the congregation and in the world involves us in the concern for Christian living. The gospel calls us to a life that is always seeking to be conformed to the truth as it is in Jesus.

4. Some forms of Christian service require very specific ministry skills. Individual Christians should be concerned to know what their God-given gifts are, and to be trained to use them effectively.

A comprehensive Christian education program, then, will be designed with an eye to the need for every Christian to be nurtured in the four areas of Bible knowledge, theology or Christian doctrine, practical issues of Christian living, and skills for particular ministries. It is clear that the differentiation of these four areas does not imply that they are completely separate. They do in fact interact, and there are other ways that we could analyze the implications of the gospel. Yet if we are to implement an effective Christian education program, we need to be analytical about it so that it does not end up being a kind of smorgasbord program with people dabbling in different things as the mood takes them.

Furthermore, in any properly functioning congregation there will be the potential for at least four kinds or levels of Christian education:

1. Basic or entry level. In this we provide for newcomers or inquirers into the Christian faith, for those seeking for meaning from Christianity, or for those who are feeling their way into involvement with a church for the first time.

2. General level. This would provide for any believers who want to grow in spiritual understanding and to mature as Christians.

3. Training level. This is designed for those whose spiritual gifts have at least been tentatively identified and who are aiming at specific areas of service involving specific skills.

4. Leadership level. This is designed for those who, through spiritual maturity and the use of gifts, display the potential to have the oversight in some specific area of ministry in the local church.

Pastors of smaller churches might seriously question whether such a scheme is workable in any but the larger congregations that have plenty of mature leadership and ministerial resources already in place. I would suggest, however, that the principles remain the same whatever the size of the local church, and that it is a matter of the ministerial priorities that we decide on. If a small church is to grow there are a number of matters to be taken care of, not the least being a strategy for evangelism. If the pastor in charge understands the various levels of need, these can be taken care of as the resources arise. Let us assume that evangelism is recognized as a chief implication of the gospel being the gospel. That is, growth for growth's sake is not what we are about; we want to grow because we believe it to be God's will that his church will grow. Consequently, we want to see people converted and saved from a Christless eternity. What kind of training do people need to be evangelists? The answer is "none" and "all they can get." That is, on the one hand, getting converted is all the start you need to evangelize; on the other hand, it certainly helps to get some basic training if it is available. We must not give the impression that one needs a diploma in evangelism before one can tell friends and relatives about Jesus. Yet we want people to reach their full potential by training them.

Let us think of an "average," moderately sized congregation of, say, one hundred and fifty adult members. It will inevitably have a children's Sunday School program, probably a youth group or two, and may well have several small groups of adults meeting at regular intervals in private homes. The old tradition of a mid-week Bible Study *cum* Prayer Meeting seems to be almost a thing of the past. At the beginning of every year the pastor makes earnest appeals for volunteers to staff the Sunday School and to do other routine jobs. Meanwhile, the home groups form and function on an *ad hoc* basis, and probably have little or no oversight or assistance from the pastor. The youth groups are probably being run by untrained young people who have zeal but little knowledge. Thus, we have a local church in which a number of people are exercising important Bible-teaching and pastoral ministries with no training and varying degrees of spiritual maturity and understanding.[10] A number of church members are also doing important ministry in the home as they seek to nurture their children in the faith, again without any training other than what they have picked up themselves.

It would seem to me that the pastor of such a congregation would need to set some priorities in ministry. Preaching must remain high on the list for, until a workable Christian education program is in place, the sermon will be the main Bible teaching that many will receive. Then, even when such a program is in place, preaching will always be a uniquely important aspect of the life of the congregation. Surely another high priority is to begin with a small group of potential leaders and teachers and to give them basic instruction in biblical theology. It is astonishing that we so readily accept the situation of an entire children's program run by volunteers who have had, for the most

---

10. Packer, "The Preacher as Theologian," p. 83, refers to the dangers of inductive studies that "tell you to 'observe' without giving you any theological orientation to help you to do it."

part, little or no training in Bible and biblical theology. Sunday School teachers need training. At the same time, some oversight should be exercised in the area of curricula and the study materials being used in Sunday School and small groups. If what is currently being used is moralistic and not gospel-centered, it should be replaced. That is not always easy to do, so at least the teachers and leaders should be made aware of the issues. What better way to do this than to instruct them in biblical theology.[11]

---

11. My book *According to Plan: The Unfolding Revelation of God in the Bible* (Leicester: IVP, 1991) was written as a course of instruction for use in the local church when I was Christian Education Minister at the Coorparoo Anglican Church in Brisbane. I used it as the text for a course in biblical theology run over some twenty-five weeks, meeting for two hours on a weeknight. It would be possible to give the rudiments of the subject in much less time, but it is important enough to spend the time. Over the five years or so that I ran the course about a hundred people took advantage of it. My *Gospel and Kingdom: A Christian Interpretation of the Old Testament* (Exeter: Paternoster, 1981) was also written for a similar purpose, more specifically to assist Christian preachers and teachers in dealing with the Old Testament. It was based on a course in biblical theology that I taught at Moore Theological College in 1973-74, and was written with the encouragement of the students.

PART 2

THE PRACTICAL APPLICATION
OF BIBLICAL THEOLOGY TO PREACHING

Christ in All the Scriptures

The Literary Genres

As we come to think now of the practical issues of biblical theology applied to sermon preparation, we need to say a few words about the various dimensions we have to deal with as we approach the biblical text. The first of these is that of the literary genre. It is not only in the technical field of biblical studies that this issue arises — it is a factor in any literary communication. We take it for granted that there are different ways to communicate through the spoken and written word and most people have little difficulty in adapting to different forms. It is so much a part of our culture that we move from one genre of communication to another without giving it a moment's thought. There are accepted conventions for scientific prose, for the short story, for a wedding invitation, or for a real estate advertisement in the newspaper, and we easily distinguish between them. When we come to the Bible, it does not take long for the new reader to grasp that a piece of historical narrative looks and sounds different from a psalm, a prophetic oracle, or a parable.

In part 2 we will consider some of the main biblical literary genres from the point of view of the literature as the vehicle for the theological truth of biblical revelation. It is less important for the preacher to be able to pin down the definition of genre, or to tabulate all the genres of the Bible, than it is to be aware that literature is used in different ways for different functions. Our aim should be to understand how the truth of God's word is variously communicated and to respond appropriately to the text in our exegesis. Within larger units that may be classified according to the predominant genre we may find various subgenres or kinds of literary expression. There will inevitably be gray areas where there may be some debate about genre and how the literary text is functioning, but on the whole we stand by the principles of the essential clarity of Scripture and its self-interpreting nature.

To illustrate, let us take as an example the theme of going on a journey. The same general concept can be dealt with using different genres or types of literary expression that produce quite different results in the significance of the passage. Compare the following passages all dealing with some kind of journey:

> The whole congregation of the Israelites set out from Elim; and Israel came to the wilderness of Sin, which is between Elim and Sinai. (Exod. 16:1)

> Even though I walk through the valley of the shadow of death, I fear no evil; for you are with me; your rod and your staff — they comfort me. (Ps. 23:4)

> Those who trust in their own wits are fools; but those who walk in wisdom come through safely. (Prov. 28:26)

> He brought me in visions of God, to the land of Israel, and set me down upon a very high mountain, on which was a structure like a city to the south. (Ezek. 40:2)

> A man was going down from Jerusalem to Jericho, and fell into the hands of robbers. (Luke 10:30)

> I know a person in Christ who fourteen years ago was caught up to the third heaven — whether in the body or out of the body I do not know; God knows. (2 Cor. 12:2)

The first comes in the context of historical narrative and purports to relate events that happened in history. The second uses metaphor to describe a hypothetical experience of serious adversity in life, and possibly death itself. The third describes a style of life as a walk characterized by wisdom. The fourth deals with a prophet's visionary experience, real or imagined, in which he visualizes being transported to a distant but real place. The fifth is the beginning of a story, the point of which does not depend upon this having actually happened in real life. The last describes some kind of spiritual experience that someone claims to have had. Whether these passages are found in the context of formally identified genres is not the most important consideration. The preacher needs to be able to identify how the particular literary expression is intended to function. If the formal identification of literary genre can assist in that process, so much the better. But, being able to label the genre is not as important as understanding the nuances of each literary expression and what the author wants to achieve by it.

Broadly speaking, by genre we mean a class or group of literary texts that are marked out by certain common features that enable us to distinguish them from other texts. As John Barton has indicated, the identification of genre enables us to avoid reading a given text as something that it is not.[1] If there are literary genres, there are also genres of speech, and it was one of the concerns of form criticism to attempt to identify speech genres that lay behind the written text. Because a genre may include a whole book, such as a Gospel or an epistle, within which other genres may occur, such as a parable or a hymn of praise, Sidney Greidanus has suggested a tiered approach to literary analysis.[2] He designates the whole Bible as proclamation. Within the Bible we have the major genres of narrative, prophecy, wisdom, psalm, gospel, epistle, and apocalypse. Greidanus suggests that we use the familiar word "form" to describe the genres that occur within these major genres. Thus, in dealing with the book of Proverbs, the genre of the book overall is wisdom. Within that broad genre we have the distinct literary forms of instruction, proverbial saying, and numerical saying. The Gospel according to Matthew belongs to the genre of gospel. As we read it we encounter first a genealogy, then birth narratives, collected sayings, the Sermon on the Mount, many parables interwoven into narrative contexts, and so on. Each of these needs to be understood for what it is intended to do within the wider literary context. In this part we shall be mainly concerned with trying to understand how different literary genres function as vehicles for theological truth.

The Historical Progression

The characteristics of the various literary genres can never be looked at apart from the historical and salvation-historical contexts in which they occur. When, for example, we examine the biblical literature for wisdom genres, we find that there are wisdom sayings that predate the major wisdom books, there are the wisdom books themselves, there are wisdom sayings in the Gospels, and there are wisdom sayings in the post-Pentecost New Testament literature, notably the Epistle of James. While it is important to understand in

1. John Barton, *Reading the Old Testament: Method in Biblical Study,* 2nd ed. (London: Darton, Longman, and Todd, 1996), p. 16.
2. Sidney Greidanus, *The Modern Preacher and the Ancient Text* (Grand Rapids: Eerdmans, 1988), pp. 22-23.

general literary terms how an aphoristic proverb functions,[3] the theological function of a proverbial saying in one of the Gospels may be very different from the function of the proverbial sayings in Proverbs. The progression of salvation history remains a key consideration in the way we understand texts and relate them to the Christian. This is particularly pertinent to our consideration of narrative text since it is the principal vehicle for the formation of the historical structure of the Bible.

The Theological Epochs

Because the Bible is the revelation of God given within the specific context of salvation history, I have sought to explain the overall structure of this revelation. This can only be done in theological terms. In diagram 8 I have suggested a right way and a wrong way of approaching the interpretation of a text. The right way involves us in a movement from the text through the theological structure of the Bible in order to make the valid link to the contemporary hearer. In this second part of the book I want to apply this principle to some of the major forms or genres of biblical literature in their historical context. If we use diagram 9 (on p. 139) as a simple outline of biblical structure, we are able to identify the position of any text that we happen to be dealing with. It is important to identify whether the text relates to epoch A, (the kingdom revealed in Israel's history), epoch B (the kingdom revealed in prophetic eschatology), or epoch C (New Testament witness to the kingdom revealed in Christ). The genre of the text will help us identify its function within that epoch of revelation. We attempt to identify that function in terms of its theological contribution to the overall kingdom revelation of that particular epoch. We then move to identify the way this theological contribution comes to its fruition and fulfillment, that is, how it testifies to Christ and is given its final significance by Christ. That the whole Bible testifies to Christ is what we mean when we say that Christ is in all the Scriptures. It is because of this that the preacher must ask the question of every sermon, "Did the sermon show how the text testifies to Christ?"

In the chapters that follow, some of the main literary genres are considered in turn for their relationship to the progression of redemptive history, with a view to providing the biblical-theological context for individual texts. A number of examples are given that are chosen purely on the basis of the desire to examine a variety of texts. There is no intention to highlight only prominent or theologically important texts. In some cases I have chosen texts

3. An aphorism is a short, pithy saying.

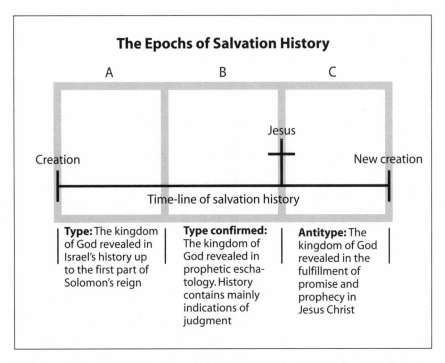

The Epochs of Salvation History

A   B   C

Jesus

Creation   New creation

Time-line of salvation history

| **Type:** The kingdom of God revealed in Israel's history up to the first part of Solomon's reign | **Type confirmed:** The kingdom of God revealed in prophetic eschatology. History contains mainly indications of judgment | **Antitype:** The kingdom of God revealed in the fulfillment of promise and prophecy in Jesus Christ |

Diagram 9: The three salvation history epochs which establish the typological context of biblical interpretation. The literary genre of the text must be identified in this framework of history and theology if a valid link is to be made with the contemporary hearer.

that might not be considered as the most productive of preaching material. My aim is, by this means, to cover a selection of texts that are representative of the whole range of biblical material.

CHAPTER 10

Preaching from Old Testament Historical Narrative Texts

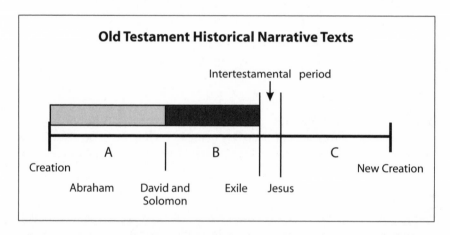

Diagram 10: Old Testament historical narrative text occurs across two epochs. In A the narrative has the primary focus on the outworking of salvation and the revealing of the kingdom of God. The secondary focus is on judgment. In B the primary focus is on decline and judgment, but there is a secondary focus on restoration and the pattern of the kingdom of God.

Historical Narrative Texts in Biblical-Theological Context

At the outset an important distinction should be made between two broad and very different approaches to preaching from narrative historical texts. In a landmark study some years ago, Sidney Greidanus looked at these two approaches in the context of a controversy in the Dutch Reformed Church (Gereformeerde Kerken) during the 1930s and early 1940s in the Netherlands.[1] The matter at the heart of this controversy is as relevant today as it was then. It has to do with whether historical texts should be treated mainly for their exemplary value or for their contribution to and place in salvation history. In exemplary preaching the characters in the narrative serve as examples of godly or godless living as the case may be. A particular character, for example, Nehemiah, may be chosen as the means of teaching principles of leadership or some other quality. Yet, to take this approach often involves the preacher in some very big assumptions about the character. Are principles of excellent leadership the only lessons to learn from Nehemiah? Biblical characters, even major ones, are frequently ambiguous as to their exemplary value. It is not always clear whether some characteristic or action is recounted intentionally as a blemish or as a virtue. We need to evaluate the biblical characters, even the great heroes of faith, in the light of the larger perspective of salvation history. In opting for a salvation history approach we do not thereby rule out any appeal to biblical characterization. It is a matter of the perspective of the text as a whole. If we must see narratives in terms of characters, then let us remember that the chief character in the unfolding drama of redemption is God himself.

Historical narrative texts in the Old Testament span the two epochs of salvation history. In the first epoch (A in the diagram), which we have designated as running from the beginning of biblical history up to and including the first part of Solomon's reign, the emphasis is on the way of salvation and the nature of the kingdom of God. The preamble to this is, of course, the creation and the fall into sin. From Genesis 4 onward there is a steady buildup of the picture of God's gracious dealings with humankind, leading to salvation and the kingdom. We have noted the way Genesis 4–11 acts as a preparatory stage to the calling of Abraham and the giving of the covenant promises. These promises to Abraham provide the basis for the unfolding of all subsequent events up to the climax with King David. The promises to David in 2 Samuel 7 find immediate, if partial, fulfillment in Solomon, who actually rounds off the glory of David's reign with the building of the temple.

Narrative historical texts dealing with the post-Solomonic decline of Israel provide overall a very negative focus (epoch B in the diagram). From the salvation-historical perspective, the nature of the kingdom of God and the way of salvation are essentially in place. The decline is not only a commentary on the effects of human sin but also a demonstration that, despite the glories of David's reign, the kingdom is not yet. We remember from our Christian standpoint that the original plan and purpose of God was the kingdom

---

1. Sidney Greidanus, *Sola Scriptura: Problems and Principles in Preaching Historical Texts* (Toronto: Wedge, 1970). Greidanus is concerned with working out the principles that should govern preaching from historical texts.

brought about through the suffering and death of his Son. We must never regard the gospel as an afterthought because things went wrong in Israel. The gospel was always God's forethought to everything, including creation, for how else can God have chosen us in Christ before the foundation of the world (Eph. 1:4)? It is important, then, to remind ourselves in sermon preparation that the gospel is God's forethought to the entire historical process in the Old Testament.

There are narrative texts that are not historical but occur as stories told within the historical narrative. These are mostly classifiable under other genres and need to be handled accordingly, though their placement within the historical narrative will always be an important consideration in preaching. For example, there is the telling of Jotham's fable, the narrative portions of Job, the recounting of dreams and visions, and, in the New Testament, Jesus' parables, all of which are different from the normal historical narrative. Mostly the narrative material can be regarded as historical writing even though it wouldn't necessarily satisfy the secular historical critic.

To sum up the salvation history perspective on narrative texts, we see that there are two main areas or epochs. In the first (epoch A) we will be looking for the text's function in the overall pattern of salvation and the kingdom of God that is revealed up to the first part of Solomon's reign. The focus of a particular text may be mainly negative, as in the judgment at the flood, the confusion of tongues at Babel, the captivity in Egypt, the judgment on Israel for Aaron's golden calf, the wandering in the wilderness, or the defeat at the hands of the Philistines. Nevertheless, in this epoch the focus is principally on the positive. The major thrust of the narrative as a whole is the revelation of blessing in the form of the promise and its fulfillment in the kingdom of David and Solomon. Bear in mind that both the positive and negative aspects are vital to an understanding of salvation since being saved is being rescued from sin and judgment. So, the positive will be seen in the salvation of Noah, the promises to Abraham, the exodus from captivity in Egypt, the constitution of the nation as the people of God at Sinai, the entry into and possession of Canaan, the kingship, and the temple.

In the second epoch (B in diagram 10), when things are going from bad to worse in Israel's history, the main focus of historical narrative is the judgment that overtakes the nation as it splits into two, and as each part in turn is destroyed. The final indignity is for the descendants of Abraham to be deprived of every material pledge of God's blessing: the land, the temple, the kingship. Yet it is not all doom and gloom in this period. Leaving aside for the moment the massive contribution of the prophets in projecting the hope for a future kingdom of God, there is still the positive side of things in the history of triumph in the face of adversity, especially as recorded in Daniel 1–6 and in the book of Esther. Then, with the Persian victory over Babylon comes the release of captive nations and the return to the homeland of a remnant of Jews as recorded in Ezra and Nehemiah. The latter two books give a tantalizing account of reconstruction that has all the promise and potential of becoming the real restoration promised by the prophets, yet all the time falling short. This potential restoration stands as a reminder to the people that their history is the context in which God has acted in the past and will again act definitively in the future.

At the risk of oversimplification, it could be said that the historical texts of the first epoch, especially from Abraham to David, are texts that come under the covenant with Abraham; it is the age of promise. However, it is also the age, as we have seen, in which the definitive pattern of salvation and the kingdom is revealed as the content of the promise. Then, those texts coming in the second epoch, from Solomon's apostasy to the end of the Old Testament, fall in the age of prophecy. It is important to recognize this. In fact, I would go so far as to say that most of the misuses of narrative text occur because this point is not appreciated. The "gospel" thrust of narrative texts comes either from the covenant promises (epoch A) or the prophetic eschatology (epoch B), both of which provide the biblical-theological context for the texts. It is impossible to understand the theological function of a given text unless we understand how it relates to the promises of the covenant or to the eschatology of the prophets. When we consider the nature of prophetic eschatology in more detail, we shall see that it is like a second-stage rocket propelling the Abrahamic covenant toward its fulfillment. Let us, then, consider a few representative narrative historical texts from the point of view of their biblical-theological context and significance.

1. The Story of Noah (Genesis 6–9)

The preacher must devise a workable strategy for a single sermon or a series of sermons and then decide how much background is necessary to set the stage for the audience. The theological context of all preaching is of course creation, fall, and God's plan of salvation, so I will not continue to reiterate that obvious point. Noah, then, is placed in the context of increasing human wickedness and the judgment of God. The saving event illustrates a number of important themes that are developed in the later redemptive history. We might mention here the election of Noah, the plan of salvation, the response of faith, and so on. But also we can see in this account an expression of the reality of the kingdom. As creation results in a "kingdom" consisting of God meeting his people, Adam and Eve, in the place he prepares for them, namely Eden, so in the flood narrative we have a "kingdom" situation as God deals with his own people, Noah and his family, in the prepared salvation context that is the ark. The story of Noah is more than one of obedient faith in that it is part of the larger picture of God preserving a people for himself in a direct line to Abraham, and thus to David and to Christ.

The references to Noah in the New Testament are not numerous, but they are significant. These passages highlight the saving function of the ark (1 Pet. 3:20-22; 2 Pet. 2:5) or Noah's faith (Heb. 11:7). Jesus refers to the Noah event as having parallels with the final day of salvation and the coming of the Son of Man (Matt. 24:36-39; Luke 17:26-27). There is more than enough in these passages to enable the preacher to link the Noah story to the final salvation and judgment and to raise the question as to how these texts testify to Christ. There is a practical question that persistently emerges in this regard. If it all has its fulfillment in Christ and the gospel, why not forget about trying to preach from the Old Testament and simply concentrate on the New? There is a short answer to that and a long answer. The long answer has to do with all that I have been discussing regarding the unity of Scripture as a book about Christ. The short answer is that the New Testament insists on sending us back to the Old Testament as part of its overall message about Christ. Who are we to argue!

2. Ruth

The human interest value of the story of Ruth is immense, and the temptation for the preacher is to treat it at the purely exemplary level. Again, let me stress that the human factor is integral to the text, and we should not overreact against a character study. The important thing is to keep it in perspective with the major thrust of the narrative. In the case of Ruth we need to try to understand the purpose of the book and to make sure that any character analysis assists in expounding that purpose. On one occasion I was asked to preach on Ruth, chapter 1. It was a one-time sermon and not part of a series. Nevertheless, I was asked to deal with the text under the topical heading of "Dealing with self-pity." Chapter 1 tells how Naomi and Elimelech go with their two sons to Moab to live because of a famine in Israel. The husband dies, and the two sons marry Moabite women. Then the two sons die, and Naomi decides to return to Israel. One daughter-in-law turns back to Moab, but the other, Ruth, returns with Naomi. When they reach Bethlehem Naomi tells of how God has dealt bitterly with her and brought calamity upon her. At the end of chapter 1, even if Naomi is expressing a certain amount of self-pity, there is no discussion of how she deals with it.

In thinking through my approach to this task I decided that I had to look at the overall message of the book of Ruth. Only then could the real significance of chapter 1 emerge. Had I been given the task of preaching a series of four sermons, one on each chapter, I would have had to follow the structure of the whole book. I now had to relate that structure and overall message in one sermon. Whichever strategy was chosen, biblical theology would still need to inform the hermeneutics of the text. In the Hebrew canon, Ruth is one of the Five Scrolls of the third section, the Writings *(ketubim).* The main consideration here is whether this placement among the five "festal" scrolls should perhaps alert us to the perceived theological significance along with the historical.

The narrative of Ruth clearly purports to be history in that the book's resolution leads to the genealogy of David. The four chapters delineate four main episodes:

1. Chapter 1 poses the problem: Naomi is left destitute. Yet the seeds of the solution are there in the young Moabite woman who forsakes her old life and embraces Naomi's life, her people, and her God.
2. Chapter 2 develops the solution as the daughter-in-law finds favor with a kinsman who can perform the role of "redeemer."
3. Chapter 3 takes up this redeemer role and develops it.
4. Chapter 4 shows the solution to Naomi's problem: Boaz will be the redeemer and marry Ruth. While the story seems to focus on Ruth, in the end the people see the solution as Naomi's. The child born to Ruth and Boaz is hailed as Naomi's son.

So much for the story, but where are the biblical-theological links to salvation history? The desolation of Naomi is removed as she becomes, through Ruth, the ancestress of King David. One aspect of the idea of redemption is filled out for us in the role of Boaz. But what of Ruth? Are we left only with her clearly attractive character of tenacity and faithfulness, of integrity and trust? Some might add foolhardiness to that list. The description of Ruth is not totally unambiguous, but one characteristic keeps on being stressed: she is a Moabite. The story moves from the introduction of the Moabite to the genealogy of the Messiah.[2] It is not too much to suggest that we see two aspects of the relationship of Israel to the gentiles. First, the restrictions imposed on dealings with the Moabites in Deuteronomy 23:2-6 appear to be overridden in Ruth. In general terms Israel's contact with the nations was proscribed, but every now and then a special case arises that shows God's purpose of including the gentiles. Second, the fact that the Messiah-king is part Moabite may seem to be unacceptable, but it clearly foreshadows one of the main themes of the Bible: the purpose of God to include a multi-

---

2. M. D. Gow, *The Book of Ruth: Its Structure, Theme and Purpose* (Leicester: Apollos, 1992).

tude drawn out of every nation, tribe, and language group in his kingdom. The preacher should not neglect the potential of the Ruth narrative as a missionary text.

3. Bringing the Ark to Jerusalem (2 Samuel 6)

Here we are reaching the climax of the epoch of historical revelation of the kingdom of God. The account of David bringing the ark to Jerusalem can be considered from at least two historical perspectives: it is part of the history of the ark and part of the history of David's rise. In 1 Samuel the ark goes on a journey from the sanctuary because of the foolishness of the Israelites in the face of the Philistine threat. The ark is first taken into battle in the hope it will guarantee success for Israel. The reverse is the result, and the ark is captured and taken to the Philistine city of Ashdod. It proves too hot for the Philistines to handle and is eventually returned to the Israelites. But it also proves too hot for the Israelites, and it is stowed in the house of Abinadab. Apart from one disputed reference to it in 1 Samuel 14:18, we do not hear of the ark again until 2 Samuel 6.

In the period from the ark's journey to Philistia and back the whole question of kingship has developed. Beginning during the ministry of Samuel the prophet and judge, the matter is raised, disputed, and eventually resolved for a time with the kingship of Saul. When Saul's kingship fails the test, David is chosen by God to succeed. The history of David's rise begins with his anointing in 1 Samuel 16. Though chosen and anointed, he is rejected and driven out. Not until the death of Saul at the hands of the Philistines is David able to make a real comeback and to establish his kingship. Throughout this process he is shown to be reluctant to do anything other than to allow Yahweh to vindicate him and bring his anointing to fruition. In 2 Samuel 5 David is anointed king over Israel at Hebron. He then captures Jerusalem, which is called Zion, the city of David. In chapter 6 the move to transfer the ark to Jerusalem signals David's intention to establish Jerusalem as the center of faith and rule.

The ark is brought from the house of Abinadab, but on the way Uzzah is killed for reaching out to touch the ark. David is afraid and leaves the ark at another house, but the owner is unexpectedly "blessed," so David decides to move it again. With great rejoicing, and with David dancing before it, the ark is brought to Jerusalem. The dynastic tension is relieved when David's wife Michal, a daughter of Saul, despises David and is condemned to be childless. The bringing up of the ark is the prelude to the events of chapter 7 in which David expresses a desire to build a temple for Yahweh. The theological highpoint is the covenant with David and the promise that David's descendants would possess the throne forever, and that David's son will be the son of God.

There are many possibilities for composing a sermon out of 2 Samuel 6. Whatever emphasis is adopted, it is important that the events be seen in their context of the wider salvation history. The history of the ark goes back to the activation of the promises to Abraham in the Exodus and the giving of the Sinai law. In this we can see the direct theological link between the covenant with Abraham, the covenant with Israel at Sinai, and the focusing of these promises on one representative Israelite as the son of God, namely, the Davidic prince. The story of the bringing of the ark to Jerusalem could be seen as the opportunity for the preacher to explore some of the secondary themes: the death of Uzzah, the blessing of Obed-edom, or the cursing of the Saulide dynasty in Michal. But if these are not seen in their redemptive-historical context, the whole point of their being in the narrative will be missed. To understand the relationship of this text to the gospel, we must be ready to pursue the great themes of kingship, the dwelling of God among his people, and the temple.

4. Nehemiah Builds the Walls of Jerusalem (Nehemiah 2–6)

I want to avoid referring only to the easy and obviously salvation-oriented texts. The fact that there are difficult texts does raise the question of choosing a text. Few preachers would aspire to preach through every book of the Bible while exercising the pulpit ministry in any one church. Few would imagine that Paul had any such project in mind when he spoke to the Ephesian elders of "declaring to you the whole counsel of God" (Acts 20:27). Given that we can only hope to preach from a somewhat limited selection of texts, would it not be better to leave the difficult and more obscure ones alone? We recognize that not all texts speak as directly of the gospel truths as others, and so the question arises whether there are some texts that we ought to just leave out of consideration for preaching programs. Elizabeth Achtemeier identifies one source of problematic in the fact that many stories in the Old Testament do not fit our preconceived ideas of God.[3] This is particularly true of the so-called moral difficulties attached to stories of bloodshed and slaughter. However, John Bright commented on this subject, "I find it most interesting and not a little odd that although the Old Testament on occasion offends our Christian feelings, it did not apparently offend Christ's 'Christian feelings'!"[4]

---

3. Elizabeth Achtemeier, *Preaching Hard Texts of the Old Testament* (Peabody, Mass.: Hendrickson, 1998), p. xii.
4. John Bright, *The Authority of the Old Testament* (London: SCM, 1967), p. 77.

In turning to the episode in question, the preacher may again be tempted to see the main human character as the principal focus for sermonizing. There is obviously much that can be learned from a study of the characters of both Ezra and Nehemiah. These are two faithful men with different strategic roles in the reconstruction of the Jewish state after the terrible devastation of the fall of the kingdoms of Israel and Judah and the exile in Babylon. It would be a shame, however, if the preacher became so involved with these personalities that the real function of the narratives of the two books were to be overlooked.

The salvation-historical context of the books of Ezra and Nehemiah involves us in a theological understanding of the historical events within the canon of Scripture.[5] The return of the Jews after the decree of Cyrus in 538 B.C. was understood in both political and prophetic terms. The theological context is the prophetic hope for the restoration of all that had been lost in the exile. Furthermore, the prophets variously described what would transpire in such a restoration as the coming of the glorious kingdom of God. Predictions such as Jeremiah's of a seventy-year exile followed by the return would be taken as evidence that the decree of Cyrus was the instrumental means of the fulfillment of this hope. By the time of this edict all the eschatological oracles of the prophets, except those of the three postexilic prophets and Daniel, would have been heard. There was no reason to suppose that the return from Babylon would not be the prelude to the great day of the Lord and the glorious restoration of all things.

The reality, as we discover from Ezra and Nehemiah, and the postexilic prophets, is another story. On the positive side there is indeed a kind of second exodus from captivity, but the returning exiles are, as some of the prophets had predicted, a remnant. With the encouragement of the Persians, the Jews are able to begin reconstruction of both the socio-political aspects of statehood, albeit under the oversight of the empire, and the religious identity focusing on a rebuilt temple and the law. The city of Jerusalem is at the center of both these aspects, hence the concentration on its reconstruction in the book of Nehemiah. There is also the intriguing figure of Zerubbabel, who is a descendant from the dynasty of David and functions in the rebuilding of the temple and as governor.[6]

On the down side, the narratives of Ezra and Nehemiah present a picture of a constant struggle to establish a Jewish identity in the face of opposi-

---

5. Many writers of histories of Israel have suggested that the biblical account has been distorted by a textual problem with dating. They propose that, contrary to the biblical text, Nehemiah actually preceded Ezra in coming to Jerusalem. However, a very cogent defense of the biblical order is presented by J. Stafford Wright, *The Date of Ezra's Coming to Jerusalem* (London: Tyndale Press, 1947).

6. Ezra 3–5; Neh. 7:7; Hag. 1:1, 12, 14; 2:2; Zech. 4:6-10.

tion from local tribes and of intrigue in high places in the Persian empire. When the temple is finally rebuilt, it is such an unimpressive building that, far from being the temple of prophetic hope, it does not even measure up to the glory that was there before the exile. All kinds of problems beset the new community, not the least of which is the flouting of the law on mixed marriages. The prophet Haggai depicts a situation in which lack of fidelity is characteristic of the population. In short, this is clearly not the kingdom of God foretold by the prophets. The major aspects of prophetic hope are in place — land, returned remnant, new temple, rebuilt Jerusalem, and Davidic leadership — but there is no glory. The shadow of Ichabod hangs over the land.[7] Thus, the books of Ezra and Nehemiah in general, and the rebuilding of Jerusalem in particular, need to be seen in this wider historical context as it is interpreted for us by the prophetic word. Preaching that is merely exemplary will almost certainly distort this perspective that points to the need for the true fulfillment to come while at the same time showing the faithfulness of God to sustain his people in the hope of the coming kingdom.

Literary and Historical Considerations

A distinction needs to be made between preaching from a narrative passage and preaching a sermon in narrative form. In the former we are concerned to respond to the nature of the biblical text and to understand how it functions as text. In the latter we are concerned about the mode of communication that the preacher will adopt in delivering the sermon. Some writers have been at pains to indicate that Greek rhetoric influenced the form of sermonizing in the Early Church. Such a rhetorical mode of address contrasts with the bulk of the biblical text that comes to us in the form of narrative. As John Holbert puts it, "Narrative is central to the Bible's own interests in communicating its message."[8] Furthermore, when we want to give expression to our experiences of life, we inevitably do so in narrative form. We recognize this in the well-tried evangelical practice of giving one's testimony. Some homileticians have taken these two points, the nature of the biblical text as story and our chief way of recounting human experience, as the basis for a homiletic revolution.

The "New Homiletic" is a phrase that is in vogue to describe this revival of interest in the narrative form of a sermon.[9] While the formal narra-

---

7. 1 Sam. 4:21-22; the Hebrew *'i kabod* means "there is no glory." As the dying wife of Phinehas, mother of Ichabod, said, "The glory has departed from Israel, for the ark of God has been captured."

8. John C. Holbert, *Preaching Old Testament: Proclamation and Narrative in the Hebrew Bible* (Nashville: Abingdon, 1991), p. 21.

tive sermon is not the only possibility canvassed, the move is to redress the imbalance that has come about by what Hans Frei refers to as the eclipse of biblical narrative.[10] Calvin Miller says, "The narrative sermon, rather than containing stories, *is* a story which, from outset to conclusion, binds the entire sermon to a single plot as theme."[11] Sidney Greidanus has endorsed a narrative approach to narrative texts and contrasts this form with the didactic form.[12] He comments, "The most serious objection to the didactic form, however, is that in reshaping the form of the text, it may unintentionally distort the message of the text."[13] At a common-sense level it may be argued that if God has seen fit to communicate his ways to us in narrative, should we submerge this narrative in our sermon form so that it comes out as a series of five abstract conceptual points all beginning with the letter P?

It is beyond the scope of this book to deal with the pros and cons of different forms of the sermon. However, in the matter of narrative texts I believe biblical theology has something to contribute to the way we will finally deliver the sermon. Greidanus has a useful analysis of the reasons for engaging with narrative text in a narrative form of sermon. He also sounds some warnings that, to the evangelical preacher, are particularly pertinent. In response to some of the "New homileticians" he warns of thinking that simply telling the story is preaching.[14] Preaching involves a transferring of the point of the passage to today's hearers. I would reinforce this caveat by pointing out that biblical theology should sensitize us to these crucial points:

1. The story is never complete in itself and belongs as part of the one big story of salvation culminating in Jesus Christ. Simply telling a story based on a piece of Old Testament historical narrative, however complete in itself, is not Christian preaching. A sermon involves the application of biblical truths to the present hearers.

2. Biblical theology is the antidote to dehistoricizing the biblical message. Story-telling sermons can easily be hijacked by an existential philosophy, as Bultmann has shown us. The value of the story according to this approach is not that it tells us what actually happened in history, but only that it increases our personal self-understanding. Once the story is

9. Eugene L. Lowry, *The Sermon: Dancing the Edge of Mystery* (Nashville: Abingdon, 1997), p. 20.

10. Hans W. Frei, *The Eclipse of Biblical Narrative* (New Haven: Yale University Press, 1974).

11. Calvin Miller, "Narrative Preaching," in *Handbook of Contemporary Preaching,* ed. Michael Duduit (Nashville: Broadman, 1992).

12. Sidney Greidanus, *The Modern Preacher and the Ancient Text* (Grand Rapids: Eerdmans, 1988).

13. Greidanus, *The Modern Preacher,* p. 147.

14. Greidanus, *The Modern Preacher,* p. 149.

divorced from the framework of history, theology will become hopelessly distorted.

Planning Sermons on Historical Narrative Texts

The nature of the biblical text, and the unity it exhibits theologically, indicates that preaching from historical narrative requires us to honor the revealed purpose of God to transform the universe with the coming of his kingdom. I have often reflected on the possible reasons why, in the heyday of Sunday School attendances, so many children graduated from programs and were never seen again. There were no doubt a host of reasons, including the lack of parental encouragement or of active ministry in the home. There is another contributing factor that I think bears consideration. While I certainly do not want to appear to be carping and critical of the multitude of faithful volunteers who prepare curricula and teach them in Sunday Schools, I get the impression that both tasks are often carried on with little or no understanding of the big picture of biblical revelation. Consequently, children are often taught a whole range of isolated Bible stories, each with its neat little application deemed appropriate to the respective age levels. So much of the application is thus moralizing legalism because it is severed from its links to the gospel of grace. By the time many of these children reach their teenage years they have had a belly full of morality, enough, they would think, to last them for the rest of their lives. They thus beat a retreat to live reasonably decent but gospelless lives.

What can the pastor do to help redress this situation? I would suggest at least two things. The first is, as mentioned in chapter 9, to institute a training program for all church members engaged in any kind of teaching or pastoral ministry. At the heart of such a program must be a basic course on the unity of the Bible as shown in biblical theology. The second is to draw up a preaching program that includes one or more series based on historical narrative texts. Such a series should be planned with an eye to the theological thrust of the particular book of the Bible within the wider context that links this to the coming of Christ. If I might borrow Greidanus's distinction again: the exemplary sermon is more inclined to lead us to ask, "How does this character (or event) testify to my existence?" By contrast, the redemptive-historical approach is more inclined to lead us to ask, "How does this event (or character) testify to Christ?" Let us never forget that our existence is only properly defined in terms of our being either in Christ or outside of Christ. If we really want to know how a text testifies to our existence, it must do so via its testimony to Christ. That is basic to any Christian sermon.

CHAPTER 11

Preaching from Old Testament Law

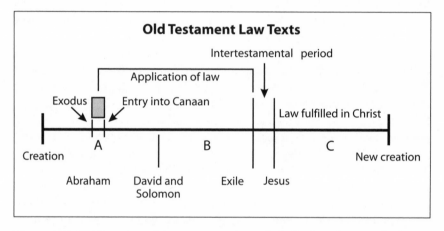

Diagram 11: Old Testament law texts occur in a relatively short but significant period immediately after the exodus from Egypt. The "Second Law," or Deuteronomy, purports to be the last words of Moses a generation later and just before the entry into Canaan. The law goes on being applied by prophets and other functionaries throughout the Old Testament period. Christ comes as fulfillment of the law.

The Law in Biblical-Theological Context

The first and obvious comment to be made about the Old Testament law is its context in salvation history. The law was given to a people who had been chosen by grace and already redeemed by grace. There can be no question of the law functioning as a way of achieving salvation by works. The second point to notice is that the word "Law" is the usual translation of the Hebrew word *Torah,* which does not necessarily carry the same narrow legal connotation that we are prone to place upon it since it strictly means "instruction." The third point is that, while the Sinai law continues to be appealed to in different ways throughout the Old Testament period, there is little direct evidence in the New Testament that it was regarded as in any way the normative expression governing Christian behavior. The fourth point, connected with the previous comment, is that the exact relationship between the law and the gospel has been a matter of controversy and concern since New Testament times.[1]

The question of what law existed before the giving of the Sinai code is a vexed one.[2] It is clear that the people of God in the period before Sinai could not be characterized as lawless. The preacher must confront this question exegetically when dealing with the book of Genesis as narrative text. It is clear that Abraham was given certain ceremonial directions, including circumcision, but it is less clear as to what it would mean for him to walk before God and to be blameless (Gen. 17:1). The question of the ethical implications of the Genesis narratives is somewhat different from that of the application of the Sinai code, which is presented formally and extensively as instruction from God to his people.

There are two possible approaches to the law-grace question. On the one hand we can start with the giving of the law at Sinai and follow through its application until we come to the New Testament. On the other hand we can begin with the gospel and tackle the matter of law from within an understanding of the gospel. We probably need to do both, though I maintain that a Christian must recognize that we never approach the Old Testament as anything other than as Christians and with Christian eyes. One thing is certain: sooner or later we have to confront not only the issue of how the law is handled in the New Testament, but also the practical homiletic question of how useful it is to try to preach from the law of the Old Testament.

When it comes to preaching the law most pastors would, understandably, give priority to the Ten Commandments. Formally, these laws function as the kernel of the whole Sinai corpus and are usually seen to sum up all the ethical principles of the law. Christians tend to favor the Decalogue as a summary of ethical instruction. After the Reformation the three major branches of the Protestant Church, Reformed, Lutheran, and Anglican, all produced

---

1. See Donald E. Gowan, *Reclaiming the Old Testament for the Christian Pulpit* (Atlanta: John Knox, 1976), chapter IV; Wayne Strickland, ed., *Five Views on Law and Gospel* (Grand Rapids: Zondervan, 1996).

2. One tradition would suggest that the law, and specifically the Ten Commandments, was given to Adam and Eve. I find the evidence for this somewhat lacking. It is clear, however, that some kind of covenantal relationship existed on the basis of creation and the spoken word of God. This relationship was transgressed in the disobedience of the human pair.

catechisms[3] based upon the Apostles' Creed, the Lord's Prayer, and the Ten Commandments. Thus, Protestant churches have tended to regard the Decalogue as the basis of Christian ethics. The Sabbath commandment has always been a sticking point because it appears to be more ceremonial than ethical.[4] The problem with the Protestant catechisms is that they do something with the Ten Commandments that the New Testament doesn't seem at all interested in doing. Nowhere in the New Testament epistles are the Ten Commandments as such expounded to teach Christian ethics; in fact, only individual commandments are mentioned, and those not very often. However, there is no doubt that the case can be made that the New Testament assumes continuity of the ethical law of Israel and nowhere repudiates it but rather sharpens the application of it.

The concentration on the Ten Commandments also highlights a distinction that has commonly been made to enable the ethical laws to remain in force while the civil and ceremonial laws are somehow discarded. The civil laws applied to the organization of a community that no longer exists. The new community is now defined by who and what it is in Christ. The ceremonial laws were mainly a matter of symbolic relationship to God, a dimension that is redefined in the New Testament in terms of Christ as the mediator. Again, the idea that we are freed from the ceremonial laws while remaining subject to the ethical involves a distinction that is also difficult to find in the New Testament. This is not to say that to inquire into the shape of Old Testament ethics is invalid or unprofitable.[5] Once again, however, redefinition has taken place as Christ becomes the mediator of all relationships. We perceive a distinction between ceremonial and ethical on the basis of personhood. The ceremonial involves symbolic actions that point beyond themselves to another reality, usually divine. The ethical involves us in questions of direct or indirect human personal relationships. The foundation of these in biblical terms is the personhood of God who has made us in his image. The Christological dimension is unavoidable once we recognize the personal relationship dimension. A Christian is defined by union with Christ and can never relate personally to God or anyone else apart from this fact. The idea that Old Testament laws relating to ethical behavior can somehow apply to Christians apart from Christ is, to say the least, a denial of who we are in Christ.

But what of the nonethical laws? How do they function, and is it worth trying to preach from them? The answer to this must surely lie in the way

3. Catechisms are manuals of basic Christian instruction.
4. Seventh Day Adventists deal with the matter by declaring the Sabbath commandment to be still in force, while the Westminster Confession modifies it and makes Sunday a Sabbath.
5. See, for example, Christopher Wright, *Living as the People of God* (Leicester: IVP, 1983).

such ceremonial prescriptions were intended to function for Israel. This brings us back to the context of the Sinai law. I imagine it would be a fairly bold preacher, some would say reckless, who would contemplate an entire sermon on the subject of, say, ritual uncleanness in Leviticus 15. Even the less contentious and less specific issue of clean and unclean foods seems so irrelevant to us today, unless we want to distort the significance of these laws and reduce them to matters of hygiene.[6]

Two major parts of the ceremonial material merge with the ethical in that they are directly concerned with interpersonal relationships, but this time with God himself. These are the related matters of the provision of the sanctuary and of the whole sacrificial system. They represent, on the one hand, the goal of all God's dealings with his people in establishing fellowship with himself. On the other hand, they show something of the "mechanics" of God's way of making this fellowship possible given the universal alienation of the human race from him through rebellion, which is sin. Reconciliation and justification are a possibility because, and only because, the just requirement of a holy God as revealed in his law is satisfied.

A biblical theology of law must take into account this paradox in the law itself, namely, that God required strict and perfect obedience but at the same time provided the means of dealing with the fact that such obedience could not be given by sinful human beings. Integral to the law, then, was the tabernacle and the whole system of propitiatory sacrifice. If God required of Israel that she should be holy, even as God is holy, and love the Lord with all her heart, soul, and might,[7] he also knew that a people as yet not fully saved could never achieve that standard. In such a context the idea of loving God takes on a new significance that is governed by God's grace.

The provisions for the tabernacle are eloquent of the grace of God. He makes this provision after the kernel of the covenant of Sinai is given. The sequence in redemptive history then is:

– election and calling (Abraham);
– captivity (Exod. 1);
– redemptive miracle in the Exodus (Exod. 2–15);
– assembly at Sinai (Exod. 19);
– the giving of the Decalogue (Exod. 20);
– the "book of the covenant" (Exod. 20:22–23:33);

6. Lev. 11. The attempt to rationalize these laws as based on principles of hygiene, which God understood even if Israel did not, is unconvincing. While some unclean foods may indeed have been hazardous, not all were. Furthermore, the laws are superseded in the New Testament on the basis of the gospel, for example, in Acts 10, and not with the advent of refrigeration and advanced methods of hygiene.

7. Lev. 19:2; Deut. 6:5.

– the ratification of the covenant (Exod. 24);
– the prescription of the tabernacle (Exod. 25–31).

The law must be understood in this redemptive context. The more detailed provisions in Leviticus, which define holy separation out of the world to Yahweh and reconciliation with fellowship through sacrifice, only serve to emphasize the significance of this context. Particularly we should notice the purpose of redemption as expressed in Exodus 19:3-6. God has brought Israel to himself that they might live before him as a treasured possession: a kingdom of priests and a holy nation. They are chosen and saved in order to be God's people and to represent him among all the nations of the earth.

Into this context the Decalogue is given and followed by some more detailed laws in the book of the covenant. The law functions to enable this new nation of redeemed people to know what kind of existence is consistent with this unique relationship with God. The law not only functions to prescribe human behavior but fulfills the very significant purpose of indicating what kind of God has redeemed them. The law is not simply a guide for human behavior; its ethics and obedience are primarily there to indicate a relationship to God. At the heart of the law is the covenant relationship with God. Relationships between individuals and groups are to reflect the relationship of the individual and the group to God, a relationship that has been established by grace. Once the book of the covenant is given to Moses, the people are summoned to assembly and told what God has said. They respond by saying, "All that the Lord has spoken we will do." The covenant is sealed in sacrificial blood in a largely unexplained but very evocative ceremony (Exod. 24:3-8). In short, it appears that the covenant can work only on the basis of the blood sacrifice. If this is so, then the covenant depends on the way God will justify the sinner who turns to him for grace in the face of the perfect requirements of the law.

Thus, the tabernacle is given because a key aspect of the character of God is his desire for fellowship with people, and this fellowship is primarily described as his dwelling among them. A common mistake that was made in some types of biblical interpretation was to allegorize all the details of the tabernacle and the priestly ministry there, in order to make each aspect say something specifically Christian.[8] There are undoubtedly details whose symbolism is quite transparent, but there are others that are difficult to understand. The function of the tabernacle for reconciliation and fellowship must control our understanding of the details. A biblical theology of the tabernacle

8. Vern Poythress (*The Shadow of Christ in the Law of Moses* [Brentwood, Tenn.: Wolgemuth and Hyatt, 1991]), in dealing with the tabernacle, draws out the important biblical data and symbolism. At times he seems to go beyond the evidence in suggesting symbolic meanings of some details, but this is not a serious fault in this excellent treatment.

would focus on the promised land as a type of the restoration of Eden, with the tent, and then later the temple, indicating God dwelling with his people in the promised land. The prophetic view of the restored temple of the messianic age includes the detailed description in Ezekiel 40–47, the climax of which is the new temple at the center of the new Eden. From prophetic eschatology we move to the new temple that is Christ, the temple in heaven, and the new temple created by the Spirit of Christ through the gospel.

Returning to the law, we find that while Moses is still on the mountain receiving the law of the tabernacle, the people engage in an act of breaking the law to which they have already assented. The incident of Aaron's golden calf illustrates the point that the lust for autonomy from the word of God still characterizes the human heart even in the aftermath of the most amazing demonstration of grace and the instruction concerning the shape of the graced life. Thus, while there will be many heroes of faith who stand as examples of godliness, the depressing truth is that Israel's existence will be characterized by faithlessness and law breaking. It is this that leads to the destruction of the kingdoms of Israel and Judah and the catastrophe of the exile.

As the curse of the law falls on the kingdoms, the prophetic threats are shown to be well founded. Meanwhile the prophetic eschatology breathes hope for those whose trust is in God. One day God will act in such a way that changes the sinful hearts of his people so that their wills become reflections of his will.

> The days are surely coming, says the LORD, when I will make a new covenant with the house of Israel and the house of Judah. It will not be like the covenant that I made with their ancestors when I took them by the hand to bring them out of the land of Egypt — a covenant that they broke, though I was their husband, says the LORD. But this is the covenant that I will make with the house of Israel after those days, says the LORD: I will put my law within them, and I will write it on their hearts; and I will be their God, and they shall be my people. No longer shall they teach one another, or say to each other, "Know the LORD," for they shall all know me, from the least of them to the greatest, says the LORD; for I will forgive their iniquity, and remember their sin no more. (Jer. 31:31-34)

> I will take you from the nations, and gather you from all the countries, and bring you into your own land. I will sprinkle clean water upon you, and you shall be clean from all your uncleannesses, and from all your idols I will cleanse you. A new heart I will give you, and a new spirit I will put within you; and I will remove from your body the heart of stone and give you a heart of flesh. I will put my

spirit within you, and make you follow my statutes and be careful to observe my ordinances. Then you shall live in the land that I gave to your ancestors; and you shall be my people, and I will be your God. (Ezek. 36:24-28)

From the point of view of biblical theology the question that must concern us is how such passages find fulfillment. It is clear that it does not happen in the postexilic period of reconstruction. I remind the reader of what I have been saying about the structure of biblical revelation so that we do not simply assume that the first point of application is the Christian believer. When the author of Hebrews expounds the law as a shadow of the good things to come, he goes on to show that what the law could not achieve, Christ has achieved for us (Heb. 10:1-18). He offered for all time a single offering for sins and sat down at the right hand of God. Only in this context does the author of Hebrews then quote Jeremiah 31:33-34. The people of God are assured that God remembers their sins no more precisely because all the requirements of the law are met in Jesus. In fact, we would have to say that Jesus is the Israelite upon whose heart the law of God is perfectly written.

Perhaps part of our difficulty in preaching from the law comes from the lumping of such a mixture of themes under the one heading of "law." If we approach the matter analytically, as well as on the basis of a synthesis of the whole concept, we can distinguish in a useful way the various elements that make up the whole.[9] Taking the Sinai covenant as a whole, we encounter in turn, in the book of Exodus, the Ten Commandments, the book of the covenant, and the laws of the tabernacle. In Leviticus we have the laws of holiness, the sacrificial system, and the laws of clean and unclean. Finally, Deuteronomy recapitulates some of the main elements of the law at the time when the next generation of Israel is about to enter the promised land.

Our overview of law in biblical theology, then, takes us from the details of the Sinai covenant, through the giving of the law as recorded in Deuteronomy, to the life of Israel in the land. The inescapable truth is that the grace of God continues to shine upon a people whose major claim to fame is the suicidal ability to break the covenant. While it is appealing to concentrate on the heroes of faith and the shining achievements of Israel, the sad fact is that it is a nation heading for disaster. The prophets stand as beacons to the law, but they must also preside over the demise of the nation. Only the eschatological promises concerning a people made new with the law of God on their hearts relieves the gloom of their message.

---

9. A useful summary of these elements is found in T. D. Alexander, *From Paradise to the Promised Land: An Introduction to the Main Themes of the Pentateuch* (Carlisle: Paternoster, 1995).

The "law" given to the first Adam, the first son of God, was broken, and mankind was thrown out of the garden into the wilderness. The law given to Israel, the son of God, was broken, and the nation was thrown out of its promised land into the wilderness of exile. A last Adam came as the truly obedient covenant partner of God, signifying his identification with a people that desperately needed his help. We can almost hear heaven's sigh of relief, "At last! A true son of God." "You are my beloved son in whom I am well pleased" is God's word of approval. Then this true Adam, this true Israel, goes out into our wilderness to be tempted and to be victorious, so that he might make for us a way back into the garden of God.

Jesus did not come to destroy or abolish the law but to fulfill it (Matt. 5:17). He is the end, the *telos,* of the law.[10] He is its ultimate reference point, revealing with unprecedented clarity what Sinai was all about. He applies it with uncompromising rigidity: "unless your righteousness exceeds that of the scribes and Pharisees, you will never enter the kingdom of heaven" (Matt. 5:20). In the Sermon on the Mount, in his parable of the Pharisee and the tax collector, and in his dealing with the lawyer's question about eternal life (Luke 10:25-29), he takes the ground of self-justification out from under those who think they can somehow climb up the ladder of the law to acceptance with God. He has come to fulfill all righteousness for us. He not only fulfills all the law in his own sinless life, but he is content to have our law breaking imputed to him so that he bears the curse of the law for us (2 Cor. 5:21). By faith we receive the gift of Jesus' law keeping, which was perfectly achieved on our behalf, and in him we become the righteousness of God. By faith we do not overthrow the law: "on the contrary, we uphold the law" (Rom. 3:31). We uphold it by turning our backs on our own warped efforts to keep the law and by putting all our confidence and trust in the one who satisfies all the law's demands on our behalf.

While the relationship of law and gospel remains an area of discussion and dispute, there are some salient points that can be made with confidence. The gospel event is not a repudiation of the law; it is its most perfect expression. The life of Jesus, what some theologians refer to as the active obedience of Christ, is as much a part of his justifying work as is his death (the so-called passive obedience).[11] Not only can we plead the forgiveness of our sins because they were borne for us by Jesus on the cross, but we have as a gift his perfect righteousness that he exercised in his life (Rom. 5:10).

The apparent ambivalence that Paul expresses about the law is surely a function of the place of law in salvation history. The Christian life bears a

10. Rom. 10:4, "For Christ is the end of the law so that there may be righteousness for everyone who believes." The Greek word *telos* suggests the goal or purpose of the law.

11. This terminology conveniently points to the fact that the life of Christ is part of his saving work. It is inaccurate in that Jesus was not entirely passive in his death.

unity with the life of Israel under the old covenant because it is a relationship with the same unchanging God. What has changed is the clarity of the revelation of God and his way of salvation. No longer is it Moses on Sinai that is the beacon to guide us; rather it is Christ on Calvary. When the Ephesians need warning over the temptation to go on living as "gentiles," Paul does not rehearse the Ten Commandments, but he says, "That is not the way you learned Christ" (Eph. 4:20). When it comes to certain ceremonial matters Paul says, "Therefore do not let anyone condemn you in matters of food and drink or of observing festivals, new moons, or sabbaths. These are only a shadow of what is to come, but the substance belongs to Christ" (Col. 2:16-17). When he tells Christians, "you are not under law but under grace" (Rom. 6:14), he does not mean the Christian life is lawless. Far from it. He goes on:

> There is therefore now no condemnation for those who are in Christ Jesus. For the law of the Spirit of life in Christ Jesus has set you free from the law of sin and of death. For God has done what the law, weakened by the flesh, could not do: by sending his own Son in the likeness of sinful flesh, and to deal with sin, he condemned sin in the flesh, so that the just requirement of the law might be fulfilled in us, who walk not according to the flesh but according to the Spirit. (Rom. 8:1-4)

1. The Ten Commandments (Exod. 20)

Notwithstanding my comments above about the comparative silence of the New Testament about the Decalogue, I want to assert that the Ten Commandments are not only eminently preachable but provide an important aspect of the Bible's teaching about conformity to the character of God. The first commandment hardly needs any comment as the principle clearly holds forever: there is only one God to be worshiped. The second commandment reminds us that God gave no visible image of himself and that any attempt to make one is idolatry because it comes from the imaginings of the human heart and not revelation. The principle, of course, applies to the attempts to depict Jesus as a stereotypical person. The only visual description of Jesus in the Bible is the highly symbolic one in Revelation 1:13-16. I find it hard to understand why some Protestants will vigorously oppose Roman Catholic three-dimensional images of Jesus while endorsing two-dimensional images of the same person in stained glass or picture books.

The Sabbath commandment needs to be dealt with in the light of the New Testament understanding of Sabbath. Even if we accept that it is a creation ordinance, the questions of how a Christian observes it and why it should or should not be Sunday are exegetical questions that need to be set-tled before preaching on the subject. The essentially ethical nature of the Ten Commandments is based on the character of God. It is this God who reveals himself finally in his Son, Jesus Christ, who then becomes the ethical model. The preaching of the commandments must always point people both to the impossibility of our being justified by works of the law and to the fulfillment of the law's demands for us by our Savior. It cannot be emphasized too much that insofar as there is lawfulness in Christian sanctification, it can only come via the prior justification by grace in Christ. I will refer to this again in chapter 17.

2. The Tabernacle (Exod. 25–30)

Little more needs to be added to what has been said already about the taber-nacle in the context of biblical theology. It is easy to understand why, in some circles, it was a popular way of preaching about Christ. It is unfortunate that this so easily leads to fanciful and false typology. The symbolism of the tab-ernacle is, in its salvation-oriented essentials, quite clear. The function of the priestly ministry in the tabernacle is also clear. From the tabernacle we move to the temple, then to the new temple of prophetic eschatology. Then comes Jesus as the true temple in which God dwells. Finally the New Testament, es-pecially in Hebrews, deals with the heavenly temple where Jesus now is. The new earthly temple is the creation of the Holy Spirit through the gospel proc-lamation. Those who are united to Christ become a new dwelling place of Christ in the Spirit.

3. Clean and Unclean Foods (Lev. 11)

As stated above, there is no obvious rationale given for the division of clean from the unclean foods. Any hygiene considerations, if they exist, are not spec-ified, and the gospel seems to dispense with the distinction altogether. Is there any point in preaching from a passage that appears to be repudiated by Acts 10:15? If our understanding of the teaching of Jesus on the wider matter of the Old Testament is correct, then this passage like all others somehow testifies to Christ. This chapter needs to be understood in the wider context of clean-unclean and holy-profane as dealt with in Leviticus 11–16. Not only certain foods but various conditions rendered people unclean. As Gordon Wenham helpfully comments about uncleanness through skin disease (Lev. 13): "Theol-ogy, not hygiene, is the reason for this provision. The unclean and the holy must not meet. The camp of Israel is holy, and in the middle of it stood the tabernacle, seat of God's most holy presence."[12] These laws, then, were an aspect of God's teaching to his people of the absolute opposition of uncleanness and profanity to holiness. It is a helpful antidote to the popular notion that the meaning of the word "holy" is self-evident. It is in fact a very elusive term, but it is finally defined for us by Christ himself. In the Old Testament it is drawn out in different ways that show the utter separateness of God and his people from a profane world. Its ultimate expression is, negatively, God's rejection of sin as seen on Calvary and, positively, in the vision of God we find in Jesus.

4. A Ceremonial Directive (Num. 10:1-10)

This is a ceremonial provision given outside the main corpus of the law. I include comment on this passage here to encourage the preaching of some sermons from the book of Numbers. The directive recorded in this text is given just before a number of real problems are recounted, climaxing in the refusal of Israel to go up and possess the promised land. Moses is told to make a couple of silver trumpets to be used for the signal to break camp or to summon the people to the tent. This should not be seen as a kind of village brass band in the making, for the trumpets have a priestly function. Nor are they simply the loudest thing available to give signals in warfare, as true as that may be. They function as signals to the acts of Yahweh in saving his people. In giving war signals they are to act as a reminder before God so that the people might be saved from their enemies (v. 9). In connection with the tabernacle the trumpets call the people to the place of reconciliation, signal the time to move toward the promised land, and signal before God that these are his people.

The trumpets[13] and the sound of the trumpet take on great significance in the Bible, and their meaning in Numbers 10 echoes their wider use. It begins with the supernatural sound of the trumpet at Sinai indicating the presence of God (Exod. 19:16, 19; 20:18). Trumpets appear in certain Sabbath rituals (Lev. 23:24; 25:9), a fact that points to the idea of rest in the promised land. They are used in the holy war by which the promised land is possessed, and for the bringing of the ark to the holy city (2 Sam. 6:15). They also turn up at the anointing of some of the kings. In prophetic eschatology the trumpets signal judgment and salvation, and it is this significance that is echoed in the New Testament. The angel with the trumpet will gather the elect to the holy place (Matt. 24:31), and the trumpet will summon the people of God

12. Gordon J. Wenham, *The Book of Leviticus,* The New International Commentary on the Old Testament (Grand Rapids: Eerdmans, 1979), p. 21.

13. There are two kinds of trumpets — the metal ones (Heb. *hatzotzerah*) and the ram's horns (Heb. *shofar*) — but they appear to be used interchangeably and are translated by the same word (Gk. *salpinx*) in the LXX.

from the dead in the resurrection (1 Cor. 15:51-52; 1 Thess. 4:16). The common feature is not the loud sound of the signaler's instrument.[14] The thread running through the use of trumpets, by God, his angels, and his priestly representatives, is the calling of his people to enter into their rest in the assurance of acceptance by God. In Christ we live in certainty of the day when the trumpet shall sound and we shall be raised imperishable to enter into our rest.

Literary and Historical Considerations

Perhaps the most significant advance in studies of the law in recent times has been the investigation of the literary structure of covenant. In earlier historical criticism, distinctions had been made between the apodictic and the casuistic laws in an attempt to get a grasp on the history behind Israel's laws. The apodictic laws are typically the straight imperative: "you shall . . ." or "you shall not . . ." These were thought to be distinct to Israel and are the form of the Decalogue laws. Casuistic laws are the conditional case laws: "If . . . , then . . . ," or law by precedent. The Sinai law contains both, and it is not clear what help the distinction gives other than to alert us to the way the law worked. Presumably casuistic or precedent law implies principles that are applicable beyond the specified case. Apodictic law seems to go more directly to the principle involved.

In the mid-twentieth century, there was interest in the formal characteristics of certain ancient Near Eastern treaty codes. It emerged that the world of the biblical patriarchs and the period of Israel's birth was one of considerable political and military activity. The study of ancient suzerainty treaties, that is, treaties imposed by a conquering ruler (the suzerain) on a conquered nation (the vassal), which was then bound into a covenant relationship, revealed what were seen to be important parallels with the biblical law code.[15] This view was vigorously applied by Meredith Kline to the book of Deuteronomy and also to the Decalogue.[16] Kline makes critical as well as theologi-

---

14. If you have ever heard a *shofar,* you will know that a ram's horn does not produce either a very loud or a very vibrant sound. It has the wrong shape and is made of the wrong material to produce anything like the sound of a brass trumpet.

15. See John A. Thompson, *The Ancient Near Eastern Treaties and the Old Testament* (London: Tyndale Press, 1964); D. J. McCarthy, *Old Testament Covenant: A Survey of Current Opinions* (Richmond: John Knox, 1972); Wenham, *The Book of Leviticus;* Peter C. Craigie, *The Book of Deuteronomy,* The New International Commentary on the Old Testament (Grand Rapids: Eerdmans, 1976).

16. Meredith G. Kline, *Treaty of the Great King: The Covenant Structure of Deuteronomy* (Grand Rapids: Eerdmans, 1963). Kline begins his discussion by presenting a case for the covenant treaty structure in the Decalogue.

cal mileage out of this proposal in that the book of Deuteronomy, usually assigned a late date by critics, is seen to have a structure that is much older than
Moses. He also suggests that the typical provision of a duplicate copy of the
treaty to be placed in the sanctuary of the god of the conquered nation, accounts for the two tablets of the law. Both would contain the full Decalogue.
Since the Suzerain and the God of the vassal are one and the same, both cop-
ies go into the one sanctuary.

The theological gain in this understanding of the covenant structure is
to reinforce the removal of the law from the realm of legalism. It is a structuring of life under the rule of the Great King. It was, as Peter Craigie says, "a
reminder to the people of their liberty in this world and of their total commitment to God."[17] The relationship has been established, and these are the obli-
gations of faithfulness that are the true expression of the gracious relationship. It is worth summarizing the structure of the treaty that has so taken the
imagination of the scholars:

1. The preamble: the word of the king or, in the case of Moses, the king's
   representative.
2. The historical prologue, which accounts for the events by which the
   present treaty relationship has been brought about.
3. The stipulations of the covenant as expressing the relationship between
   the king and his people.
4. The sanctions of blessings or curses depending on the response of the
   people to the covenant.
5. The disposition: the requirement of a duplicate copy, and the provision
   for renewal at the point of transition of power.

The Decalogue as Covenant Treaty

Preamble
   "I am Yahweh your God"
Historical prologue
   "Who brought you out of the land of Egypt . . ."
Stipulations
   "You shall have no other gods before me," etc.
Sanctions
   "The Lord will not hold him guiltless . . ."
   "That your days may be long . . ."

17. Craigie, *Deuteronomy*, p. 37.

Disposition
   Two tables of the law
   Covenant renewal before Moses dies, and at Joshua's accession

One other literary feature is worth noting. John Sailhamer has emphasized the literary unity of the Pentateuch both in its form and in the history of
its acceptance as canonical Scripture.[18] Placing the Sinai covenant in its literary narrative context leads him to suggest certain things about the intention
of the author of our finished Pentateuch. The outlook is eschatological and
anticipates a time when that which the law did not achieve in Israel will be
the reality.

> As a literary document, [the Pentateuch] is fundamentally different
> from a document of the Sinai covenant. The Pentateuch is a docu-
> ment that looks at the Sinai covenant from a perspective that was not
> the same as that of the covenant itself. Like the other OT historical
> books, the Prophets, and the NT, the Pentateuch represents a look
> back at the failure of Sinai and a look forward to the time of fulfill-
> ment (e.g., Deuteronomy 30).[19]

In preaching from the Pentateuch we should pay attention to its overall
structure. Sailhamer proposes narrative typology within the Pentateuch that
has the purpose of showing how the events of the past shape what happens in
the future. This, as we have already noted, is characteristic of the way the
prophets model their eschatology on the historical experience of Israel.

   The narrative element provides a framework for the law giving at Sinai.
As Sailhamer points out, it is not until the incident of the golden calf that we
are given the more detailed priestly code. This suggests a strategy that is related to the purpose of showing a contrast between Abraham, who lived by
faith before the law, and Moses, who failed under the law and died in the wilderness. The Pentateuch, on this reading, performs a similar function to
Galatians in showing the impotence of the law.[20] However, we must be careful not to detract from the positive significance given to Moses in Scripture.

---

   18. John Sailhamer, *The Pentateuch as Narrative: A Biblical-Theological Commentary*
(Grand Rapids: Zondervan, 1992).
   19. Sailhamer, *The Pentateuch,* p. 27.
   20. Sailhamer, *The Pentateuch,* pp. 61, 77.

Planning Sermons on the Law

There is enough material in the law that is relatively straightforward to keep us going for a long time. The rich variety in the law contains many important theological dimensions that find their goal in the gospel. Once we have established the fact that the law of Sinai did not provide a way of salvation by works, we are a good way along the track to making it clear that the essence of being a Christian is not being good. The law-grace relationship in the Old Testament is important for establishing the relationship between the grace of justification and the lawfulness of sanctified living. The possible topics for sermons on the law are virtually endless, but for the preacher who wants to go beyond using the Ten Commandments as a means of expounding the ethical implications of the gospel, there is much to be gained by taking the various segments of the law and showing how they functioned for Israel.

The crucial thing for the preacher is to reach some consistent hermeneutic that enables the congregation to apply the significance of the law as it is fulfilled in Christ. Preaching from the Old Testament adds texture to the terminology of the New Testament. It is too easy to assume that people will understand concepts such as holiness and righteousness, whether with reference to God or to his people. The Reformers referred to the three uses of the law that we might consider in planning our preaching. First, the law acted to restrain human wickedness; there is a God in charge who cares and who makes demands on all hymankind. The law declares that we are responsible to acknowledge him as Lord. Second, the law convicts of sin. Let any person oriented to righteousness by works declare, in the face of this law, that he or she keeps all God's laws all of the time. Expounding the law should show something of the seriousness of sin. Then we can tell people how to come to Christ for forgiveness. Third, the law instructs the people of God in righteousness. This is perhaps the area of most contention among Christians, and I won't repeat what I have already said about the matter. Obviously, however, it can only function this way if it does so in the framework of the gospel.

In planning sermons on the law, one way would be to have a long-term plan. As part of one year's program you might plan to preach a series on the Decalogue; the next year a series on the tabernacle; then one on the law of holiness; and so on. Show how these various aspects enrich our understanding of Christ the fulfiller of the law and, through him, inform us of the nature of Christian living.

CHAPTER 12

Preaching from the Old Testament Prophets

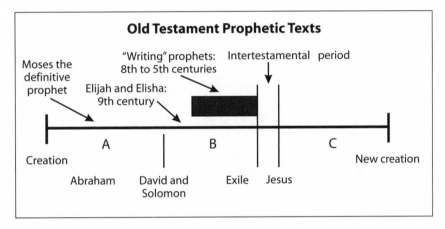

Diagram 12: Prophecy begins with Moses. Elijah and Elisha recall Moses' ministry in the Sinai covenant. The so-called writing prophets function in the period of decline, exile, and postexilic reconstruction.

Prophetic Texts in Biblical-Theological Context

In chapter 8 I looked at prophecy in the context of salvation history and specifically its role in the development of eschatology. We saw how the prophetic view of the future salvation that God would effect, despite the faithlessness of Israel, was cast in terms that recapitulate the structure of salvation experienced in the period from Abraham to David and Solomon. However, the biblical prophetic books contain more than eschatology, and preaching from the prophets can involve us in a wide range of perspectives and topics.

Prophecy in Israel needs to be seen as a whole. The first person to be referred to as a prophet is Abraham in the divine address to Abimelech (Gen. 20:7). This incident tells us little about the specific meaning of the word other than, in this case, that God is on Abraham's side. Next, Aaron is designated by God as Moses' prophet in the coming conflict with Pharaoh (Exod. 7:1). This was a concession to Moses who argued that his poor speaking abilities would be a disadvantage when it came to confronting the king. Aaron's prophetic responsibility is to be the spokesperson for Moses, but it is clearly Moses who exercises the primary role since he was to be "like God to Pharaoh." Next, Miriam, the sister of Moses and Aaron, is designated a prophet (Exod. 15:20). There is little to indicate why she should be called a prophet other than the fact that she leads the women in dancing and in singing the refrain from the Song of Moses, which celebrates Yahweh's victory over the Egyptians. The main function thus far attributable to the prophet is that such a person in some way represented God.

With Moses the picture becomes clearer, although the name prophet is not applied to him until the book of Deuteronomy (Deut. 18:15-22; 34:10). The two relevant passages in Deuteronomy are important for our understanding of the office and suggest that we must see Moses as the truly definitive prophet. In the first, Moses promises that the office of prophet would not cease with him. The prophet functions as the mediator between God and the people specifically to convey the word of God:

> "I will put my words in the mouth of the prophet, who shall speak to them everything that I command. Anyone who does not heed the words that the prophet shall speak in my name, I myself will hold accountable." (Deut. 18:18-19)

The last words of the book of Deuteronomy indicate that such a prophet as Moses, at the time of writing, had not yet arisen in Israel. The dating of Deuteronomy is not as important to understanding these words as might at first be thought. In whatever way we consider Moses to be involved in the authorship of the bulk of Deuteronomy, he clearly did not write the account of his death and this final comment. Furthermore, the fact that a prophet such as Moses had not arisen at the time of writing chapter 34 does not indicate there had been no prophetic activity. Rather it is stated that:

> He was unequaled for all the signs and wonders that the Lord sent him to perform in the land of Egypt, against Pharaoh and all his servants and his entire land, and for all the mighty deeds and all the terrifying displays of power that Moses performed in the sight of all Israel. (Deut. 34:11-12)

The signs and wonders go hand in hand with the mediation of God's saving word and become themselves instruments of salvation. Furthermore, it is clear from the Sinai corpus and the book of Deuteronomy that Moses was also unequaled as the mediator of God's Torah. He was above all the prophet who spoke the words of God to the people of God.

The unnamed prophet in Judges 6:8-10 is sent by Yahweh to remind the Israelites of the "gospel" event of the Exodus. On the basis of this past demonstration of the faithfulness of God, they are exhorted to stand firm in the face of the threat of the Midianites. Gideon is then sent as a savior to deal with the Midianites. The next prophet named is Samuel, who is not only a prophet but a judge and a king maker. The mediatorial role of Samuel is clear, and he acts as the conscience of the first king and of the nation as a whole. Yahweh sends him to anoint David to be the king chosen to head the dynasty of rulers who are called to represent the rule of Yahweh among his people. For David the prophetic office continues particularly through Nathan and Gad.

When we come to Elijah and Elisha the narrative writer gives a great deal of attention to their respective ministries that, in terms of significance, really merge into one. These two prophets operate at a time when the nation is on the verge of complete apostasy, particularly under the concerted efforts of the pagan consort of King Ahab. Jezebel is depicted as one who deliberately sets out to destroy Yahwism and, in the process, comes into conflict with Elijah. But, the real conflict is seen to be between Yahweh and Baal, each represented by their respective prophets. From the biblical-theological perspective, then, Elijah and Elisha are sent to call Israel back to the covenant of Sinai and to do battle with the forces seeking to seduce the people of God into apostasy. There are two features of the combined ministry of these prophets that are relevant to placing them in the context of salvation history. The first is the prophetic challenge to Israel to return to a faithful acceptance of the covenant. The second is the concentration of signs and wonders performed by these two men. As with the miracles of Moses before them, and the miracles of Jesus yet to come, these are miracles that signal the coming of the kingdom of God.

Elijah begins his ministry by proclaiming to the king that a drought will overtake the land (1 Kings 17:1). This contradicts the covenant promises to Israel concerning the fruitfulness of the land and reenacts the scene of Moses standing before Pharaoh and announcing plagues on the land. Elijah then is sent into the wilderness to be sustained there as Israel was (1 Kings 17:2-7). When Elijah's water supply fails, he is sent to a Sidonian widow, a Canaanite, for sustenance. Elijah works a miracle, providing meal and oil in endless supply for this widow and her child. When the child dies, Elijah raises him from death. Thus the Israelite savior-prophet goes to a gentile, when Israel is turning against the covenant, and shows that God is able to raise up children from the "stones" of the gentile races if he should so wish.[1] Elijah's conflict with the priests of Baal on Mount Carmel is clearly a call to Israel to return to the prophetic word given through Moses; a call to the covenant. Not only is the form of the Sinai law reinforced in the way Elijah orders the sacrifice on a legitimate altar, but the summoning of fire from heaven recalls the similar occurrence at the institution of the first burnt offering for sin.[2] Elisha also performs miracles that reflect the promises of God to sustain his people in the land. But, perhaps his best known, and most preached on, miracle is the healing of the Syrian general Naaman. Again we see the reaching out of God's grace to the gentiles at a time when Israel is in danger of turning its back on its responsibility to become the vehicle of blessing to the nations.

To sum up thus far: the covenant of grace mediated by Moses structures the life of the people who are elect and redeemed in the Exodus event. All prophecy after Moses reinforces and reapplies this definitive Mosaic ministry. Prophecy and Torah (law/instruction) go together since the function of the prophet was to be the mouthpiece of God as he gave his instruction to his people. Samuel's role is significant in that he acts as God's instrument and mouthpiece in setting up the kingly rule in Israel according to the regulations of the covenant. The king, like the prophet, is to be a guardian of Israel's covenant status and behavior. Things go badly astray, however, and the kingdom is broken into two parts. At the start of this decline, Elijah and Elisha are sent to demonstrate the grace of God to a wayward people and call them back to Sinai to live as those redeemed by grace. This is to no avail; the kingdoms slide into oblivion as the judgment of God falls first on Israel, then on Judah.

Elisha's ministry extends into the eighth century and is therefore followed soon afterward by the earlier writing prophets.[3] The writing prophets, which make up the section of the Hebrew prophetic canon usually called the "latter prophets," cover an extensive period of history. It is convenient from an historical point of view, and for understanding the local and historical references of each book, to group them as preexilic, exilic, and postexilic. It is reasonable to speculate that a theological basis exists for the words of these latter prophets being preserved in writing while notables like Samuel, Elijah,

---

1. Compare Matt. 3:9.

2. 1 Kings 18:38; see also Lev. 9:24. The same phenomenon is recorded in 1 Chron. 21:26 when David makes a burnt offering, and in 2 Chron. 7:1 at the dedication of the temple by Solomon.

3. The question of who wrote the prophetic books is not an issue for our purposes. I refer to them as "writing prophets" because we have books that were written under their names. Some opinions place Joel as the earliest of the writing prophets and a contemporary with Elisha. Other scholars place Joel in the postexilic period. The wide diversity of opinion here suggests that its date cannot be achieved by a consideration of the nature of the message, and thus its placement within the salvation history of the Old Testament must remain a broad one.

and Elisha are known to us only from historical narrative text. We have no record of the oracles of these three men that match the collection of sermons and pronouncements in the latter prophets. Could it be that the reason lies in the fact that God is announcing a new thing through this new breed of prophet? The earlier ones typically called Israel back to the great prophetic oracles of Moses. Now the blessings of the covenant, which obedience to the Sinai law was intended to preserve, are slipping away. Destruction looms, and any attempts at reform are shallow or, in the case of Josiah's, undone by successive apostate kings.

The writing prophets span the entire period of Old Testament history from the accelerating decline of the divided kingdom to the end of the Old Testament period. As Sidney Greidanus says, "prophetic literature openly declares its immediate relevance by presenting itself as preaching."[4] Each has a distinct message that has largely to do with the historical situation into which the prophet must speak. Yet, all of them contain three main ingredients to their message:

1. They address the covenant breaking of the people in oracles of stinging indictment and accusation.
2. They warn of the consequences of this folly as they speak of the judgment that has come and will yet come.
3. They remind people of the covenant faithfulness of God, who will yet act in some conclusive way to bring about his purposes. These oracles of restoration are the linchpin of Old Testament eschatology. They take the patterns of salvation history established in the period from Abraham to David and project them into a future of unparalleled glory and splendor when God will act on his great day to save his people. On that day the nations of the earth will see the light of Israel, and out of them will come a multitude to find salvation through the blessings of Israel.

The preacher should be careful to place the prophets into this redemptive-historical framework. There is a tendency among some to use the word "prophetic" exclusively to characterize a style of preaching that is directed toward a critique of our modern social structures and injustices. There is no doubt that the prophets and the gospel do address these issues, and the preacher must try to understand how. However, to use the word "prophetic" in a way that suggests that its meaning is essentially found in such a sociological orientation is very misleading. The older popular notion that the essence of prophecy was to predict the future was simplistic, yet it was not without merit. The writing proph-

4. Sidney Greidanus, *The Modern Preacher and the Ancient Text* (Grand Rapids: Eerdmans, 1988), p. 228.

ets are characterized by the development of an eschatological perspective that does not exist in the earlier prophets. I have already discussed this in chapter 8, and thus it will suffice to say that the eschatology of the prophets exhibits the following characteristics relating to salvation history:

1. It recapitulates the structures of salvation history already in place from the epoch of Abraham to David.
2. This recapitulation is not a mere repetition of the former in that, when it transpires, it will be perfect, glorious, and forever.
3. Eschatology, both of judgment and of restoration, involves two main foci: a more immediate one affecting the nation of Israel, and a more universal one involving the whole of creation. This makes room for more than one point of fulfillment and prepares the way for the three-fold fulfillment in the New Testament.[5] Let us now consider some representative passages from the prophetic books in the context of redemptive history.

1. The Marriage of Hosea (Hos. 1–3)

There is no doubt that the account of the marriage of Hosea has potential for some sermons on marriage itself, but that is not its main purpose. Hosea prophesies in the northern kingdom of Israel at the time when its history was nearing a chaotic end. His ministry begins in a period of relative calm during the reign of Jeroboam II. The book opens with the word of the Lord to Hosea telling him to marry a harlot. Children born to Gomer, Hosea's wife, are given symbolic names, again at the Lord's command, each of which relates to the covenant violations of Israel.[6] At the end of chapter 1 there is an oracle reaffirming Yahweh's faithfulness to the covenant and his intention to reverse the situation of doom and destruction. Chapter 2 is an oracle in which the marriage drama of Hosea's own life is applied to the "marriage" relationship of Israel and Yahweh. Israel, like Gomer, is a harlot. Although she is under judgment, God will woo her back so that the symbolic names of Hosea's children no longer apply: he will have pity on "Not pitied," and to "Not my people" he will say "you are my people." The story is completed in chapter 3, where Hosea is commanded to love the adulteress and to win her back as Yahweh will do to his people.

The whole account of Hosea's marriage is not without problems, as

---

5. See the discussion of this point in chapter 7.
6. Hos. 1:4-8. Jezreel is a direct reference to the murder at that place of the house of Ahab by Jehu (2 Kings 10:1-14); *Lo-ruhammah* and *Lo-ammi* are Hebrew for "not pitied" and "not my people," respectively.

most commentaries indicate. But the fact that God tells Hosea to do an unlikely and seemingly immoral thing in marrying a harlot must be accepted at face value. The relationship of chapter 3 to chapter 1 is another area that presents exegetical problems, but overall the thrust of these three chapters seems reasonably straightforward. It presents a magnificent illustration of the seriousness of Israel's covenant breaking, and of the covenant love and faithfulness of God. These oracles are the more poignant for their historical context of the decline of Israel and the impending devastation at the hands of the Assyrians. Hosea provides the last word of hope to the northern kingdom that has always been under the shadow of the apostasy and schism of Jeroboam I. Yet, while the purposes of God continue to be focused on the Davidic dynasty in Judah, Israel always remains an integral part of God's plan for the coming of his kingdom.

The heart of this account in Hosea 1–3 is recalled in two notable places in the New Testament. Paul in Romans 9:25-26 quotes Hosea 1:10 and 2:23 in connection with God's election and the mystery of Israel's unbelief. 1 Peter 2:10 quotes Hosea 1:9-10 and 2:23 along with a number of other Old Testament allusions and quotations that characterize the people of God under the new covenant. To put the texts into a more comprehensive redemptive-historical framework we need to recognize that the path from old people of God to new people of God is via the person of Jesus. Matthew recognizes this when he applies Hosea 11:1, which recalls God's kindness to Israel in the Exodus, to the return of the infant Jesus from Egypt after the threat from Herod has passed (Matt. 2:14-15). Israel was God's firstborn son brought out of Egypt in the redemptive event, but because of faithlessness Israel is called "not my people." One day, according to Hosea 1:10–2:1, this will be reversed. The subsequent history of Israel does not support this contention until we come to the one who *is* the true Israel coming from Egypt and who, at his baptism, is addressed by God as, "my Son in whom I am well pleased" (Luke 3:22). All that the New Testament says about the Church as a new people of God stands on the fact that faith unites us to the one true Son of God, and we become joint heirs with him (Rom. 8:14-17).

The marriage theme is not ruled out by this wider perspective symbolized by marriage. If a preacher should approach this part of Hosea as saying something about marriage, it is important to do so by recognizing that Christian marriage according to Paul in Ephesians 5:25, 32 is a relationship that speaks of, and is derived from, the relationship of Christ to the Church. The consummation of this is the eschatological marriage of the Lamb in Revelation 19:7; 21:2, 9.[7]

---

7. In Rev. 21:2, 9, Zion is spoken of as the bride. As in the Old Testament, Zion can be either the city or those who dwell in it as the people of God.

2. Isaiah's Missionary Vision (Isa. 2:1-4)

From the perspective of biblical theology a couple of points need to be made about this passage. First, it is clearly a piece of Zion eschatology that has a missionary perspective in that it refers to the day of salvation when the gentile nations will come flocking to the restored temple in Jerusalem. Second, we need to consider this oracle in terms of its significance within the entire book of Isaiah. It is a fairly advanced piece of eschatology in terms of its vision of the function of the new Jerusalem at the center of the world.[8] This literary wholeness and structure of prophetic books is considered below.

If we are going to avoid the view that Isaiah consists of an unruly collection of oracles with no real thought for plan or structure, we must ask why this oracle appears in this place. Isaiah 1 presents a very gloomy introduction to the covenant faithlessness of Judah and the already experienced results in the judgments of God. Then, suddenly, we are given this magnificent vision of restoration. Barry Webb is surely correct in his assertion that this oracle completes a movement from the negative situation in chapter 1 that "anticipates the movement of the book as a whole, from the Zion that is to the Zion that will be, via purifying judgment."[9] The eschatology of Isaiah 2 anticipates that of the latter part of the book that climaxes in the vision of the new heaven and the new earth in Isaiah 65:17-25.

The two major themes in this oracle are the restored Zion and the ingathering of the nations. Temple theology is at the heart of the redemptive revelation because of its implications that God wills to dwell among his people. The temple is linked to the priestly ministry of Israel as the place of sacrifice and therefore of reconciliation with God. It is also linked with the kingly ministry by association with David and Solomon and the chosen dynasty. The destruction of the Jerusalem temple in 586 B.C. by the Babylonians is a paramount catastrophe, but one that God enables the exiles to surmount by means of an ongoing prophetic ministry and the hope of a new beginning with a new temple.

While the attempt of the returning exiles to rebuild the temple is only moderately successful, the postexilic prophets focus in different ways on the reality that is yet to come. For many, this may seem to be realized in the extraordinary accomplishment of Herod in redeveloping the second temple. The Christological significance of the theme is developed in the Gospels as the true temple is shown to be Jesus himself. The theme of the impending destruction of the temple, which probably stems from the "abomination that

8. See Barry G. Webb, "Zion in Transformation: A Literary Approach to Isaiah," in *The Bible in Three Dimensions,* ed. D. Clines et al. (Sheffield: JSOT, 1990); *The Message of Isaiah* (Leicester: IVP, 1996).

9. Webb, *The Message of Isaiah,* p. 45.

desolates" in Daniel 9:27 and 11:31, is picked up in the apocalyptic sayings of Jesus.[10] For some reason many commentators take this as being fulfilled in the literal destruction of the Jerusalem temple in A.D. 70, an event which seems to be of very little interest to the New Testament writers. Far more significant is Jesus' sign of cleansing the temple, which in John's account provides us with a very different interpretation.

> His disciples remembered that it was written, "Zeal for your house will consume me." The Jews then said to him, "What sign can you show us for doing this?" Jesus answered them, "Destroy this temple, and in three days I will raise it up." The Jews then said, "This temple has been under construction for forty-six years, and will you raise it up in three days?" But he was speaking of the temple of his body. After he was raised from the dead, his disciples remembered that he had said this; and they believed the scripture and the word that Jesus had spoken. (John 2:17-22)

The destruction of this temple is clearly the crucifixion, for its rebuilding is the bodily resurrection of Jesus. In the light of this we can understand why Stephen was adamant that the Jews needed to move on from the old temple made with hands (Acts 7:47-51).

Our passage in Isaiah 2 links the temple's restoration to the ingathering of the gentiles. The apparent discrepancy between this ingathering in the Old Testament and the outreach of Christian mission is explainable in terms of the new temple. The real temple is where Jesus is for he *is* the temple, the place where God and humankind meet, the place of reconciliation and of the kingly rule. Jesus is in heaven, but he makes himself present among us by his Holy Spirit. Where the Spirit is, there the gospel is being preached and the people of God, both Jews and gentiles, are brought in to fellowship with God at the true temple. The Spirit is not confined to one physical and geographical location, which is why modern pilgrimages to "The Holy Land" are a misnomer.[11] The only biblical pilgrimage to the Holy Land is to go to Jesus by faith, for he represents for us the real Mount Zion.[12] The nations are coming to the temple wherever the gospel is preached and applied to human hearts by the Spirit of Jesus.

---

10. Mark 13:1-26. See Peter Bolt, "Mark 13: An Apocalyptic Precursor to the Passion Narrative," *Reformed Theological Review* 54.1 (1995).

11. While modern Israel or Palestine is emphatically not the Holy Land, I would not want to suggest that visiting these parts has no value for Christians who wish to gain some feeling for the context of the biblical story. Jesus' comments on the abolition of all "holy" places are worth considering (John 4:20-24). Referring to church buildings, or to certain parts of them, as sanctuaries is a similar misnomer to that of calling Palestine the Holy Land.

12. This is clear from the reference to Christian faith in Heb. 12:22-24 as a coming to Jesus and Zion.

One other point should be noted. There is a definite structure to the Jew-gentile relationship in the Old Testament that needs following up in the New. Jesus said to the Samaritan woman that salvation comes from the Jews. As Japheth is to share in the tents of Shem (Gen. 9:26-27), so the gentiles will be blessed through the Shemites, who are Abraham's descendants. The true descendant of Abraham to whom the promises apply is Jesus, and the children of Abraham are those who belong to Christ (Gal. 3:16, 29). Yet Paul's treatment of Israel in Romans 9–11 would seem to be unnecessary if the essential Jewishness of the gospel were not to be maintained.[13] Revelation 7, using the very Jewish imagery of apocalyptic, envisages two distinct though not separate groups of the redeemed. The perfect number redeemed out of the twelve tribes of Israel is complemented by the numberless multitude from every nation, tribe, and language group.

3. Amos's Vision of the Basket of Fruit (Amos 8:1-14)

Amos, the other writing prophet ministering to the northern kingdom, was sent from the south. Like Hosea his ministry begins in the time of Jeroboam II. The relatively stable political situation of this time was accompanied by a great deal of social injustice that is seen by the prophet as a reckless repudiation of God's covenant. Jeroboam sends Amaziah, the priest from the sanctuary at Bethel, to rebuke Amos for his condemnation of Israel. This only serves to stir Amos to proclaim more words of condemnation from the Lord (Amos 7:10-17). The vision of the basket of fruit is placed next to this biographical account in the book of Amos. The fruit is described as "summer fruit" and is interpreted as symbolic of the end that is coming on Israel.[14] It is followed in Amos 9:1-10 by a vision of the Lord standing by the altar uttering words of final judgment on Israel. The almost unremitting gloom of Amos is relieved in the final oracle of the book, which gives a brilliant picture of restoration on the day of salvation.

The hermeneutical questions raised for the preacher by such a passage as Amos 8 are similar to those we have considered in chapter 11 in relation to the law. Covenant breaking is law breaking irrespective of how it is specifically expressed in the social and religious life of the people. We must try to

---

13. The case for the ongoing distinction between Jew and gentile in the New Testament is carefully and, I believe, convincingly argued by Donald W. B. Robinson, *Faith's Framework: The Structure of New Testament Theology* (Sydney/Exeter: Albatross/Paternoster, 1985), chapter 4. The oneness in Christ argued by Paul in Gal. 3 is a oneness of acceptance with God as a new humanity in Christ, and does not obliterate the distinctions.

14. So, as NRSV margin indicates, "summer fruit" (Heb. *qayits*) and "end" (Heb. *qets*) involve us in a pun based on the sound of the two words.

understand how this oracle functions theologically in the context of this epoch of redemptive history, and on this basis work out the path by which it leads us to a valid application to a Christian congregation. One hermeneutic has involved a simple transfer from the covenant-based society of Israel to the modern society in which we live. If God thunders against Samaria or Jerusalem, then God is at the same time thundering against New York, or London, or Hong Kong, or Sydney. Put in those terms it is simple enough, for God also has words of condemnation for pagan nations in a number of the prophets.[15]

The liberal hermeneutic is commendable in its concern to address the ills of society. It goes astray when it applies the prophetic judgment directly without concern for the pathway of redemptive history in the Bible. Covenant breaking and covenant keeping in Israel converge on the one who both kept the covenant and was content to be counted among the transgressors and to pay the full penalty for covenant breaking. The central fact that Jesus bore the curse of the covenant in his death on the cross simply cannot be omitted from the equation. God has made a full end, but in so doing he has provided the way for the renewed life of the people of God. The concerns of Christians for social justice must be worked out in the framework of the gospel. This of course raises a number of issues as to the mode of our action and what we seek to achieve. While it is true that modern evangelicals have often reacted against the social justice issue because of the liberal agenda that confuses social action with the gospel, it ought to be recognized that evangelical religion has been one of the greatest motivations for social action in modern history. The prophets never see the answer to the social issues in any way other than through the saving work of God and faithfulness to the covenant.

4. Jeremiah's Letter to the Exiles (Jer. 29:1-14)

In the face of the Assyrian threat to Jerusalem at the end of the eighth century, the prophet Isaiah has counseled steadfastness on the grounds of faithfulness of Yahweh to protect the city and its people. A century later, in the face of the Babylonian threat, Jeremiah counsels the opposite. His was the heart-rending task of presiding over the doom of his people and nation. To him had been given the most unpopular message imaginable: Jerusalem is finished. When the blow fell and the king of Babylon took the Judean king and a large number of others into exile, Jeremiah continues to hammer home the theme that exile must be endured until the Lord is pleased to act. His vision of the two baskets of figs (Jer. 24), one of good fruit and the other of bad

---

15. For example, the oracles against the neighbors of Israel in Amos 1:3–2:3.

fruit, was interpreted to mean that the good figs were those who had been re-moved from the land. He foretold a sojourn of seventy years in Babylon (Jer. 25:11-12; 29:10).

The letter of Jeremiah 29 written from Jerusalem to the exiles in Baby-lon reinforces this curious message of reversal. He counsels them to settle down and to make the best of the situation; to build, plant, marry, and repro-duce. They are to seek the welfare of the city almost as if they were still pray-ing for the peace of Jerusalem.[16] This would be unthinkable under the terms of the covenant promises if it were not for the promise of restoration to come. For the purposes of God to be centered in the great harlot city of Babylon must have been inconceivable to most Jews. However, it stands as the climax of the history of judgment on covenant breakers that pagans should be the in-strument of God in the chastisement of his people. It is also an amazing ex-pression of grace that God would sustain a remnant of the faithful until the right time should come for their restoration. As Isaiah sees it, the eventual re-turn would be like a second exodus from captivity, and signal the favor of the Lord in salvation.[17] The second part of Jeremiah 29 returns to the theme of the rotten figs, which are those left in Jerusalem.

This passage, then, functions in its context to highlight the purposes of God and his faithfulness in the midst of judgment. There are lessons to be learned from the way God deals with his people insofar as they show us the holy righteousness of God who must judge sin but who is a compassionate and saving God. An important principle of prayer is given expression in Jeremiah 29:10-14. While God acts to save in response to prayer, the prayer of the exiles is founded on the revealed word of God. Another dimension of this letter that needs following through is that of the blessing of God coming outside the ex-ternal structures of the kingdom, but always in the hope of the restoration of the kingdom. When Israel walks through the valley of the shadow of death, God is with her and his rod and staff comfort because his rule cannot fail.

5. The Last Oracle (Mal. 4:1-6)

The three postexilic prophets minister to the restoration community that is in danger of losing hope. The reason for this is the discrepancy between the hope of restoration that would be the signal for the establishment of God's glorious kingdom, and the reality that exists in the new nation. These proph-ets need to be read in conjunction with the books of Ezra and Nehemiah. The salvation-history context is that of the rebuilding of Jerusalem and the tem-

---

16. Compare Ps. 122:6.
17. Isa. 40:1-5; 43:1-7, 15-21; 48:20-21; 51:9-11; see also Jer. 23:7-8.

ple, but also of the disappointment of expectations for the coming of the promised day of the Lord. The fulfillment of the prophetic hope of restoration from the exile is, at best, only partial. The postexilic nation and its structures are a pale reflection of the promised glory, and there are two reasons for this. The immediate reason is the one given by the postexilic prophets, namely, the continuing faithlessness of the people. The theological reason is the one that we can understand only in hindsight, namely, the Messiah-king and savior has not yet come.

The immediate cause for the lack of blessing is, then, the disobedience of the people, and specifically their profaning of the temple (Mal. 2:10-17). If they long for the Lord's coming, they should be warned that none will be able to endure such a coming because it will involve a cleansing judgment (Mal. 3:1-5). But the day of the Lord is coming. Evildoers will be consumed, and those who revere the name of the Lord will find blessing (Mal. 4:1-3). The last part of the oracle promises the return of Elijah to call people back to the covenant, and then the great and terrible day of the Lord will come.

Our Old Testament canon, then, ends with a frank recognition that the story is not complete.[18] There is no room for complacency among the postexilic Jews, but neither is there need for despair. The promise of a new Elijah reminds us of the way that particular prophet functioned in the whole scheme of things. The New Testament takes up the story after a gap of nearly four hundred years. John the Baptist is seen as the one who fulfills the role of Elijah to turn the people back to God in repentance. We might note in this regard that the baptism of Jesus is portrayed as the identification of Jesus with Israel in repentance. We need to remember that the goal of repentance is to be turned to God. While Jesus had no sin to turn from, he shows himself to be the perfectly God-oriented Israelite, and hence the son in whom God is well pleased. We should also note in passing that it is the incompleteness of the Old Testament that makes a Christological interpretation necessary.

Literary and Historical Considerations

The old literary criticism or, more strictly, historical criticism, dealt fairly harshly with the prophets. There was a greater emphasis on source analysis that led to fragmentation. Perhaps the most notorious example was the critical decision to make at least three Isaiahs out of the book and to date chapters 40–66 to the exilic and postexilic periods. Evangelical preachers found little

---

18. The Hebrew canon places the Prophets before the Writings, and the last book is 2 Chronicles.

help in this approach since it tended to naturalistic explanations of the message, especially the eschatology. The idea of God actually speaking through the prophets was not particularly popular among the critics, and the notion that God would or could cause a prophet to predict the name of Cyrus two hundred years ahead of his time was simply unthinkable.

The advent of form criticism did not change the skepticism of many toward the biblical texts, but form criticism did focus on the way literary forms were used, often as stereotypes, to convey different kinds of messages. So, for example, the prophetic indictments, threats of judgment, and oracles of salvation helped focus the critic on the main dimensions of the message. The oracle of salvation was particularly associated with the phrase, "Fear not," which led some to propose that Jesus deliberately used this term as the introduction to oracles of the salvation he was claiming to bring. Donald Gowan nominates three main kinds of speech in the prophets: biographical narrative; prophetic speeches; and words from man to God such as hymns, laments, and prayers.[19]

More recently still, a new literary criticism has focused on whole books and sought to understand the creative urges that brought about the finished texts as we have them. Thus, while many of these new critics would not accept that Isaiah, the eighth-century prophet, was responsible for the whole book of Isaiah, they have found a new interest in the unity of the book and its message.[20] This new emphasis is a very healthy one insofar as it seeks to understand the books not as amalgams of fragments from different sources but as deliberately crafted, unified texts. The weakness in much of this is a tendency to regard lightly the historical and theological claims of the text. We need to keep all three dimensions in view.

In chapter 15 we shall consider apocalyptic literature. It is perhaps worth remarking at this point that there is a certain amount of scholarly discussion about the relationship between apocalyptic literature and prophetic eschatology. The distinctiveness of biblical apocalyptic warrants a separate treatment of the subject, but we should bear in mind that some parts of the prophetic literature are in a gray area, and it is difficult to say with certainty if these parts are or are not truly apocalyptic. In the final analysis, however, that is not the most important consideration. Placing a label on a literary form or genre is not the issue. The preacher is under constraint to try to understand how the particular text functions as a vehicle for God's word. The identification of the genre is important only if it helps us in this task.

19. Donald E. Gowan, *Reclaiming the Old Testament for the Christian Pulpit* (Atlanta: John Knox, 1976), p. 121.

20. There are evangelical scholars who maintain both the literary and authorial unity of Isaiah. See J. A. Motyer, *The Prophecy of Isaiah* (Leicester: IVP, 1993), and Webb, *The Message of Isaiah.*

One other aspect of prophetic literature should be commented on, and that is the language of much of the eschatology. I have suggested that the definitive fulfillment of eschatology is found in Jesus Christ. If, then, he is the new land and temple, and so on, does this mean that all the prophetic terminology has only symbolic value? The answer is no. All kinds of metaphor may be used, and one of the tasks of the interpreter is to try to understand when language is being used in symbolic fashion. I will discuss this further in the chapter on apocalyptic literature. The fact that Jesus is the fulfillment of prophecy in himself does not exhaust the fulfillment.[21] While it is clear that the fulfillment of prophecy cannot be pushed into a literalistic mold, it is also clear that it cannot be relegated exclusively to an "in Christ" fulfillment. Thus, for example, the description of the messianic age in Isaiah 11 involves a return to harmony among the beasts and man. This belongs to the wider hope of a new Eden, new heavens, and a new earth.[22] The whole point of God fulfilling every element of promise in Jesus is so that it may have its eventual universal consummation. It is not fanciful to propose that since animals are part of the original scene in Eden, these nature prophecies point to a reality of the new earth where humans will once again dwell in harmony with the animal kingdom.

Planning Sermons on Prophetic Texts

I have already indicated some dissatisfaction with the approach to preaching from the prophets that moves from the indictment of Israel and Judah for covenant breaking to an indictment of the ills in contemporary society. As Donald Gowan says, "The most dubious move is to apply to America what was once spoken to Israel, as if America were the new covenant nation."[23] This is a timely warning that we should not plan sermons on the prophets for some preconceived purpose, such as tackling social ills, unless we are sure that it is a legitimate application of the texts chosen. Expository preachers are more inclined to be inductive in their approach; to take a prophetic book because it is there, because it is about the gospel, and then to see where it leads us.

We are more likely to stick to an inductive plan when preaching from the minor prophets. They are regarded as "minor" only for their comparative brevity, and it is this that makes a comprehensive series more manageable.

21. See chapter 7 on the fulfillment of all prophecy for us, in us, and with us.
22. Isa. 65:17-25. Note the repetition of the animal theme in v. 25. See also the Eden themes in Isa. 51:3; Ezek. 36:33-35; 47:1-12.
23. Gowan, *Reclaiming the Old Testament,* p. 126.

When preaching from any of the three major prophets, again so named because of their length, the selection process is more difficult. The preacher is prone to select well-known or favorite passages. Whatever method of selection is applied, the chosen passages or oracles should always be placed in both the literary and the redemptive-historical framework. This can be done quite briefly in the actual sermon, but it helps in understanding if something of the theological unity of the book can be highlighted. At some stage the passage needs to be placed in its canonical context so that its relationship to the gospel can be drawn out.

One of the most important services the preacher can perform in the preaching of prophetic texts is emphatically to avoid any attempt to predict the exact details of time and events of a future fulfillment. We will achieve this if we are careful to place the gospel of Jesus Christ into its relationship to the prophetic message as the focus of fulfillment. By speaking into a contemporary historical situation with a hope for the future, the prophets provide a vital link between the coming of Jesus of Nazareth and the past history of God's people. We need to hear the prophetic text in its own context if we are to understand its impact on ancient Hebrew society before we move to hear its fulfillment in Christ. We can only achieve this if our selection of passages to preach on is done with care. If possible we should deal with a complete oracle or, if choosing a smaller unit, interpret its meaning as part of the complete oracle.[24]

---

24. Greidanus, *The Modern Preacher,* chapter 10, gives very useful guidelines for the practicalities of preaching from the prophets.

CHAPTER 13

Preaching from the Wisdom Literature

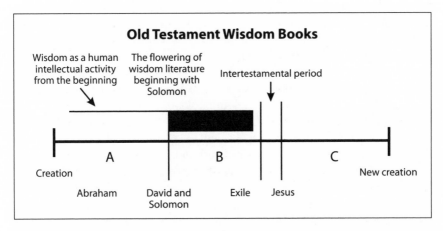

Old Testament Wisdom Books

Diagram 13: Wisdom as a human activity is as old as humanity. The wisdom of God revealed to his people begins when God first speaks to humankind. Ongoing revelation continues to be the framework of God's wisdom within which human wisdom can be developed. True wisdom is a response to human experience in the light of God's wisdom.

The Wisdom Books in Biblical-Theological Context

There are two kinds of wisdom in the Bible: the wisdom of God and the wisdom of men. The latter can be divided into pagan wisdom, or wisdom gained through human thought and experience without reference to the wisdom of God, and godly wisdom, which applies the perspective of divine revelation to human thought and experience. Some Christians work with the mistaken idea that godly wisdom involves God, or the Holy Spirit, simply pouring his thought into ours or working directly through our minds. This is seen to relieve us of the task of thinking through issues and making considered decisions for which we are entirely responsible. This is not a biblical view of wisdom. That God did directly inspire certain people with revelation is without doubt, although the psychology of this process is largely unknown to us. The subject of wisdom as a human pursuit is the topic of the biblical wisdom literature, and this literature would be superfluous if God made all our decisions for us.[1]

The wisdom literature includes the books of Proverbs, Job, Ecclesiastes and, some would add, The Song of Songs. There is also a list of psalms, by no means unanimously agreed on, that are classified as wisdom literature. The identification of wisdom outside of the main wisdom books became a matter of concern for biblical scholars, and the preacher should be aware of the possibility of wisdom idioms turning up in all kinds of places in the Old Testament.[2] One problem of the three main wisdom books, as well as the identifiable wisdom psalms, is the difficulty of dating them. However, it is reasonable to say that wisdom literature begins to flower with Solomon and continues for most of the remainder of the Old Testament period. The nature of wisdom is such that a precise dating is neither possible nor necessary.

In order to place Israel's wisdom books into biblical-theological context, it is helpful to understand that the general historical and cultural context of this literature involves a very ancient intellectual and literary activity among Israel's neighbors. This is not surprising because human beings are characterized by the gathering and classifying of knowledge. As a species we have always learned in various ways from experience. That is the basis of scientific and cultural progress or change. It was usually done in ancient societies with some sense of the religious element involved, whether it was through divine revelation or providential assistance. Thus, the ancient Egyptians had the sense of universal order overseen by a divine being named *ma'at*. Long before Israel became a nation at the exodus from Egypt there was a flourishing wisdom literature in both Babylon and Egypt. According to Stephen, Moses was schooled in all the wisdom of Egypt in his upbringing at Pharaoh's court (Acts 7:22).

We have to say, then, that religious orientation was not the distinctive

---

1. The burning issue of guidance in the Christian life is closely related to that of wisdom. See Gary Friesen, *Decision Making and the Will of God* (Portland: Multnomah, 1980); Phillip D. Jensen and Anthony J. Payne, *The Last Word on Guidance* (Homebush West, Sydney: Anzea Press, 1991).
2. See Graeme Goldsworthy, *Gospel and Wisdom: Israel's Wisdom Literature in the Christian Life* (Exeter: Paternoster, 1987), chapter 9. This matter is also discussed in Donn F. Morgan, *Wisdom in the Old Testament Traditions* (Atlanta: John Knox, 1981).

feature of Israel's wisdom, any more than was religion itself distinctive to Israel. Israel's wisdom was distinctive and superior to that of its neighbors only because Israel knew the one true and living God. A biblical theology of wisdom takes us back to Adam and Eve to whom God spoke and revealed the divine order as the framework within which they were to think and act.[3] From that point on we see that the revelation of God constitutes the grounds for all proper human thinking and willing. Yet this revelation is progressive and moves from the promises to Abraham, through the captivity and Exodus, and then to the entry into the promised land. As we have seen, the climax of this first epoch of redemptive historical revelation comes with David and Solomon. It is no accident that wisdom begins to find expression under David and flourishes at the hands of Solomon.

Solomon's wisdom is really the theme of the whole narrative section in 1 Kings 3–10, for thereafter problems of Solomon are stressed and "anti-wisdom" takes over. We are familiar with the story of Solomon's request for wisdom in 1 Kings 3, and the first evidence of it in his handling of the dispute between two women over a baby. It is important to note that the whole glowing description of Solomon's reign and the glory and riches of his kingdom come within this context. Solomon asked for an understanding mind and, in response, God gave it to him along with riches and honor. It becomes clear from this narrative that these other gifts are closely linked to the gift of wisdom. The magnificence of the temple is also an aspect of Solomon's wisdom, as the queen of Sheba clearly perceives (1 Kings 10:4-5).

Solomon's wisdom not only surpasses that of all the wise men of the east, but the period of his rule is seen, in this first part of the narrative, as echoing the kingdom of God.[4] That these wise people, including the queen of Sheba, flock to hear the wisdom of Solomon is suggestive of the eschatological blessing promised to the nations and to come through Abraham's descendants. In the context of biblical theology, then, wisdom comes to its maturity at the end of the first epoch of kingdom revelation. This seems logical in that with David and Solomon the entire pattern of redemption and the kingdom of God is in place. In other words, the framework of divine revelation that enables human beings to make sense of the world and of human experience is established. This epistemological (how we know) and noetic (how we think) framework is vital for the interpretation of our existence in the world.

Wisdom drawn from human experience is sometimes referred to as empirical wisdom. However, it should be distinguished from modern empiri-

---

3. Friesen, *Decision Making,* pp. 165-67, has an amusing and pointed parable of this matter in which Adam and Eve learn that they have to use their God-given freedom to make decisions for themselves.

4. 1 Kings 4:20-34. Note the echoes of v. 25 in the eschatology of Jer. 23:6; Mic. 4:4; and Zech. 3:10.

cism. There is a modern scientific empiricism that mistakenly assumes its own objectivity and works on the presupposition that knowledge gained through our senses is the only valid knowledge. Since this presupposition is not empirically demonstrable, it involves a "religious" leap of faith, which is a denial of the very thing it asserts. Biblical empiricism, however, recognizes its dependence on the self-revelation of God for a right understanding of reality. This is emphatically not the Thomist view of nature plus grace, which posits the possibility of true, even though partial, understanding through nature without grace, that is, without the gift of special revelation. According to this view grace complements and completes natural knowledge. The biblical view of empirical wisdom is not nature *plus* grace, but nature *through* grace. The gracious revelation of God is the prism through which every fact is viewed and understood. In biblical terms: "The fear of the Lord is the beginning of knowledge," and "The fear of the Lord is the beginning of wisdom."[5]

Wisdom, then, has to do with a right perception and understanding of reality. It presupposes that there is a divinely ordained order in the universe that can be perceived. It directly contradicts the relativism of postmodernism, for wisdom assumes the coherence of God's created order. The book of Proverbs is characterized by the assumption that, given the right start with the fear of the Lord, a person is able to develop a perception of the created order through observation and instruction in a way that makes for the good life, a life of wisdom and righteousness. The message of Job is that in this pursuit of understanding we may encounter deep mysteries that cannot be penetrated and that throw us back onto trust in the goodness of God. Ecclesiastes, a complex book, reflects on how human wickedness confuses the order to the extent that a rigid application of empirical wisdom to life's experiences is likely to lead us astray. All three books complement one another in encouraging the believer to use mind and faculties to try to understand life in God's universe, but also in rebuking the arrogance of those who would claim to have it all together. Trust in the goodness of a sovereign God is the underpinning of all intellectual endeavor.

We may place all the wisdom literature of the Old Testament in this general area of history beginning with Solomon's contribution to Proverbs. The significance of Solomon is seen in the way his name is associated with the subject of wisdom — which, given his track record as narrated in 1 Kings 11 and afterward, is perhaps a little surprising. A biblical theology of wisdom needs to take into account the distinct features of the books themselves while bearing in mind that the reason they are linked as a common genre is

---

5. Prov. 1:7; 9:10. The fear of the Lord here could be described as the appropriate response of faith to the self-revelation of God. This revelation can only be the covenant, redemption, and the law.

not so much the literary characteristics they share as the subject matter of wisdom as how we make sense of the world. During the period of Israel's decline wisdom literature, so it would seem, continues to be produced. Its focus, however, is not on the fortunes of the nation as such. In fact, one of the problems for biblical theologians regarding wisdom literature has been its lack of national concern and its comparative silence about such matters as redemptive history and the covenant.

One suggestion favored by many biblical theologians is that wisdom is focused on creation rather than salvation. Certainly questions of covenant and salvation history are not prominent in the literature, but it would be a mistake to imagine that such a creation orientation was somehow a different mind-set altogether. The sages of Israel were not a separate sect with a different theology. Wisdom is not unrelated to the major concerns of Old Testament theology. The Solomon narratives in 1 Kings 3–10, along with a number of other passages that link wisdom to the king or messiah, surely indicate that wisdom and salvation are closely related. This is borne out by other passages, not of the wisdom genre, which see the goal of salvation as a new creation. A different emphasis there may be, but the lack of explicit salvation history in wisdom is hardly the problem it is sometimes made out to be. Thus, Solomon, the accepted patron of wisdom, is the messianic son of David in his capacity as temple builder. Though in the end Solomon fails to live up to expectations, the prophetic eschatology maintains the wisdom theme. Isaiah 11:1-3 describes the messianic prince to come in wisdom terms:

> A shoot shall come out from the stump of Jesse, and a branch shall grow out of his roots. The spirit of the LORD shall rest on him, the spirit of wisdom and understanding, the spirit of counsel and might, the spirit of knowledge and the fear of the LORD. His delight shall be in the fear of the LORD.

Wisdom is not prominent in prophetic eschatology, but there is enough of it to help us complete the picture. The main link between wisdom and salvation history is Solomon and the temple. While the wisdom literature has the common theme of understanding what is in life so that one might be better able to take charge of the good life, this, like law keeping, is something that ultimately eludes perfection. The kingly figure who is the great sponsor of wisdom himself fails the test, but he stands in the line of the promise given to David. The eschatology of wisdom points to the wise rule of the Messiah-king to come. Finally, of course, this expectation is only fulfilled in the New Testament. Jesus of Nazareth comes and is revealed as the wise man of God. Even as a child he is described in wisdom terms as increasing in wisdom and years and in divine and human favor (Luke 2:52). We note here that this is recorded in connection with the boy Jesus at the temple. It is appropriate, given the relationship of wisdom to the temple of Solomon, that Jesus is revealed both as wisdom and the new temple. In his teaching he uses the wisdom forms of proverb and parable. To the classic Reformation Christology based on the offices of prophet, priest, and king, we need to add wise man. So, Paul asserts that Christ became for us wisdom from God (1 Cor. 1:30). In Jesus divine and human wisdom meet perfectly. Furthermore, as we see from the biblical books, from the narratives of human failure, and from our own experience, we are prone to do foolish things, even as Christians. Wisdom points to our responsibility to try to understand life and reality in the light of Christ so that we might make wise decisions. We know that just as our actions are tainted by our sinfulness so they are tainted by our foolishness. The two failures are really one, and both are dealt with through our being justified by Christ. His righteousness is attributed to the believer, and there is no condemnation for those who are in Christ Jesus. For Jesus to be made our wisdom means that we are accounted truly wise in him. When our wisdom has been lacking there is always room for repentance and the assurance that there is no condemnation.

1. Proverbs 1:1-7

No series of sermons on Proverbs should be attempted without at least making clear reference to the prologue to the book. This passage is important for indicating a purpose for the whole collection, which otherwise might seem to be a rather arbitrary gathering of miscellaneous wisdom passages. This is manifestly a composite book, but the prologue shows that there is a plan to the way it has been put together. We should not ignore the title that, although the whole book is clearly not by Solomon, places the entire collection under his name. It links Proverbs with this key person at the climax of the first epoch of salvation history. After stating what the collection is intended to achieve, the ruling principle is given in v. 7: the fear of the Lord is the beginning of knowledge. The idea of the fear of the Lord is not unique to the wisdom literature, but it is often a good indicator of the wisdom idiom. We note further that it is the fear of the *Lord,* that is, the fear of Yahweh, the God of the covenant. This is also a link with salvation history. When so many of the individual sayings in Proverbs contain no reference to God at all, it is important to stress this connection to the fear of Yahweh.

2. Proverbs 8:22-31

This passage has been traditionally interpreted as a reference to Christ, which of course in the Old Testament it isn't. The passage consists of a poetic personification of wisdom. It is not a divine personification like the Egyptian *Ma'at* but rather a metaphor for the place of wisdom in the planning of God for the shape of the universe. Wisdom is portrayed as the beginning of God's work; it attends creation and rejoices over it. Thus, the order established by God in creation is that which can make for order in the lives of God's people. While this passage, then, is not about Christ directly, it certainly foreshadows the role of Christ as the wisdom of God in creation (Col. 1:15-17).

3. Proverbs 10:1-32

It is important that the context of salvation history is not ignored when the preacher tackles some of the individual sayings in Proverbs. They can easily be treated as if they had a validity on their own, and indeed they can make sense even if treated as simple examples of worldly wisdom. Empirical wisdom is drawn from human observation and experience, and thus for many of the sayings there is nothing that would distinguish them from secular proverbs or the empirical wisdom sayings that come out of another religious context.[6] Pagans and secularists are, after all, part of the same human race and are seeking to understand the same kind of human experience in the same world as believers. Non-Christians and pagans can do clever things and, on a certain level, make wise decisions. The differences come in the presuppositions about the reason for the observable order and how to evaluate experience and behavior. Proverbs 10 is a collection of sayings that mainly contrast wise and foolish behavior or, alternatively, righteous and wicked behavior. It would appear that these two pairs of opposites are synonymous. There is a cumulative effect to this chapter that works on the assumption of the character of God as the basis of assessing what is wise and righteous. Insofar as a natural retribution operates in the world, it is because God has made it so.

The empirical wisdom of Proverbs makes an important contribution to the understanding of the biblical word "righteousness." Because it is virtually synonymous with wisdom, and because wisdom involves perception of the order in the whole of creation, righteousness is seen to be far more than ethi-

---

6. Most commentators agree that Prov. 22:17–23:14 is heavily dependent on the Egyptian wisdom of Amen-em-ope. The fact that Solomon could be compared to pagan sages, including the queen of Sheba, suggests a certain commonality in ancient Near Eastern wisdom.

cal conformity. It encompasses a person's relationship to God, to people, and to the world of nature. Thus, a passage like Isaiah 11 that focuses on the wisdom of the Messiah-king moves to contemplate the restoration of order in nature. Isaiah 32 looks toward the day when justice and righteousness will characterize nature. Righteousness is acceptance with God because we are restored to harmony with the order he has created. When Paul refers to Christ as our wisdom and righteousness, he is focusing on the all-embracing nature of our justification in Christ. Jesus is the restored order for us. That is why Paul can then go on to eschew worldly wisdom and to express his determination to know nothing among his hearers but Christ and him crucified (1 Cor. 1:30–2:2).

4. Job 28

If any passage sums up the message of Job it is this one. While there is truth in the common assumption that Job deals with the problem of suffering, it can be asserted that the real theme of the book is: Where is wisdom to be found? Placing Job as a whole in the context of salvation history is difficult especially since the narrative portions provide no links with the other narratives of the Old Testament. It is not even clear that the narratives intend us to take the person of Job as a historical character. Given that this is a wisdom book, the bulk of which is written in poetry with a very stylized structure, it is arguable that the purpose of the book is served whether or not the account is historical. In this regard we might compare it with the parables of Jesus.

5. Ecclesiastes

The book of Ecclesiastes presents certain problems to the preacher because of the difficulty in understanding its structure. As far as its placement in the context of salvation history and biblical theology in general, there is little that can be added to what has already been said. It belongs to the period somewhere between Solomon and the end of the Old Testament period. Some scholars see it as containing an apologia against certain pagan philosophies and would consequently date it relatively late. It is more likely that it is intended to be a broadside against the distortion of Israelite wisdom and thus continues the kind of protest that we find in Job. The rigid application of natural retribution (as with Job's friends) cannot account for human experience, which faces the double confusion of divine mystery and human sinfulness.

6. The Song of Solomon

The only clue to the salvation-history context for this book is its association with Solomon, which also reinforces the conviction that it belongs with the wisdom literature.[7] Traditional attempts to give the Song of Solomon an allegorical interpretation seem largely to have been motivated by a dissatisfaction with the idea that a book of the Bible could deal with the love of a man and a woman. Commentators differ in their views of the unity of the book, and opinions range from seeing it as a collection of separate love poems to a well-structured drama of true love. The theme is timeless, and from the perspective of biblical theology the question is how it testifies to Christ. This work more than any other part of the Old Testament might seem to defy the claims of Jesus that the Scriptures testify to him, especially as we have no record of his ever entering into a sexual relationship with a woman. Modern commentators have quite rightly been at pains to reassert the view that the book is primarily about human love, the love of one man for one woman, and not an allegory of God's love for his people. Such human love is an entirely proper concern for Scripture, and such love also is revealed as having its foundations in the love of God for his people, and specifically in the love of Christ for his Church. The allegorical approach was not wrong in seeing this connection but erred in bypassing the face value of the text's concern for human love.[8]

Literary and Historical Considerations

The literary questions relating to the wisdom literature include which major literary forms are found and how they function. Questions of the theology of wisdom are often closely related to the literary matters. Starting with Proverbs we note that there are perhaps three main literary types. The first, the instruction, occurs mainly in the first nine chapters and in the "Amen-em-ope" section.[9] The instruction is a longer wisdom saying usually beginning with an address.[10] What follows is then either a direct imperative instruction or

---

7. While not sharing many of the literary characteristics of wisdom, the book does express concern for significant factors in our human existence: love and marriage. At the same time there is little to link its concerns with Israel's salvation history.

8. See Barry G. Webb, "The Song of Songs as a Love Poem and as Holy Scripture," *Reformed Theological Review* 49.3 (1990): 91-99.

9. Prov. 22:17–23:14. Instruction forms are also found in the rest of chapter 23 and chapter 24.

10. The Hebrew usually addresses "My son," but the NRSV changes this to the inclusive "My child."

conditional and result clauses. Typically the instruction exhorts the pupil or child to strive after wisdom, or it gives moral instruction and warning against evil pursuits.

The second literary type is the two-lined proverbial saying that usually contains some form of parallelism. While there is some evidence that an editorial hand has been at work to arrange these in some thematic and formal order, the indications are that the individual sentences had their own origin in human experience. The questions, then, are how much do we try to penetrate the meaning of the individual sayings, and how much are we led by the canonical arrangement in the finished book of Proverbs?[11] An important theological question relates to the way the proverbs were intended to function.[12] It must be emphasized that, while law and wisdom may overlap in their stated concerns, wisdom sayings are not presented as law. We mistake the function of Proverbs if we see the individual sayings as the fine print of Sinai. Sinai functions as the revelation of the infallible wisdom of God. Proverbs functions as divinely inspired human wisdom that reflects on individual concrete situations of experience. They are not general rules with divine sanctions like the laws of Sinai. The sanctions in wisdom are those built into the nature of things. While God graciously reveals his wisdom in the lawful framework for understanding reality, he expects his people to express their humanity by using their reasoning and thinking powers within that framework.

One other form in Proverbs is the numerical saying, which is characterized by grouping a number of things with the formula n, n+1.[13] These appear to function in the same way as many of the sentence proverbs by simply placing things together and leaving it open to the reader to perceive what is the common feature, and even to add more items (n+2, n+3, etc.). These sayings appear to group things in order to show that, contrary to first appearances, there is in fact an orderliness to the world and to human experience.

The literary questions relating to the book of Job concern the status of the prose sections in relation to the poetic center of the book, and the structure of the poetic section. The preacher must decide how a series of sermons on this very long book might be attempted. Some scholars have suggested that the prose prologue and epilogue constituted an original tale in which Job loses all and subsequently has everything restored. As interesting as such speculation might be, we have to deal with the canonical book of Job and not some theoretical antecedents. Thus we must treat it as a unity and try to understand the contents of the unity. Any good commentary will aid in under-

---

11. See my comments above on Prov. 10.

12. Goldsworthy, *Gospel and Wisdom,* chapter 6.

13. Here n = any number; Prov. 6:16-19 (n = 6); 30:15-16, 18-19, 21-23, 24-28, 29-31 (in all but one n = 3). Amos uses this form in his oracles against the nations (Amos 1:3–2:6).

standing the literary structure. For the preacher, a more pressing question is that of how the arguments of the four friends of Job are to be taken. Since their approach is finally rejected, can we say that everything they utter is false? Bear in mind that Job also has much of his discourses contradicted. The preacher faces the task of trying to determine the truth of the individual speeches and even of the individual utterances within each speech. There is a good case to be made that the friends of Job are not so much mistaken in their specific statements as in the rigid application they make of their point of view. Some scholars have referred to this as the "crisis of wisdom."[14] As I have said elsewhere concerning the intellectual struggle between Job and the friends:

> There is never a head-on clash of ideas which leaves one or other the clear winner. We may suggest that this clever arrangement underlines the fact that the friends are never wholly wrong. In this lies the appeal of the book. It is an exercise in making contact between two aspects of wisdom. The one stresses the observable patterns of cause and effect, while the other stresses the mysteries of life's experiences.[15]

If Job represents some tensions between the norms of human experience, the relationship of deeds to outcomes, and the inexplicable mysteries in life, Ecclesiastes certainly involves more of a head-on clash. This is not to disqualify proverbial wisdom, for there is quite a bit of it in Ecclesiastes, but only to question its rigid application in a way that contradicts experience. The literary problem of Ecclesiastes is in trying to discern some plan or development.[16] In view of the apparent pessimism of Qohelet and his view that everything is breath (Heb. *hevel*), the preacher must find some way of understanding the message as a positive contribution to our view of reality. In the final analysis, Qohelet does not despair; he acknowledges the mysteries in life, but at the same time recognizes life as a good gift from God.

Both Job and Ecclesiastes are important for their development of a theme that is already there in Proverbs, if not so prominent. This is the theme of the limitations of human wisdom. While Proverbs may seem to be the most optimistic in this regard, the limits of wisdom are clear. God's revealed wisdom is always the framework of true human wisdom, and God's good providence is the object of trust and confidence when human wisdom fails.

14. Goldsworthy, *Gospel and Wisdom,* chapter 7.
15. Goldsworthy, *Gospel and Wisdom,* p. 95.
16. One theory even suggests that our version of the book came from an original codex whose pages had been shuffled. Perhaps the value of this fairly unlikely theory is that it underlines the apparent lack of development in the book's argument.

The literary concerns for the Song of Solomon lie mainly in the area of the unity and structure of the book. There is a certain difficulty encountered if we try to deal with it as a kind of dramatic poem, and yet to treat it as simply an anthology of love poems does not really do justice to it. The preacher is faced with a choice about the main characters: Are we dealing with the king and his lover, or is the king an intruder in the love between two of his subjects? One thing is clear: the perspective of the book on human love is realistic. It extols the mysteries and the pleasures of love freely expressed and yet is without a hint of salaciousness. It also recognizes the dangers of passion and even the perils that human sinfulness can introduce into true love. It is neither prudish nor lustful.

Planning Sermons on Wisdom Texts

Probably the biggest pitfall in dealing with wisdom in sermons is the temptation to isolate a small portion of text from its literary-canonical context and its redemptive-historical context. There is so much practical material in Proverbs and Ecclesiastes that we might be tempted to deal with a wisdom saying, or a group of them, selected for the topical relevance to a behavioral or ethical issue faced by our congregation. I can see no real problem in dealing with a topic in the light of such wisdom sayings provided that we do not use the opportunity to put our hearers under the law with no gospel. Proverbs is as much about how one goes about gaining wisdom as it is about particular topics of wisdom.

A sermon series on Job is a challenge. How much do we need to cover in order to penetrate to the real message of the book? Furthermore, how can we use a series to build up to the understanding of the message without isolating parts and thus distorting them? Finally, as with all our sermons, how can we show its relationship to the Christian? Ordinarily, a series on Job would need to start with the prose prologue. This sets the scene and gives the reason for the dialogues with the friends. Furthermore, it establishes that Job's fortunes are not, as the friends assert, due to some terrible sin he has committed. Depending on the length of the series, some attention would need to be given to some or all of the friends, in order to try to crystallize their arguments and Job's responses to them. While the presenting problem is Job's suffering, the issue is the wider one of the limits of human wisdom and the need to trust a sovereign and benign God.[17] No series would be complete

---

17. An excellent discussion is given in Gerhard von Rad, *Wisdom in Israel* (London: SCM, 1972), chapter 12.

without dealing with God's address to Job (Job 38:1–42:6), which is the real solution to the problem. Some commentators have suggested that the prose epilogue, in which the friends are told off and Job is vindicated and restored, contradicts the solution of the poetic section. However, it is the only outcome of vindication that can be presented in the Old Testament context of blessing in the here and now. The New Testament would have us hope in eternal life, but this is beyond the view of the Old Testament.

A series on Ecclesiastes is conceptually more difficult because of the apparent lack of structure in the book. A number of different concerns are dealt with within the wider framework of *hevel* or vanity. There is little doubt that the epilogue plays an important part in conveying the message of the book.

The Christian preacher has great flexibility in dealing with a series of texts from any one book, provided the treatment of the texts is true to their significance in the framework of the whole book. The ultimate concern of the preacher should be to preach the meaning of the text in relation to the goal of all biblical revelation, the person and work of Christ. Can I maintain my integrity as a Christian preacher if I preach a part of the Bible as if Jesus had not come? Can I really fulfill my calling in preaching from the wisdom texts of the Old Testament if I fail to make clear that the whole significance of these texts hinges on the fact that Jesus has been made our wisdom, that he has suffered for us, and that he has risen from the dead to provide the justification of all our failures to live as wisely and as righteously as we should?

CHAPTER 14

Preaching from the Psalms

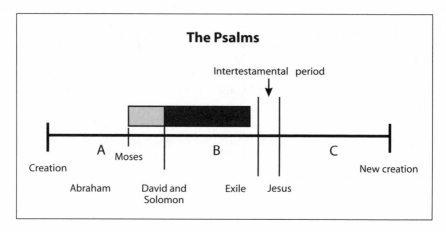

Diagram 14: Psalm 90 is attributed to Moses, and there is no reason why early psalmody could not have emerged at that time. Most of the psalms were written in the period from David to the exile.

The Psalms in Biblical-Theological Context

The significance of the Psalms for preaching rarely hangs on the question of the date of composition. It is more to the point to try to understand the theological perspective of the individual songs, and to do this within the context of the canonical book as a whole. The Psalms, along with the wisdom literature, provide us with the best evidence of how the faithful Israelites were encouraged to relate their covenant faith to the business of daily life. A cursory reading of the narratives of the Bible may leave one with the impression that life in Israel was a matter of miracles or spectacular events occurring six times a week and twice on the Sabbath. Someone has estimated, though I have never tried to verify this, that if we averaged out all the signs, wonders, and miraculous events recorded in the Bible over the whole period of Israel's history, we would find evidence for one event about every thirty years. Certainly we need to step back a bit from the individual narratives in order to appreciate the large time span of biblical history. There must have been many Israelites who lived long lives without ever witnessing an event that was out of the ordinary. Meanwhile the life of faith went on.

The earliest traditional reference in the Psalter would seem to be to the Song of Moses as the title to Psalm 90. Given the tradition of Moses as the one who sang the psalmlike "Song of the Sea" in Exodus 15, there is nothing to cause doubt that psalm activity is as old as Moses.[1] The attributing of a number of psalms to David need not be rejected despite the suspicion that many commentators have expressed toward this traditional ascription. In general we may say that the genre developed in the epoch of Israel's historical rise and achieved some prominence in the time of David. Even if the canonical form of the Psalter is relatively late, and it must be exilic or postexilic given the manifestly Babylonian provenance of Psalm 137, individual psalms provide a variety of perspectives on Yahweh's dealings with his people throughout the whole Old Testament period. In fact, the Psalms provide us with an enormous amount of material for constructing a biblical theology of the Old Testament. The great themes of creation, redemption, covenant, law, Yahweh's holy war, the land, the temple, the king, human suffering and persecution, the faithfulness of God, and the hope of future salvation are all to be found in abundance.

The Psalms, then, reflect upon the saving deeds of God and upon human failings. They, like the narrative history and the prophets, describe the disintegration of the kingdom and the longing for the day when God will act to save his people. Some of the psalms rehearse salvation history, others simply extol God's greatness, and still others cry out in distress with a longing for restoration. The great themes of prophetic eschatology are to be found in the Psalter along with the main subjects of the historical books.[2]

What was daily life like for the Israelite, and how did the structures of Yahwistic religion impact society, family life, and individual piety? The Psalms and the wisdom books provide some of the clues needed to answer these questions. There are various theories on the origin and use of the Psalms in Israel that may or may not help the preacher in the exegetical

---

1. See William J. Dumbrell, *The Faith of Israel* (Grand Rapids: Baker, 1988), p. 208.

2. See "Athanasius' Letter to Marcellinus on the Interpretation of the Psalms," printed as an appendix to *St. Athanasius on the Incarnation: The Treatise de Incarnatione Verbi Dei* (London: Mowbray, 1953).

stages of sermon preparation. We also need to take account of the use that the Christian Church has made of the Psalms in the context of formal worship. The assumption seems to be that if the Psalter was used as a kind of hymn book in the temple worship of Israel, should it not function as the basic hymn book in Christian worship? The Psalms have been an important part of Christian liturgical worship since earliest times. Furthermore, the Psalter provided the impetus for modern hymnody in the Christian Church. Many of the earlier hymns in the Protestant churches were either metrical forms or paraphrases of the Psalms. Some of the paraphrases recognize the hermeneutical problem of simply using the Psalms as they stand as Christian hymns.[3] The use of the Psalms in Anglican worship involves the assumption that Christian congregations are able to make this hermeneutical leap from Old Testament to Christian perspective.

The background to this Christianizing of the Psalter is the biblical use of Psalms. First, the Psalter itself has been variously estimated as a finished collection. It is commonly held that the Psalter took its final form as the hymn book of the second temple, that is, as an integral part of the worship of the postexilic Jewish community. Placing the Psalms in the context of biblical theology, then, must be based upon the subject matter of each psalm, although the canonical shape of the book as a whole must also be considered. Even if this is the case, it tells us little about the dating of the individual songs. Second, the poetic nature of the psalms and the prominence of hymns of praise in the collection makes the Psalter attractive as a source of Christian praise.

When we come to the New Testament we find the Psalms to be one of the most frequently quoted or alluded to books of the Old Testament. According to Henry Shires[4] the Psalms have influenced the New Testament more than any other Old Testament book (Isaiah would run a close second). His tally records 70 New Testament quotations of Psalms introduced by formulas,[5] 60 quotations with no introductory formula, and another 220 identifiable citations and references. While the Psalms as a whole collection seems to have been accepted as canonical, there are twenty-nine individual psalms

---

3. The Tate and Brady paraphrase of Psalm 34 is well known today as the hymn:

> Through all the changing scenes of life,
> in trouble and in joy,
> the praises of my God shall still
> my heart and tongue employ.

In order to Christianize the otherwise unadjusted Old Testament expression, the Trinitarian doxology was added in some versions as the final verse.

4. Henry Shires, *Finding the Old Testament in the New* (Philadelphia: Westminster, 1974), pp. 126-27.

5. These are statements that identify what follows as a quotation from Scripture, for example, "As it is written," "David says concerning him."

that are not referred to in the New Testament. However, silence does not allow us to deduce that these psalms were somehow regarded as suspect or unsuitable.

C. H. Dodd has proposed that there was a group of texts from the Old Testament that were used as primary testimonies to form the foundation of New Testament theology.[6] Included in these testimonies are a number of psalms, for example: Psalms 2:7; 8:4-6; 90:1; 118:22-23. These testimonies involved an interpretative procedure that gave the Old Testament passages Christological significance. Both Dodd and Shires remind us that a quotation can, and sometimes clearly does, imply the whole passage from which the extract is taken.[7] The psalms most frequently referred to in the New Testament are Psalms 2, 22, 33, 34, 35, 39, 50, 69, 78, 89, 102, 105, 106, 107, 110, 116, 118, 119, 135, 145, and 147. The top eight are Psalms 2, 22, 34, 69, 78, 89, 110, and 118.[8]

The evidence of the Gospels is that Jesus used the Psalms in prayer, and as a source of authoritative teaching. He saw himself as fulfilling certain aspects of the Psalms, especially in his passion. He is recorded using the Psalms more than any other Old Testament book. As well as indicating that Jesus himself constantly used the Psalms, the Gospel writers use and apply the Psalms in their account of Jesus and his ministry. A number of times events are seen as the fulfillment of prophecy in the Psalms: for example, Matthew 13:35 quotes Psalm 78:2 as fulfilled; John 19:24 fulfills Psalm 22:18; and John 19:36 fulfills Psalm 34:20. In Acts we find many quotes from Psalms: for example, in Acts 2:25-35 Peter refers to Psalms 16:8-11; 132:11; and 110:1, which suggests how important the Psalms were in the apostolic preaching of the gospel.

It is true of course that the Psalms are used in the New Testament in direct reference both to Christ and to people. For example, Paul uses a number of quotes from Psalms, along with one from Isaiah, with cumulative effect in Romans 3:10-18 to show the sinfulness of the whole human race. Hebrews 1:5-13 quotes both Psalms and Isaiah with reference to Christ. Non-Christological uses do not contradict the assertion of the general principle that all Old Testament texts point to Christ. Those that deal with human sin testify to the sinful nature that was imputed to Jesus in his death on the cross. Conversely, the horrors of the cross show the real nature of the problem in that it took the death of Jesus to fix it. Once again, to say that our interpretation must go via the person and work of Jesus does not imply that it stops there with nothing to say to us

---

6. C. H. Dodd, *According to the Scriptures* (London: Nisbet, 1952).

7. During the formation of the New Testament there were, of course, no chapter and verse divisions of the text as we know them. To quote a passage from the Scriptures it appears that it was customary to quote a prominent portion of it, but the whole unit would be implied.

8. Shires, *Finding the Old Testament,* p. 131.

about ourselves. Indeed, for it to speak the truth about ourselves it *must* go via Jesus.

The question of identity, then, is important: Does the Christian simply identify with the psalmist (in praise of God or in cry for help)? If we identify with the psalmist, to what extent and on what grounds? To ask the latter question is to inquire of the biblical-theological link between the psalm and the Christian believer. The danger of the Psalms to the preacher is the easy applicability of so many of them to the contemporary listener. But we should not be seduced into thinking that the Psalms can speak from and of themselves to us. If they speak to us of God, they must speak to us of the God who has finally revealed himself in Jesus Christ. If they speak to us of sinners, they speak to us of those who are outside of Christ. If they speak of the judgment of God, they speak to us of the curse of the law that Christ suffered for his people on the cross. If they speak to us of the faithful, the godly, or the righteous, they speak to us first of Christ, and only then of those who are redeemed in Christ. In the light of what I have said in chapter 9, I believe we should make this abundantly clear to our hearers and not leave it to chance. The preacher must constantly ask of the Psalms, "How do they testify to Christ?"

To sum up our survey of the Psalms in biblical-theological context, William Dumbrell makes the point that "the Book of Psalms is a compendium of biblical theology, and issues touching every aspect of Old Testament thought and life are taken up within it."[9] He agrees that Psalm 1, which treats two ways to live, has been placed at the head of the corpus to give a formal introduction in terms of *torah* (God's instruction). Again, he comments, "The Psalter is . . . a book of praise proclaiming that God, as Creator and Redeemer, has given to Israel through the Torah, through the revelation of himself in history, the possibility of new life and a complete indication of how it is to be lived."[10] If he is right in these observations, we are faced with the task of placing the Psalms as a collection and individually in the context of Old Testament theology. The intuitive approach to the Psalms may seem edifying, but it does not help us understand the hermeneutical principles applying to the Old Testament.

The fact that many of the psalms are praises in response to what God has revealed of himself in his great saving acts for Israel suggests that the theological expression will be salvation oriented. It is likely that the understanding of the nature of God will be historically based in a way that helps us to avoid clichés in describing the attributes of God. In other words, the characteristics of psalm praise stem from the revelation of God in his sav-

9. Dumbrell, *The Faith of Israel*, p. 211.
10. Dumbrell, *The Faith of Israel*, p. 212.

ing acts in history. In New Testament terms, this is to say that the gospel, the revelation of God in his saving acts in Christ, defines the terms that are used as the attributes of God. The historic nature of biblical revelation presents a God who is Lord of creation, savior, covenant maker and covenant keeper, judge of all, ruler of the nations, and so forth. The preacher needs to constantly bring his hearers back to this gospel-centered biblical perspective on God.

The response of Israel, then, is to worship God in historical terms (e.g., Psalms 78, 105, 106, 107, 114, 136). The concern for the glory of Yahweh is not philosophical or speculative but grounded in the demonstration of the *ḥesed* or covenant faithfulness of God (e.g., Ps. 92:1-2; 100:4-5). The Hebrew word *ḥesed* occurs some 130 times in the Psalms.[11] The name of God is another frequently occurring theme open to examination by the method of biblical theology. Exodus 6 indicates the covenant faithfulness element in knowing the name Yahweh. To call on the name of the Lord is a response to the saving acts of God (e.g., Ps. 63:4; 79:6; 80:18). Yahweh is the living God who is thus the source of life (e.g., Ps. 90:2-6; 102:25-27). He shows himself to be the Holy One.

Note the problem of defining exactly what the word "holy" denotes. If we start with the popular notion that the holiness of God is goodness that is perfect, we have the problem that people will tend to fill in the blank space with their own, rather than the biblical, view of goodness and holiness. The psalmists understand that this attribute is manifested in God's acts of deliverance of his people (e.g., Ps. 22:3-5; 30:1-4; 33:18-22; 71:22-24; 98:1-3; cf. Ezek. 36:22-23). Any picture of holiness is incomplete without a sense of the wrath of God. Other themes include the wonderful deeds of God, the glory of God, and the only God.

Preaching the Psalms involves the same basic hermeneutical principles that we should employ in preaching any other part of the Old Testament. In the process of exegesis we will seek to understand the unique features of the individual psalms and their significance in their canonical and historical context. Exegesis of the passage leads us to relate it to the immediate theological horizon. Then we need to relate the text to the overall pattern of redemptive history as it finds its fulfillment in Christ.

Bruce Waltke[12] writes as an evangelical scholar and proposes a type of canonical approach to the interpretation of the Psalms. He says that in the

11. There is no single way of translating this technical term. English versions variously use terms and phrases like "steadfast love," "loving kindness," "mercy," and so on. In most cases the word has a covenant connotation, and thus "covenant love" or "covenant faithfulness" would be appropriate.

12. Bruce K. Waltke, "A Canonical Process Approach to the Psalms," in *Tradition and Testament,* ed. J. Feinberg and P. Feinberg (Chicago: Moody, 1981).

Psalms we see four distinct points in the progressive perception and revelation of the text occasioned by the enlarging of the canon:

1. The meaning of the psalm to the original poet.
2. Its meaning in the earlier collections of psalms associated with the first temple.
3. Its meaning in the final and complete Old Testament canon associated with the second temple.[13]
4. Its meaning in the full canon of the Bible including the New Testament.

In applying his view to the Psalms, Waltke sees the king as the principal human subject, both in the original intention of the individual psalms and in their early canonical collections. In the postexilic period such royal concerns would have been interpreted as messianic eschatology, although in the intertestamental period they were domesticated in the synagogue. With the advent of Christ the true significance of the Psalms emerges. Waltke concludes that the Psalms now stand as the prayers of Jesus Christ who, as the corporate head of the church, represents all believers in their own prayers. It is because we are in Christ that we can appropriate these prayers as our own.

Waltke's thesis is important here for he raises the Christological significance of the Psalms. Whether or not we accept the notion that the psalmist is consistently the king and, therefore, the forerunner of the Messiah, the Old Testament notion of the "one and the many" or the representative function of king and priest is important. Waltke's move to make all the psalms utterances of the king is, in my opinion, unnecessary. Jesus is not only the Davidic king-Messiah, he is Israel, he is (by imputation) the people of God. We do not need to press all the psalms into the royal category in order to understand the messianic significance. If we allow that the Psalms are part of the Scripture that testifies to Christ, the question to be answered concerns the link between any psalmist, or the subject of any psalm, and Christ, for only when that is dealt with can we take the next step and link the psalmist with ourselves. There is surely no real difficulty in principle in doing this. Obviously the theology of kingship is one that points straight to the Christ. But Jesus is also the true and faithful Israelite, and thus whether or not the individual psalm is by or about the king is not the issue. We will pay attention to the hermeneutical issues as we deal with some selected individual psalms.

---

13. Note the assumption here that the canonical Psalter was essentially the hymnbook of the second temple, an assessment that some scholars have questioned on the basis of the instructional introduction to the Psalter in Ps. 1.

1. Psalm 1, a Didactic Psalm

This psalm is often classified as a wisdom or didactic psalm. Its place in salvation history is not specific. Its main theological concern is the contrasting of two ways to live. This is expressed in the *Torah* orientation that contrasts the preoccupation of the righteous with that of the wicked. The remarks in chapter 11 about the relationship of law and gospel are relevant to this psalm. In the final analysis the righteous, *Torah*-oriented person who is the object of God's care and preservation is a foreshadowing of the righteous Man for us, Jesus Christ. We need to make that connection because the Psalms typically speak of the ideal that in our experience is unattainable apart from the experience of being justified in Christ. The canonical placement of this psalm at the beginning of the collection that makes up the five books of the Psalter may be significant. Some commentators see it as evidence that, whatever the use of the Psalms in the temple, the finished book as we have it was framed as a compendium of instruction.

2. Psalm 2, a Royal Messianic Psalm

A number of psalms refer directly to the king, but their exact occasion is not necessarily clear. This has led to quite an amount of scholarly speculation about the original situation of the royal psalms, and theories of otherwise unknown festivals of enthronement have enjoyed some popularity. Being able to identify some cultic situation that occasioned these psalms is not as pressing as placing them in the theology of kingship and the Messiah. Psalm 2 indicates that God's way of dealing with the rebellion of the nations against him is to set his king in Zion. This is completely consistent with Old Testament eschatology that sees the restoration of Zion and the Davidic kingship as the time of judgment and salvation. The reference to the son of God in v. 7 is important. The covenant with David named his princely son as son of God.

The New Testament quotes and alludes to Psalm 2 some seventeen times.[14] These references basically apply the psalm to the baptism and the transfiguration of Jesus, his resurrection, final rule, and judgment. This is not an adoptionist theology at work, but rather a recognition of the multifaceted function of the messianic Son of God. Essentially, he is Israel and he is the ruler of Israel. While the theme of son of God is not prominent in the Old Testament, it is significant in the few places it occurs. Israel is son of God in Exodus 4:22 and Hosea 11:1. The Davidic prince is son of God in 2 Samuel

---

14. Kurt Aland et al., eds., *The Greek New Testament* (London: United Bible Societies, 1966), p. 906.

7:14 and here in Psalm 2:7. Jesus is then declared to be this princely Israel at his baptism (Matt. 3:17) and through his resurrection (Rom. 1:4). It is by union with Christ that we are sons and heirs with him.[15]

3. Psalm 19, a Creation Psalm

Whether or not the two halves of this psalm were originally separate poems, the fact is that they form one psalm in the canon. We must take account of these complementary aspects of God's revelation, the one in nature and the other in his revealed instruction. As Artur Weiser has suggested, perhaps we can see the common feature here being the revelation of divine order.[16] The question of natural theology needs to be addressed, for this psalm along with Psalm 8 may suggest on first sight that a purely natural theology is possible. It is incontrovertible that the character of God is stamped onto his creation. Paul makes that clear in Romans 1:18-20. But he also makes it clear that the human race has rebelled against the God who is so in evidence in nature, and that people suppress the truth in wickedness. We can say, then, that every fact in the universe is eloquent of God, but people are without excuse because the nature of sin is to pervert this clear evidence and to install idols in the place of God. Natural revelation speaks of what God has revealed of himself in the creation, and of this the psalm speaks. Natural theology is ruled out because of what sinful humans do with this evidence. Here the psalmist speaks as a believer and of the mind-set of believers who see the truth in nature because of special revelation. To the regenerate mind every fact in the universe is once again a witness to the glory of God. When God reveals himself to us in salvation we soon see his glory in the heavens and in the world of nature.

How does this psalm testify to Christ? It does so in that it speaks of the clear revelation of God in creation, which vision, having been blurred by sin, is now renewed in the firstborn of all creation (Col. 1:15). Some commentators have referred to Paul's perspective as that of the cosmic Christ. The fact that Paul in Colossians 1:15-17 speaks of all things being created in him, through him, and for him is significant. It indicates that the gospel is not an afterthought but is in fact the reason for the creation in the first place.

15. Sonship of course becomes daughtership for female believers, but it is important to recognize that women, like men, are indeed sons by virtue of their union with Christ the Son.

16. Artur Weiser, *The Psalms* (London: SCM, 1962), p. 201.

4. Psalm 22, a Lamentation

Psalm 22 is notable because of the fact that Jesus quotes its opening verse in his cry of despair from the cross (Matt. 27:46). It is also interesting because there is an unexplained change of mood within the psalm. It begins as a lament or cry for help (vv. 1-21), then becomes a thanksgiving (vv. 22-26), and ends with a hymn of praise (vv. 27-31). Neither the occasion nor the exact nature of the persecution of this faithful Israelite are specified. Some have suggested that the change in mood indicates that the lament was uttered in the context of the temple; a kind of formal confession and cry for help. Then a priest would have given a word of assurance, something like the prophetic oracle of salvation that began, "Fear not." The thanksgiving and praise would then have followed. We have no way of verifying this theory but, clearly, something has prompted the change of mood.

In the context of biblical theology we have to say that this psalm could come from almost any part of the Old Testament period. It involves an individual expression of what was a frequent experience in the nation of Israel: the deliverance from oppression and the turning in praise to God. The psalm is full of the confidence that comes from the covenant, for even in the initial lament there is the reference to the way God cared for the people of old who cried to him and were saved. The use of the animal images in vv. 12-21 is suggestive of the reversal of dominion over nature. Because of sin, the dominion of human beings over the animals is challenged. As a consequence, human godlessness can be depicted here in these animal images in a way that foreshadows the beast images of Daniel.

The psalm, then, deals with the real problem of godlessness and the attack it makes on the godly, on those who put their trust in God. There is reason for confidence because of God's faithfulness to save in the past. Covenant and salvation are the grounds for turning from the cry of despair to confidence. Whether the psalmist has actually experienced deliverance before he turns to praise, or simply assumes it will happen because God is faithful, is difficult to determine. When we come to Jesus' use of the psalm on the cross, we realize that it certainly expresses something of the darkness of the moment. The sinless Son of God felt utterly forsaken as he bore the wrath of the Father on sins not his own. However, the other side to this is the very real possibility that Jesus was in fact identifying with the whole psalm. His blackness was real, but he also knew that his Father in heaven was faithful and that he would ultimately be vindicated. On a number of occasions he had foretold of his suffering as leading to the resurrection. The psalm, then, is a paradigm of Israel's suffering and final vindication. It thus foreshadows the redemptive suffering of the true Israel and his final exaltation to everlasting praise of the Father. This paradigm is vital to the Christian's understanding of the sufferings of this present life and the confidence we have that we share in the vindication of Christ. That is the message that Paul so eloquently stated in Romans 8.

5. Psalm 78, a Salvation History Psalm

The recital of salvation history in the Old Testament for a long time has caught the attention of biblical scholars, especially those concerned with the discipline of biblical theology. With a loosening of the tie between Scripture and revelation that was an inevitable result of Enlightenment thinking, there emerged the idea that historical events constituted revelation while the scriptural records concerning this sacred history were reduced to the status of theological reflection on the events. The problem with this is that it undermines the historical and revelatory, or theological, value of Scripture itself. Salvation is indeed accomplished through historical event, but the event needs the authoritative interpretation of the word of God for us to know what is happening. Israel's coming out of Egypt is one migration among thousands. Its revelatory value lies in what God says he is doing in this event. Jesus' death on the cross was one Roman execution among thousands. The word of God interprets to us its unique significance.

Salvation history recitals in the Psalms may have a different function from that of chronicling the events, but that should not be taken to imply that the events are unimportant or that the psalms are not important for their historical claims. Psalm 78 belongs with others (e.g., Pss. 105, 106, 114, and 136) in focusing on the historic events of Israel's redemption. But there are important differences that make this psalm unique. It deals with the great redemptive events in the context of wisdom. It begins like a wisdom instruction and states that what follows is a parable and a riddle.[17] We need to consider the possibility that Psalm 78 was deliberately constructed as a piece of wisdom literature sharing with wisdom an altogether different purpose from a more overtly hymnic, salvation history psalm such as Psalm 136.

When we compare this with other salvation-history recitals (Exod. 15; Deut. 26:5-9; Josh. 24:1-13; Pss. 105; 106; 136; Neh. 9:6-31) there are some notable differences as well as similarities. The recapitulation (in vv. 42-43) of the theme of Israel's ingratitude returns us to more detailed treatment of the plagues in Egypt. The final stirring of God to reject Ephraim and to establish Judah, Zion, and David is unique in the salvation history recitals. It ap-

---

17. Features that might be said to be characteristically wisdom include: (a) the title *maskil,* (b) the call to hear and the phrase "I will open my mouth," both suggesting a didactic purpose, (c) *mashal* (proverb or parable) and *hidah* (riddle or dark saying) in v. 2, and (d) the phrase in v. 4a, "we will not hide them from their children . . ."

pears that the first section (up to v. 42) concentrates on Israel's rebellion, with five separate references to it (vv. 9-11, 17-20, 32, 35-37, 40-42). The second section stresses the activity of God, beginning with the detailed account of the plagues that shows the power of God over the enemy, and ending with David's rule. The similarities of vv. 70-71 and 2 Samuel 7:8 are striking. The royal ideology is worth comparing with Isaiah 11:2-3, which shares similarities with Proverbs 8:12-15. In v. 72 *tebunah,* a wisdom word meaning skill or astuteness, probably refers to the manner of David's exercise of power (his "hand"). Thus, the cure for Israel's continued apostasy is said to be the messianic wisdom of David's rule.

The theme of messianic wisdom in the salvation of God has clear Christological implications. If we are right about the wisdom nuances in this psalm, we see a significant amalgamation of wisdom and salvation history. As in the history of Solomon (1 Kings 1–10), the anointed king is the wise man. The convergence of empirical wisdom (Solomon's proverbs and songs) with the theology of the temple (1 Kings 8) and the light to the gentiles (1 Kings 10) has its antecedent in David, who is seen also to be the wise man. Luke affirms this link by including reference to the wisdom of Jesus (Luke 2:40, 52) in his account of the boy Jesus with the teachers in the temple. Thus one theological strand in Psalm 78 is that of the failure of Israel to be wise and to fear the Lord, a problem that is met by the gracious act of God in the election of David as the anointed, wise savior-king of Israel. The Christological significance of this is obvious. The fact that the psalm concludes with the rule of David can lead us only in one direction. The negative tone of the psalm points us to the wickedness of the human heart that, in the sight of God's saving wonders, still rebels against his gracious acts.

6. Psalm 96, a Hymn of Praise

For obvious reasons this psalm is classified by many commentators as a hymn of praise. It does not address God directly as many praise hymns do, but calls upon the people to praise him. The repeated call to praise is based on what God has done and how this reveals him in his greatness. The focus is first on the salvation he has wrought and on the sanctuary. Another call to worship is based on the fact of God's sovereignty in the world and his coming to judge. Once again we see that the salvation that God works for his people is inseparable from his deeds as the mighty judge. Salvation and judgment in the Bible are the two sides of one coin. This psalm involves the reader in a personal identification with the mighty deeds of God. It contributes to the combined witness of the Old Testament texts to the reality of salvation and judgment. The significance of this biblical-theological perspective that moves through the Old Testament to the gospel is that it ties the gospel events to the whole process of salvation history. It leaves us in no doubt as to the reality of the wrath of God endured by our Savior on the cross as the way of salvation for all who believe.

Literary and Historical Considerations

Mercifully, we have moved on from the days of the old liberal historical criticism that was preoccupied with questions of authorship and date, and with what lay behind, rather than in, the finished text. The advent of form criticism produced some gains in the study of the Psalms and also resulted in some very strange theories about the origins of the individual poems. We can gain some benefit by considering the classification of individual psalms proposed by form critics because it helps us to realize that different kinds of life situations are involved. Furthermore, it will enhance the appreciation of the richness of the Psalter when we recognize the different ways psalms worked. Form critics set out to classify items of literature by formal similarities, which included the content of the units as well as the literary idioms used to express them. The theory was that similarity of form indicated similarity of original use. Gene Tucker suggests that the purpose of form criticism is "to relate the texts before us to the living people and the institutions of ancient Israel."[18] Many recent commentaries have followed some kind of form-critical classification of the Psalms, the most common categories being: hymns, laments, royal psalms, thanksgivings, didactic and wisdom psalms, and liturgies. Some early form critics made much of the distinction between psalms of the individual and psalms of the community. Attempts were made to assess the original situation in life in which the psalm was used. The results of such approaches are inconsistent.

Another approach in contemporary scholarship is to try to understand the significance of the shape of the Psalter as it now stands in the canon of Scripture. How did the Psalter as a book function in Israel? This is a different question from that of the origin and function of the individual psalms. The Psalter is a collection that goes under the loosely descriptive title "praises."[19] Not all the compositions fit this description, and it is not obvious what a "psalm" really is. The titles of some of the psalms may help us understand

18. Gene M. Tucker, *Form Criticism of the Old Testament* (Philadelphia: Fortress, 1971), xi.
19. Hebrew: *tehillim,* songs of praise.

how they functioned. As Peter Craigie notes, the various titles contain five different types of information:[20]

1. Identifying the psalm with a person or group of persons.
2. The purported historical situation of the psalm.
3. Musical information.
4. Liturgical information.
5. The type of psalm.

The titles were known and used by New Testament writers (Mark 12:35-37; Acts 2:29-35). We don't know how the titles came to be fixed to the various psalms, but they do suggest the way they were understood in the canonical Psalter.

Brevard Childs[21] has commented that critical study of the Psalms had not been interested in the canonical shape of the book. He refers to Claus Westermann's work and comments that some genres have been grouped (e.g., the complaints), while the royal psalms have been scattered throughout the Psalter. Westermann[22] suggests that the collection of psalms in the book of Lamentations shows that Israel had a collection of psalms uniform in subject matter. What the old form critics, such as Hermann Gunkel, overlooked was the grouping. In book 1 of the Psalter the lament of the individual is predominant. Furthermore, Westermann proposes that Psalm 1 and Psalm 119 formed a frame around the intervening psalms, thus showing that the collection no longer had a cultic function[23] but rather formed a tradition devoted to the law.

Westermann, thus, sees a number of collections in the Psalter: the psalms of David (3–41) and the Elohistic Psalter (42–83), which includes the psalms of Korah (42–49) and the psalms of Asaph (73–83). The psalms of Asaph are framed by two psalms that are different from the community psalms that are between them. Westermann goes on to describe in more detail groupings and frames that suggest the Psalter's editorial purpose.

Gerald Wilson investigated the editing of the Psalter and notes five indicators of its shape:[24]

1. The five-book division. It would appear that the doxologies that conclude each of the five books were, at least in part, the reason for this in-

20. Peter C. Craigie, *Psalms 1–50,* Word Biblical Commentary (Waco: Word, 1983).

21. Brevard S. Childs, "Reflections on the Modern Study of the Psalms," in *Magnalia Dei: The Mighty Acts of God,* ed. Frank M. Cross, et al. (New York: Doubleday, 1976), p. 380.

22. Claus Westermann, *Praise and Lament in the Psalms* (Edinburgh: T. & T. Clark, 1981), chapter 6.

23. That is, related to the organized and formal worship of the community.

24. Gerald H. Wilson, "The Shape of the Book of Psalms," *Interpretation* 46.2 (1992): 129-42.

ternal division of the Psalter (see Ps. 41:13; 72:18-19; 89:52; 104:48). Psalm 150 was seen as the conclusion of the fifth book and the entire Psalter.[25]

2. Two segments distinguished by organizational technique. Psalms 1–89 use author and genre designations to group the psalms, but in Psalms 90–150 boundaries are indicated by groupings of thanksgiving and praise psalms. This suggests the two sections had discrete developments.

3. An introduction and a conclusion. Many scholars now accept that Psalm 1 was intended to be the introductory song to the whole Psalter. Others suggest that Psalm 150 was similarly intended as the grand finale. Wilson argues that 146–150 fulfill this role as a group of *halleluyah* psalms.[26]

4. A central pivot point. Walter Brueggemann notes the move from Psalm 1 and its call to obedience, to Psalm 150 and its call to praise. Transition from obedience to praise is marked by the one explicit indication of editorial shaping, namely, the postscript to Psalm 72. This royal psalm interrupts the flow of the Elohistic psalms (42–83), and it appears that it has been purposely placed to provide meaningful shape to the Psalter.

Wilson goes on to suggest the implications of such a shaping of the Psalter:

1. Psalm 1 invites us to meditate on the whole Psalter as *Torah*, which is the guide to life rather than to death.

2. That Psalm 1 is the introduction to the Psalter explodes the common view that the Psalter was the hymnbook of the second temple. Whatever their original purpose, the psalms are no longer to be sung as human response to God but are to be meditated on as the source of the divine word of life to us.[27] If he is right in this, it marks a move in emphasis from the psalms as response to a canonical sense of revelation in God's word.

3. A dynamic from lament to praise. Brueggemann[28] has described a dynamic in the psalms from orientation (creation) to disorientation (sin, etc.) to reorientation (salvation). It is noted that the first half of the Psalter is dominated by lamentations, and the second half, by praises.

4. A related shift from individual to community. The dominant lamenta-

---

25. Wilson, "The Shape of the Book of Psalms," p. 131.
26. Wilson, "The Shape of the Book of Psalms," p. 133.
27. Wilson, "The Shape of the Book of Psalms," p. 138.
28. Walter Brueggemann, *The Message of the Psalms* (Minneapolis: Augsburg, 1984).

tion in the first half is usually individual; the dominant praise in the second part is usually communal.

5. Yahweh is enthroned on the praises of his people. The title of the Psalter, *tehillim* (praises), does not reflect the nature of all the individual psalms, but it does reflect this dynamic of movement to triumphant praise. This, says Wilson,[29] is confirmed by the central message of book 4 (90–106). This section stands at the juncture of the two major segments, and it indicates the interpretative response to the cry of dismay at the end of Psalm 89. Wilson sees this as a crisis of faith that calls forth the response of books 4 and 5.

Planning Sermons on the Psalms

The Psalms lend themselves to sermons either as a series or an occasional sermon on an individual psalm. The important thing, once the preparatory exegesis is done, is to carefully place the central message and theology of the psalm into its own theological horizon. In other words, we ask how this psalm functions theologically in its own historical context. We should never leave the application of a psalm to chance. The Christian congregation is not made up of ancient Israelites living in hope of a future salvation promised by the prophets. The biblical-theological perspective is necessary to tie a psalm into the broad sweep of biblical revelation and to show how it speaks of our life in Christ.

In planning a series there are many creative possibilities. One that should never lack appeal and interest is to give some examples of the different kinds of psalms and how they function. We do not need to become overtechnical, but a brief overview of the different types could be useful. The preacher will need to determine if a series will be enhanced by introducing something of the overall shape of the Psalter.[30] The advantage to this would be the combined testimony to the spiritual life of the faithful Israelite and its foreshadowing of the rich texture of Christian existence. I stress again that the latter is the by-product of understanding how the Scriptures foreshadow the rich textures of the person and work of Christ for us.

---

29. Brueggemann, *The Message of the Psalms*, p. 139.

30. If you are preaching to a congregation that still sings hymns out of a hymnbook as against following the words of choruses from an overhead projector, a useful analogy can be found in the way most hymnbooks group hymns according to type or subject.

CHAPTER 15

Preaching from Apocalyptic Texts

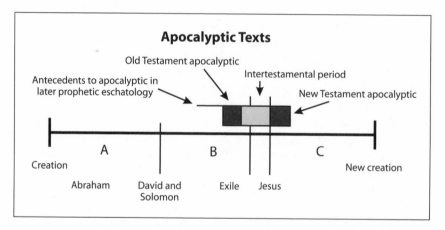

Diagram 15: Biblical apocalyptic stems from prophecy. In the Old Testament it is found mainly in the book of Daniel and some prophetic oracles. This overlaps with a wider phenomenon of Jewish religious literature, which continues into the first and second centuries A.D. In the New Testament it is found in the apocalyptic discourse of Jesus and the book of Revelation.

The Apocalyptic Texts in Biblical-Theological Context

There are some passages in the Bible that share certain distinct features of literary idiom and theological perspective, and that warrant separate consideration. These are often referred to as apocalyptic passages, and the reason for this label will be discussed later. As a basis for working I shall at this point nominate sections of Daniel, principally the second half of the book, some of the visionary material in Zechariah, the so-called Olivet discourse of Jesus, and a large amount of the book of Revelation. A great deal of scholarly discussion has revolved around the origins of this apocalyptic genre, mainly focusing on the literary and theological links with the eschatology of the prophets. Consequently there has been a tendency to see elements of early apocalyptic in some of the prophetic oracles that share a particular theological emphasis. Theories linking apocalyptic with wisdom literature no longer find much acceptance, and the attempts to account for the genre in terms of foreign influences cannot explain the theological perspective.

It will certainly be helpful for the preacher to be aware of the problems of accurately designating the genre of apocalyptic and of accounting for its characteristics. The preacher should be able to respond to the nature of the text and to rightly assess its intention whatever label we give its literary genre. The texts I have designated as apocalyptic share certain characteristics, the principal one being a perspective on eschatology that goes beyond the general emphasis of prophetic eschatology. The problem with designating apocalyptic as a genre is that the more we try to gather distinctive characteristics, the more we find that none of the candidates that we might assign to the genre share all of these characteristics. It is better if we recognize some texts as containing literary idioms that require special understanding, and then leave it at that.

The book of Daniel provides all kinds of interesting problems for the preacher, not least of which is the unity of the whole. The first six chapters with their narratives of the fortunes of certain Jewish exiles under pressure in Babylon and Persia seem quite different from the last part of the book, which contains a series of visions that, to say the least, are rather strange. Taken at face value the book originates in the sixth century B.C. in exile.[1] The theological significance lies first in the clear teaching that the God of Israel has not forsaken his people even though he has allowed them to be driven from the promised land. Second, there is the emphasis on the triumph of the kingdom of God over all godless powers in the world. Perseverance in covenant faithfulness on the part of the Jews is matched by the demonstration that God is powerful and faithful to save. The early chapters of Daniel, though cast as narratives, anticipate the apocalyptic visions of the later chapters. The humbling of the godless kings of the world by the King of Kings, as he reveals his

---

1. Critical opinion generally favors a second-century date because it avoids having to accept the idea that prophecy actually foretold future events, and because the fortunes of the Jews under the Seleucid king Antiochus Epiphanes are seen to explain the emphasis of the book. I reject this skeptical attitude to prophecy and suggest that the sixth-century dating explains the tone of the whole book far better than the second century. See Joyce Baldwin, *Daniel*, Tyndale Old Testament Commentaries (Leicester: IVP, 1978); D. W. Gooding, "The Literary Structure of the Book of Daniel and Its Implications," *Tyndale Bulletin* 32 (1981).

presence and rule, leads to the visions of the coming of the universal rule of God and the deposing of all godless power in the world. In this regard, whatever its literary distinctiveness, the book of Daniel stands in continuity with the eschatology of the latter prophets.

The consideration of the place of Daniel in biblical theology must, in the end, take account of the central vision of chapter 7, not simply because of its function in Daniel, but because of its prominence in the New Testament. The more difficult passages in the visions of chapter 8 and chapters 10–12, along with the numerology of chapter 9, make more sense if we see the visions in chapter 2 and chapter 7 as providing the broad sweep of salvation history from the Babylonian exile to the establishment of the kingdom of God. At the heart of this is the coming of the Son of Man on the clouds of heaven to God, and his receiving of the kingdom on behalf of the saints of the Most High. There is little doubt that this vision is the basis of Jesus' self-designation as the Son of Man. This suggests that Jesus clearly understood his coming in the flesh, his first coming, as the eschatological event of the coming of the kingdom of God.

The visions of Zechariah belong to the period of postexilic reconstruction in Judah. The main concern of the visions is the rebuilding of the temple. As we know, a temple was rebuilt in Jerusalem, but even in its later heyday as Herod's temple it never reached the glory anticipated by the prophets as the focal point of the kingdom of God in the coming of final salvation for the people of God. These visions in Zechariah, then, form part of the larger biblical theology of the promised land and the temple that finds no real resolution in the Old Testament. We must be careful to place these prophetic passages firstly in their own historical context of the disappointing reconstruction period, and then in the wider context of the solution to that disappointment in the coming of the true temple.

When we come to the Olivet discourse of Jesus, or the so-called "little apocalypse," we note the topics raised.[2] These have to do with the destruction of the temple, the coming end of the age accompanied by persecution, desolation, and sacrilege, and then the coming of the Son of Man. I have referred to these matters in the chapter on the prophets.[3] It is important that these eschatological texts be soundly placed in the overall scheme of the coming of the kingdom. The section on "The gospel and the End of the World" in chapter 7 is also relevant to these texts. It is unfortunate that these and other parts of the apocalyptic literature have been misused by some in the attempt to forecast the time when Jesus will return. Notwithstanding his assertion in Matthew 24:36 that this pursuit is useless, people persist in trying to predict

---

2. Matt. 24; Mark 13; Luke 21.
3. See the comments on Isa. 2:1-4 in chapter 12.

the second coming on the basis of signs of the times that they claim to see in contemporary history. I suggest that the structure of New Testament eschatology and its Christological focus mean that we must see these eschatological events as being fulfilled in the first coming of Jesus. Opinions will differ on this matter, but it seems to me this approach best accounts for the data. This, as stated earlier, does not mean that there is no reference to the second coming, only that it cannot be the exclusive reference.

Finally, in turning to the book of Revelation, we note that there are a number of different approaches to the interpretation of the book. The preacher's approach will at least in part, if not mainly, be determined by the particular eschatological stance adopted. Thus, a dispensationalist will read it one way, a historic premillennialist another, a postmillennialist another, and an amillennialist in yet another. A number of methodological factors are involved, and each preacher will probably have decided on his or hers long since. My own views about Revelation are discussed elsewhere.[4] I believe Revelation is essentially a book about the gospel, and, insofar as it describes the coming of the end, I recognize the end coming in the three ways I have discussed in chapter 7. The book is written to John's contemporaries who, like him, are suffering hardship and persecution for the faith. He writes using the apocalyptic idiom already familiar to Jews, and he uses it in the way it occurs in the Old Testament, that is, with the perspective of the one coming of the Lord at the end of the age. The apocalyptic visions that present this undifferentiated view of the Lord's coming are then contextualized by the hymnic passages that give a gospel-centered perspective. This means essentially that the end has come with the gospel events, is coming now in the life of the church, and will come with the return of Christ. Christian confusion about the reference of the visions exists because of the failure to see this gospel orientation. Of course Revelation is a book of eschatology, but the first coming of Christ must be seen as *the* eschatological event upon which all else hangs.

1. Zechariah 4

This is not the place to try to explain all of the imagery in this vision. It is clear that it is oriented to the temple and its rebuilding. We know Zechariah was a prophet of the postexilic period when the Jews struggled to reestablish their community in the face of opposition.[5] The central figure of this vision

---

4. Graeme Goldsworthy, *The Gospel in Revelation* (Exeter: Paternoster, 1984); published in U.S.A. as *The Lamb and the Lion* (Nashville: Thomas Nelson, 1985).
5. The postexilic prophets should be read in conjunction with Ezra and Nehemiah.

would seem to be Zerubbabel, who was a descendant of David.[6] The opposition to the building of the temple is, according to this vision, to be overcome by the achievements of the Davidic scion, but it will be a supernatural achievement, "not by might, nor by power, but by my Spirit, says the Lord of hosts" (Zech. 4:6). This passage, then, forms an integral part of the biblical theology of the temple. Such a supernatural building by a Davidic prince was never achieved until the new temple was raised up on the third day by the Spirit of God.[7]

2. Daniel 9

Following the central vision of Daniel 7 of the Son of Man establishing the kingdom of God, Daniel 8 presents another vision of beasts in battle. One interpretation understands this vision as a reference to the conflict between Medo-Persia and Greece. It would seem, then, that this vision refers to one aspect of the broader sweep of Daniel 7. Then in chapter 9 we have Daniel's penitential prayer and confession, the heart of which is in vv. 15-16. Daniel reflects on the prophecy of Jeremiah 29:10 that after seventy years God would restore the exiles. Here Daniel recalls the grace of God to Israel in the exodus from Egypt and asks that the same grace might now be shown to restore Jerusalem and the temple. The response to Daniel's prayer is a visionary visit from the angel Gabriel in which the seventy years of Jeremiah is projected as seventy weeks, usually understood to mean seventy times seven years (= 490). One way we can make sense of this is to see first that Jeremiah's seventy years was symbolic of the period from 597, or 586, to the edict of return in 538.[8] This vision, then, serves to prepare the way for the fact that the return from Babylon was not the occasion for the full revealing of the kingdom of God. These visions of Daniel belong with the eschatology of the postexilic prophets. If the abomination that desolates (Daniel 9:27) finds fulfillment with the desecration of the temple by Antiochus Epiphanes, only a skeptical attitude to the lordship of God over history and the writing of his word would require us to date Daniel after that event. Furthermore, the reference to this event in Jesus' Olivet discourse suggests that the cross of Christ should be understood as the principal fulfillment.

---

6. See Ezra 3–6; Hag. 1–2; Matt. 1.

7. John 2:19-21; Rom. 1:4; 8:11.

8. One suggestion is that seventy is simply a rounded figure; another is that it represents two generations.

3. Matthew 24

In view of what has already been said about eschatology, little more needs to be added with regard to the Olivet discourse or "little apocalypse." If the emphasis of the apocalyptic idiom is on the coming of the kingdom of God at the end of the age, the primary fulfillment is the first coming of Christ. The attempts to divide prophecies of the first coming from those of the second coming miss the continual emphasis in the New Testament that all the promises of God are "Yes" in Christ (2 Cor. 1:20). As with the book of Revelation, so with the apocalyptic elements of Jesus' teaching, they are presented with the basically Old Testament perspective of one and only one end event. Yet there is this difference: in the New Testament the end begins to be spoken about both as now and as future. Matthew 24 should not be shunted off into the distant future. Nothing will happen at the second coming that has not already happened in his first coming. The distinction lies in the comprehensive and consummative way it will happen when he returns. Allowing for its apocalyptic idiom, Matthew 24 does not describe anything that does not happen in his death, resurrection, and ascension.

4. Revelation 3:14-22

My reason for including one of the letters to the seven churches is not that it is written in the apocalyptic idiom; it isn't. But I want to protest against the tendency to take these letters out of their apocalyptic context and to treat them as if they existed independently. They make a fine sermon series and provide a lot of good material about life in the local church, but their real significance in the book of Revelation is often ignored. Certainly John addressed seven different congregations in Asia Minor on the basis of his knowledge of their progress, or otherwise, in the gospel. Yet Revelation 1:4 tells us that the whole of the book is addressed to these churches, and that fact alone means that the letters are not intended to stand alone and apart from the whole book. It also means, in my opinion, that the rest of Revelation was intended as a word relevant to these struggling churches in their situation then. As interesting as much of the end of the world speculation of some might be, it is more likely that John wrote the whole book to encourage first-century Christians in their struggle. It is a book about the gospel and the triumphs of Christ in his gospel. This has ramifications for the end of this age, but we don't have to wait till then for the truths of this book to apply to us. The great cosmic battles described in the visions are the reality behind the present struggles of local congregations, and continue to be until Christ returns.

5. Revelation 7

In an earlier consideration of this great vision I suggested that the two parts were different views of the same reality.[9] It seemed to me that John was describing the company of the redeemed both as a perfect number (not one of the elect is missing), and as an innumerable multitude (election does not restrict the grace of God). While I think that these are valid observations, I am inclined on further reflection to see another biblical-theological emphasis here. The first part of the vision is carefully phrased as including the redeemed out of the twelve tribes of Israel, while the second part points to the ingathering of a vast company of people from the nations. Even though under the gospel there is no distinction as to our acceptance with God — there is neither Jew nor Greek — this does not obliterate all distinctions. The Old Testament eschatology is so clear that through Abraham's seed all nations will be blessed, that it is the salvation of Israel that leads to the ingathering of the gentiles. It would seem that, in using the apocalyptic idiom, John has continued this perspective of biblical theology to describe the glorious scene of God's salvation at work.

Literary and Historical Considerations

For some preachers it would seem that preaching from apocalyptic texts is a case of fools rushing in where angels fear to tread. For others it is a case of avoiding a task that is daunting because of the difficulties in making sense of the texts. Most preachers would work on the assumption that the major apocalyptic texts are found in the second half of the book of Daniel and the bulk of the book of Revelation. I have included the so-called Olivet discourse of Jesus recorded in the Synoptic Gospels in this discussion because it is often classed as apocalyptic. The generally held view is that apocalyptic is a class of Jewish religious writings most of which are outside the canon of Scripture. The fact that most of what is usually classed as apocalyptic is not in the Bible raises the question of how much energy we need, as preachers of the Bible, to spend investigating the wider literature. This in turn directs us to the difficulty in defining apocalyptic as a genre.

What is an apocalypse? It seems that an apocalypse is what scholars and other experts decide to refer to as an apocalypse! It is not a biblical term for a genre, and it derives its name from the use of the word in Revelation 1:1, where it is translated as "revelation."[10] This suggests that the use of the

9. See Goldsworthy, *The Gospel in Revelation,* pp. 42-46.
10. Ἀποκάλυψις Ἰησοῦ Χριστοῦ.

name presupposes that the book of Revelation is somehow normative for determining the characteristics of the genre. Some of the later works found in the apocryphal New Testament bear the name Apocalypse.[11] Since the word simply means "revelation," we recognize that the genre use of it is a specific type of revelation. An apocalypse, then, is a literary work that has some affinity with the book of Revelation. This is a modern designation. There are works that are not called apocalypses but that share the genre characteristics, and there are some that bear the name of apocalypse but do not share the genre characteristics.

So, what is meant when a text is referred to as apocalyptic, and how does it help us in the task of preaching? The difficulty is in deciding what constitutes the genre. If we start with a definition involving certain literary or theological characteristics observed in one document, every other document we add to the list threatens the definition with its own distinctiveness. William J. Dumbrell comments, "The problem stems from the circularity of the mode of definition."[12] There is a similar problem in deciding what books of the Bible can be regarded as wisdom literature. Dumbrell, following Paul Hanson and John Collins, distinguishes three applications of the word:

a. *Apocalypse* (type of literature);
b. *Apocalyptic* (the eschatological perspective of a certain group of writings); and
c. *Apocalypticism* (the sociological ideology that stamps the literature as distinct).

Collins proposes a definition of the genre:

Apocalypse is a genre of revelatory literature with a narrative framework, in which a revelation is mediated by an otherworldly being to a human recipient, disclosing a transcendent reality which is both temporal, insofar as it envisages eschatological salvation, and spatial, insofar as it involves another, supernatural world.[13]

Collins sees the key word in his definition of the genre as "transcendence."[14] The manner of revelation requires mediation of an otherworldly being and

---

11. For example, The Apocalypse of James (from Nag Hammadi in Egypt, a Gnostic work translated from Greek into Coptic); The Apocalypse of Paul (in Latin, probably translated from Greek); and the Gnostic book the Apocalypse of Paul (also from Nag Hammadi). See M. G. Reddish, ed., *Apocalyptic Literature: A Reader* (Nashville: Abingdon, 1990).

12. William J. Dumbrell, *The Search for Order: Biblical Eschatology in Focus* (Grand Rapids: Baker, 1994), p. 131.

13. J. J. Collins, "Towards the Morphology of a Genre," *Semeia* 14 (1979): 9.

14. Collins, "Towards the Morphology of a Genre," p. 10.

implies the existence of another world superior to our own. An apocalypse looks beyond this world to another.

> In all the apocalypses the expectation of salvation is based on other-worldly revelation. The emphasis on the transcendent in the apocalypses suggests a loss of meaning and a sense of alienation in the present which tallies well with current views of the social milieu of apocalypticism.[15]

Collins's method of arriving at a definition of the genre is to start with the writings called apocalypses and those designated as apocalyptic by modern scholars. The scope is confined to those writings of the period from about 250 B.C. (which would include Daniel, regarded as a second-century document) to about A.D. 250.

In the final analysis, being able to pinpoint the genre characteristics of apocalyptic is hardly the issue for the preacher. The main advantage in being aware of the subject of this discussion is that we may be less inclined to force the literary form of a text into a mold to which it doesn't belong. Having some feeling for the general nature of Jewish apocalyptic will enable us to be more in touch with an apocalyptic text and its idiosyncrasies. In order to deal with a text fairly in the task of preaching, the important thing is to respond to the nature of the text and its content. Thus, for example, recognizing the Old Testament perspective of one coming of the Lord in these texts will enable us to avoid applying them exclusively in the New Testament to the second coming of Christ. Caution needs to be exercised in the matter of apocalyptic symbolism. One common, but by no means universal, characteristic of apocalyptic is the existence of an interpreting angel or other authority. In the book of Daniel it is noteworthy that the interpreter focuses on certain salient features of the vision and completely ignores others, particularly details. The important principle we should observe is to interpret Scripture by Scripture. Some apocalyptic teachers feel they must provide sure interpretations for every detail, but these usually fit their preconceived systems. There is no *a priori* reason why every detail of a vision should mean something any more than every detail in a parable should require interpretation. The principle of the analogy of Scripture suggests that the visions should yield what the immediate context allows, and finally they must be regulated by their fulfillment in the gospel. Some details we may have to be cautious about or put down to the texture of the verbal painting.

15. Collins, "Towards the Morphology of a Genre," p. 11.

Planning Sermons on Apocalyptic Texts

The important thing in many of these texts is to preach on them in a way that demystifies them for those who are not familiar with apocalyptic or who are scared off by the apparent difficulty in making sense of them. Many people seem to be either hooked or repelled by the strangeness of the idiom. Fortunately, all the biblical texts that could be classified as apocalyptic occur in some wider context that, if we pay attention to it, enables us to relate these texts to the broader sweep of biblical theology and salvation history. Above all, the preacher should resist the ever-present temptation to become a "second-coming" guru. The important doctrine of the return of Christ should never be allowed to become the happy hunting ground of self-styled prophets and interpreters of contemporary world events. The tying of eschatology to the gospel goes a long way toward preventing this kind of error.

In planning a series of sermons on Daniel the unity of the book should be considered. It is a pity that the heroic deeds of Daniel and his friends are so often isolated from the book's grander vision of the final and total victory of God and the coming of his kingdom. A series on the book of Revelation likewise should be careful to relate the future to the past. One-time sermons on any part of the Bible are, of course, permissible, but a taste for the perspective of biblical theology cannot but commend expository preaching and more concerted efforts to expound the message of whole books. One can achieve this and still be selective in the portions of the books chosen. The point to remember is that our preaching should make it plain to all who hear us that our chosen passage is part of a book that is part of the whole Bible. It should also make it plain that the message of the Bible is Jesus Christ in his gospel. As Kevin Vanhoozer notes, "The clarity of Scripture is neither an absolute value nor an abstract property, but a specific function relative to its particular aim: to witness to Christ."[16]

16. Kevin Vanhoozer, *Is There a Meaning in This Text?* (Grand Rapids: Zondervan, 1998), p. 317.

CHAPTER 16

Preaching from the Gospels

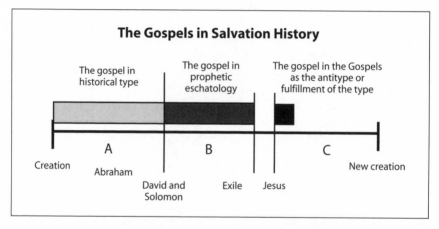

Diagram 16: The Gospels complete the salvation history picture of the Bible by presenting Jesus Christ as the fulfillment of the Old Testament promises and hopes for the future salvation of God's people. Despite the historical gap in the intertestamental period, the Gospels are anchored to the redemptive framework of the Old Testament.

The Gospels in Biblical-Theological Context

Many preachers may consider that when we come to the Gospels we are, at last, on home territory. This can be something of a mistake and can lead to problems in the way we preach and apply the text. Diagram 16 above probably states the obvious and could be regarded as superfluous. However, I have used the diagrams at the beginning of each chapter in this second section of the book because many of us need constant reminding of the biblical-theological context of the part of the Bible we are dealing with. If you are not a person who thinks visually, or if these diagrams seem patronizing or irritating, please ignore them.

The placing of the Gospels in biblical-theological context is not something that automatically happens. There is a prevalent tendency not only to divorce the gospel event from the salvation history of the Old Testament, but also to treat the Gospel narratives as historically flat within themselves. By that I mean that texts from the Gospels can be chosen and preached on as if they automatically and self-evidently all belonged to the same portion of redemptive history, namely, to our contemporary segment of it. That is why I include a second diagram in this chapter (diagram 17) to remind us of the structure of salvation history within the Gospels and Acts. As with all these chapters on the application of biblical theology, this one should be read in the light of the discussion in chapter 8 on the structure of biblical revelation.

When we come to a close-up view of this part of the Bible, we find that the gospel event, the saving event, undergoes development within the Gospel narratives. There is a history to the unfolding of the message and the events within the Gospels. No one would, I think, presume to present the account of John the Baptist, or that of Zechariah in the temple as anything other than preparatory for the main gospel message. It is clear from Acts 19:1-5 that people who have responded to the message of John the Baptist still need the full gospel about Jesus. Even the gospel as stated at the beginning of Jesus' own ministry, recorded by Mark, is framed in words that do not tell the whole story (Mark 1:14-15). We need to consider what are the points of contact between the narratives of the Gospels and ourselves, and what are the main biblical-theological differences. In chapter 8 I have pointed out the significance not only of the death and resurrection of Jesus but also of the ascension. It is obvious that we do not live in Jesus' time, nor in the same place where he lived. This creates not only a time and culture gap but a theological or redemptive-historical gap. Of first importance is the fact that Jesus is no longer here in the flesh. The way he dealt with his contemporaries is not necessarily the way he now deals with us. He spoke to them face to face. He speaks to us now through his word in the Bible, and he makes himself present to us by his Holy Spirit. We must take care not to simply read ourselves back into first-century Palestine and into the presence of Jesus of Nazareth. A framework of biblical theology is as important here as in any other part of the Bible.

A further consideration in preaching from the Gospels is that everything Jesus says up to his death is said in anticipation of his death and resurrection. Some of his sayings can be seen to be preparatory to these events. Jesus taught his Jewish disciples who came from a background different from ours. He came into conflict with Jewish opponents such as the Pharisees and

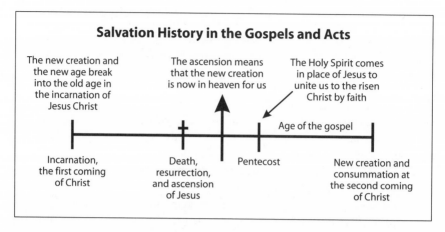

Diagram 17: The Gospels provide a close-up of the process of fulfillment of the Old Testament. The theological significance of the ascension must not be underestimated. The new age has come in Jesus Christ, but the ascension and Pentecost mean that the new age now comes through the preaching of the gospel until Jesus returns at the end of the age.

the Sadducees, and many of his sayings are directed at them. Even those sayings of Jesus aimed at his disciples must be looked at for their context. Instead of simply assuming that the teachings of Jesus stand for all time as instruction to the Church, we have to exercise some care in the way we move from the narrative to ourselves. Perhaps the worst form of neglect is preaching from the teachings of Jesus in a way that reduces their significance to moralism. On one occasion I asked a group of elderly Christians to state what they considered to be the essence of Christianity. It was not long before the discussion arrived at the notion of following the teachings of Jesus and, specifically, observing the golden rule! Of course the teachings of Jesus are important, but care is needed to understand the objectives and the intent of his words.

As the diagram above illustrates, the biblical-theological structure within the Gospels shows us a very significant modification from the Old Testament eschatological perspective of the day of the Lord. Within the Gospel narratives we move from the expectation of the fulfillment of Old Testament hope, through the critical events in the life and ministry of Jesus, to the distinctively New Testament perspective on eschatology that clearly differentiates the first and second comings of Christ. It would be difficult on the basis of Old Testament texts alone to arrive at this structure of two comings with the overlap of the ages between them. It could perhaps be argued that the same could be said of the Gospel narratives until we arrive at the Last Supper and postresurrection discourses. The two major aspects of these texts are the fact that the death of Jesus will mean that he will be leaving them, and that the coming of the Spirit means that he will always be with them. The ascension is the bridge between the resurrection and Pentecost.

Major points of unity between the Gospel narratives and our contemporary situation include the fact that the first coming of Jesus was the coming of the end, the beginning of the last days, and the start of the new age being with us. We have moved definitively from expectation and hope, or type, to the fulfillment of this, or antitype, in Jesus. Provided that we take in the whole of the story of Jesus, we have the completed gospel for the first time. From this point on we can never tell the Bible's story without showing its fulfillment and meaning in Jesus.

There are major points of discord or difference between our situation and that portrayed in the Gospels. We are not first-century Jews, and we do not have Jesus here with us in the flesh. Unlike the disciples in the first part of the narratives, we do not look forward to events that will complete the gospel. We belong to the age of the Spirit and the proclamation of the gospel in all the world. Jesus made it clear that he had to go away before this situation would eventuate. Our experience of the Holy Spirit is contingent on Jesus' finished work of obedience and his going away into heaven.

1. The Genealogies of Jesus (Matt. 1 and Luke 3)

Some may regard the use of the genealogies in preaching as reckless bravado. Add to this the sheer difficulty in reading them aloud in an interesting way and maybe we can understand why they will rarely, if ever, turn up in lectionaries and programs of daily Bible reading. I have heard a truly brilliant sermon delivered by a preacher who chose to focus on Matthew 1. On the one hand it showed some courage, and on the other hand it expressed the conviction that Matthew must have regarded this information as very important. We cannot believe that he set out to frighten away his potential readers by starting his book with a boring precursor of the telephone directory. In fact, as we have already seen, Matthew's whole biblical theology is bound up in the way he moves from Abraham to David, from David to the exile, and from the exile to Jesus. And, incidentally, on the way through he gives us a clue to the biblical-theological significance of the book of Ruth (Matt. 1:5-6). The genealogy is the perfect antidote to a moralizing character study. Here is the reason why exemplary sermons on biblical characters can easily miss the point. It is not their exemplary value but their place in the theological plan of God culminating in Jesus of Nazareth that is the most important thing. Matthew's genealogy points us to a theological structure that is reinforced by the apostolic preaching. Matthew is in effect saying to us on the one hand that we should never try to understand the New Testament apart from the Old, and on the other hand that we cannot understand the Old Testament without its fulfillment in Christ.

Luke's genealogy creeps up on us. We are well into the more interesting aspects of the narrative before he springs it on us. Once again the purpose is clearly theological. While Matthew starts with Abraham and works forward to Jesus, Luke starts with Jesus and works back to Adam. While Matthew shows us that Jesus is the seed or descendant of Abraham in whom all the promises to Abraham are fulfilled, Luke shows us that Jesus is the last and most significant in the lineup of the sons of God. The first son of God is Adam, the last is Jesus. Since the genealogy of Jesus, the son of God, comes between the baptism with God's word, "You are my Son, the Beloved, with you I am well pleased," and the temptation with Satan's opener, "If you are the son of God," it interprets both these addresses. His sonship is his true humanity, lost by Adam, repudiated by Israel, but faithfully maintained by Jesus in his redemptive life.

2. The Temple Cleansing

Some conservative commentators have proposed that, since John records this event in chapter 2 of his Gospel and Mark places the event at the end of Jesus' ministry, there must have been two such events.[1] However, might not the apparent discrepancy be simply a function of the respective theological structures? It would make sense if Jesus did cleanse the temple toward the climax of his ministry and before his arrest and execution. Mark's linking of it with the entry into Jerusalem and the last discourses sets the scene for his showdown with the Jews, which led to his death. John, however, has a different emphasis. His prologue introduces us to a focus on the new creation through Jesus. At the heart of the old creation and the promised land was the temple; now the Word of God has become flesh and taken up his residence in a tabernacle among us. John places the cleansing of the temple soon thereafter and includes the comment that Jesus' statement about building the temple again in three days was a reference to his resurrection. Then follows the discourse with Nicodemus about birth from above by the Spirit. Another temple reference is occasioned in John 4 in the discussion with the Samaritan woman. In this sequence of narratives the emphasis is on the newness of the kingdom structures as they come with Jesus. While there is continuity with the old, to the point that Nicodemus as a teacher in Israel should have understood what

1. John 2:13-22; Mark 11:15-19; cf. Matt. 21:12-17; Luke 19:45-48.

Jesus was talking about, there is an emphasis on the discontinuity, on the radical newness of what Jesus has come to bring.

Thomas G. Long has commented on the Markan account of the temple cleansing within its context of the cursing of the fig tree on the one side, and the discussion of faith and prayer on the other.

> The text then exposes the central clash of Mark's Gospel: the old order vs. the new, the powers-that-be vs. the kingdom, the limits of human (and natural) possibility vs. the unlimited divine possibilities, the ordinary season of history vs. the evergreen season of the kingdom.[2]

The point is, of course, that it was not the season for fruit, yet Jesus still curses the tree. Then he proceeds to the temple and throws out the traders and money changers. Then the fig tree is reintroduced, and Jesus comments on faith and prayer, which both the fig tree and the temple episodes help explain. The coming of the kingdom of God produces the unexpected, while the expected, the normal, must be destroyed.

In view of this, it seems reasonable to suppose that the different placements of the temple-cleansing episode in Mark and John serve different theological purposes. This conclusion highlights the fact that the Gospels, while it is clear that they are intended to be biographical, are not mere biography. They do more than simply chronicle events in the life of Jesus the carpenter's son. They are called Gospels because the Early Church understood them to be expressions of the gospel. The gospel is event, but not uninterpreted event. Sometimes interpretation can be in the form of a commentary statement, and sometimes interpretation can come through the way the narrative is put together to tell a larger single story, which is more than a collection of anecdotes. The Gospels contain both, but perhaps we should recognize that the shape of the Gospel narrative as much as the direct commentary is what interprets the parts of the whole.

3. The Parable of the Good Samaritan (Luke 10:25-37)

A great deal of work has been done on the interpretation of the parables in recent times, and it is not my aim to try to deal with all the theories.[3] Our specific purpose in these concrete examples of biblical texts is to look at them in

---

2. Thomas G. Long, "Shaping Sermons by Plotting the Text's Claim Upon Us," in *Preaching Biblically*, ed. Don M. Wardlaw (Philadelphia: Westminster, 1983), p. 92.
3. A useful treatment is Craig L. Blomberg, *Interpreting the Parables* (Leicester: Apollos, 1990).

the context of biblical theology. The exegete will need to do other tasks in the process of preparing a sermon. The parables, by their very nature as self-contained stories, can easily be separated from their context and end up saying something that seems to fly in the face of the gospel emphasis. If the discipline of redaction criticism has taught us anything it is that the biblical documents in general, and the Gospels in particular, have been carefully crafted to convey a message. It is inconceivable that Luke would have included a parable within the complex but clearly gospel-oriented structure of his work that said something entirely opposite his main thrust. Yet, when the parable is treated as if its main point is that we should go around looking for people less fortunate than we are in order to do good to them, it has lost the sense of its whole context of Jesus bringing salvation and the kingdom for us. If the parable is a body blow to the lawyer's attempt to justify himself, how can we preach it as indicating that we can justify ourselves by doing good?

No part of any Gospel should ever be preached on before we have at least given some consideration to the whole Gospel as a theological statement. In the case of the parable in question, we should, in our own thinking, place it in the context of the Gospel's linking of Jesus to the salvation history of the Old Testament, and all that such a link implies. We should remind ourselves that Luke has put his parables within a narrative framework of Jesus turning to go to Jerusalem for the express purpose of dying and rising so that the kingdom of God would come. The preacher should read and reread the several chapters that surround the parable and note how impossible it is to deal with it in any other way than as part of the message of what Jesus has come to do for us. Then we will understand why some of the great exegetes, commentators, and preachers saw that it was the Samaritan who was the neighbor and that before we can love other neighbors we must love and receive the one who came to be our Samaritan Neighbor and to rescue us. Pertinent to this point is the statement by Thomas Long in which he sees sermons as literary parallels to their progenitor, which is, "the 'gospel' genre itself, a literary form in which virtually every element of plot is shaped by its denouement, the passion."[4]

4. The Postresurrection Appearances (John 20)

There are two quite distinct perspectives in John's account of Jesus' appearances after his resurrection. These indicate something of the context of biblical theology and the dimensions that pertain to the postresurrection period. First, we find Mary Magdalene standing outside the tomb after Peter and

4. Long, "Shaping Sermons," p. 88.

John have left the scene. Mary mistakes Jesus for a gardener, but, when he addresses her by name, she realizes that it is Jesus risen from the dead. It would appear that she was so utterly convinced that it was her Lord that she tried to embrace him, but he says, "Do not hold me, because I have not yet ascended to the Father" (John 20:11-18). That evening Jesus appears to the disciples. Thomas was not there and is told later of the event. He is skeptical and insists that he would want to touch and see for himself before he would accept that Jesus is alive. A week later they are together again, Thomas with them, and Jesus appears and addresses Thomas: "Put your finger here and see my hands. Reach out your hand and put it in my side. Do not doubt but believe." Thomas is immediately convinced and believes. Jesus indicates that those who believe without seeing are blessed (John 20:24-29).

It was the same Jesus who appeared to Mary and to Thomas. Yet Mary is forbidden to touch him, while Thomas is invited to conduct a careful physical examination by touching. The gentle rebuke of Thomas leads to John's statement of purpose in writing the Gospel for those who come after and will not see Jesus but will be drawn into eternal life through believing the word about Jesus. Mary's perspective is of one who immediately believes; there is no doubt that the one who addresses her is Jesus. It seems that what she doesn't understand at first is that the resurrection is not merely the signal for business as usual, as if he had never died. Things are different now and Mary's relationship to Jesus will be by word and Spirit. No longer can she relate to him in the flesh as before. So, after the Mary episode, John recounts how Jesus breathed on the disciples and said, "Receive the Holy Spirit."

Thomas, however, cannot believe that Jesus has really risen, and thus Thomas needs to be convinced of the continuity of things, not the radical discontinuity. So, the invitation to touch him is to convince him that the Jesus that stands there is the same Jesus he knew before, the Jesus who had died on the cross. As was true of the disciples who thought Jesus was a ghost (Luke 24:36-43), Thomas needs to know that Jesus is a physical reality and not a ghost or apparition. As the crucifixion had been bodily, so the resurrection is bodily. The resurrection, then, signals both continuity with the past and discontinuity. The same Jesus is alive, but henceforth they will relate to him differently. The age of the Spirit as the agent of the word is about to begin.

Literary and Historical Considerations

The main literary consideration is that a Gospel is a new and distinctive literary genre that came about because of the nature of the gospel event and of the impulse to communicate it. There are no Gospels in the Old Testament, but there is an Old Testament testimony to the gospel, and, thus, we find certain aspects of both literary and theological continuity. The historical continuity is also a characteristic of the relationship of the Gospels and the Old Testament. Historical narrative in the Old Testament was always recognized as having the dimension of theological interpretation, and hence the bulk of it that is not in the Pentateuch belongs to the section of the Hebrew canon known as the Former Prophets. As Sidney Greidanus says, "it should come as no surprise that similarities exist between the genre of gospel and that of prophecy and Hebrew narrative."[5] I would go further and say that one thing that contributes to the distinctive nature of the genre of Gospel in the New Testament is the bringing together of the whole range of Old Testament texts in their fulfillment in Jesus. This does not necessarily require all the literary genres of the Old Testament to turn up in the Gospels, but it is understandable that many of them do. Thus, not only do we find prophetic sayings linked with statements of fulfillment, there is also the use of prophetic sayings by Jesus in a way that suggests his role as *the* Prophet. This helps make sense of the account of the mount of transfiguration, where Jesus is glorified in the company of the two great prophetic figures of the Old Testament, Moses and Elijah.

When we are familiar with the wisdom genres of the Old Testament, we are more predisposed to recognize them when they turn up in the Gospels and to inquire into their purpose. While the Old Testament wisdom literature does not contain anything quite like the parables of the Gospels, there are reasons to see some connection. Not only does Jesus blend the typical wise-foolish dichotomy into his sayings, but in its use as the conclusion to the Sermon on the Mount there is the further implication that he is the very embodiment of all wisdom (Matt. 7:24-29). He uses proverbs and parables, which some have seen as extended proverbs in narrative form.

The literary structure of the Gospels is a prime consideration for the preacher.[6] This is because, as I have indicated above, the literary structure serves a theological purpose. Yet there is a related matter to be considered. The development of the new literary criticism and its impact on hermeneutics has brought new contributions to the study of homiletics. Of course being a conservative evangelical breeds in one a certain reserve about these continual developments. Nevertheless, evangelicals should, I believe, be prepared to exercise an amount of eclecticism and never be too proud or conservative to

5. Sidney Greidanus, *The Modern Preacher and the Ancient Text* (Grand Rapids: Eerdmans, 1988), p. 263.

6. See Greidanus, *The Modern Preacher,* pp. 277-84. There is much help to be gained from reading carefully the whole of chapter 11 of this work. See also Sidney Greidanus, "Preaching in the Gospels," in *Handbook of Contemporary Preaching,* ed. Michael Duduit (Nashville: Broadman, 1992).

learn from whomever we can. In order to avoid simply being swayed by every new fad or trend that comes along, we should carefully examine what is offered and ask what principles and presuppositions are driving any new approach. An evangelical such as Greidanus has argued that we should rethink the subject of sermon form.[7] There is a logic to the suggestion that if Jesus proclaimed using, among other things, narrative form, and if the bulk of the Bible is in a narrative framework, then we should be very careful before we recast narrative text into a totally different form.

According to Eugene Lowry it was Fred Craddock's 1971 publication, *As One Without Authority,* which brought us to a new era in (North American) homiletics.[8] This was partly motivated by new literary hermeneutics that focused on the shape and nature of the text and how it was used to communicate, and partly by a serious questioning of the viability of the practice of sermonizing as a communication medium in modern society. Lowry's discussion centers on Craddock's idea of inductive preaching, which is sometimes referred to as narrative preaching. We do not have to follow the new philosophy of preaching in order to benefit from some of the questions raised about the traditional mode of sermonizing.

Planning Sermons on the Gospels

I do not want to become merely repetitious in these planning sections of each chapter. It should be obvious that I am suggesting that biblical theology should be a driving force in the practical issue of how we plan sermon series. One of the things we want to avoid is choosing favorite passages and ones that we feel more at home with, while ignoring difficult ones and ones that do not speak to our particular concerns or preoccupations. There is so much in the Gospels that a series of sermons will be limited only by our lack of understanding or creativity. It should also be obvious that the shape and purpose of the Gospels themselves should not be obscured by our rearranging events or isolating parts from the whole.

The structure of the Gospel should at least be in our thinking when planning a series. The series might aim to highlight this structure by showing the succession of emphases and critical points. A series on a group of parables or miracles should bring out their function in the overall plan and purpose of the Gospel. This really is just the application of biblical theology, by

7. Greidanus, *The Modern Preacher,* pp. 141-56.
8. Eugene L. Lowry, "The Revolution of Sermonic Shape," in *Listening to the Word: Studies in Honor of Fred B. Craddock,* ed. G. R. O'Day and T. G. Long (Nashville: Abingdon, 1993).

which we place the Gospel narratives into their canonical context, and by which we observe the critical structure of revelation within the Gospels. Let us bear in mind that John has given the lead in stating clearly his purpose in writing the Gospel. It is evangelistic but not merely evangelistic. Believing that Jesus is the Christ, the Son of God, so that we might have life in his name is about more than conversion. It is about life, about living by faith, about living with God, about knowing who Jesus is and what he has done, about what God is like. You can hardly get anything more comprehensive than that. But the point is that John put his material together with care and according to plan. The authors of the four Gospels do not invite the preacher to treat their brilliant assembling of the events in Jesus' life, death, and resurrection as if they were a collection of unconnected texts.

CHAPTER 17

Preaching from Acts and the Epistles

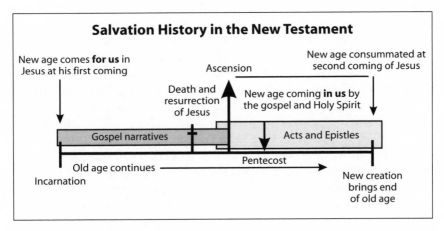

Diagram 18: The gospel event brings about the overlap of the new age with the old age. This occurs in two different ways. First, the kingdom age breaks into the old age in Jesus as he comes in the flesh. Second, the ascension of Jesus and sending of the Holy Spirit brings the new age into the lives of those who believe the gospel.

The Acts and Epistles in Biblical-Theological Context

It is a common understanding in biblical theology that the nature of the gospel event causes some modifications in the prevalent expectations among believing Jews. The general eschatological pattern in the Old Testament prophets was that of the old age coming to a full end with the advent of the final act of salvation on the day of the Lord. The great saving event would mean the end of the old and the immediate and full inauguration of the new. According to the New Testament, however, the one great event of the last day turns out to embrace the whole of history between the first coming and the second coming of Jesus. Commentators have often used the illustration of the foreshortened view of one looking at a vista of mountain peaks. In the distant view the peaks appear to merge into a single range, but as we come closer to the range we discover that there is in fact a considerable distance between the peaks and that we must travel further to reach the most distant. In the same way, the prophetic view is said to be foreshortened so that all the events of the end, separated by unspecified time, appear as one event. When we arrive at the fulfillment, however, we discover that the coming of the Son of Man is not a single peak but two, or three if we include his coming by his Holy Spirit. I refer again to the discussion on the structure of revelation in chapter 8.

Now, such an illustration tells only a part of the story, as do our diagrams, but these serve to give us a sense of the basic structures of reality that underlie the message of the Bible. In diagram 18 above I have attempted to represent the way in which the gospel brings the new age to us. It is important that we understand the context of the various New Testament texts in biblical theology. They do not all stand in the same relationship to the key gospel events of the life, death, and resurrection of Jesus. Therefore, they do not stand in the same relationship to the contemporary reader and hearer of sermons.

It might be asked if Paul the apostle stood in the same biblical-theological situation as we do today. After all, we are both post-Pentecost; Paul addresses real Christian churches made up of believers, as ours are today; he lives between Pentecost and the second coming as we do; and he addresses problems that stem from the same human sinfulness as we know and experience. Is there any difference? Certainly it is clear that the New Testament epistles are the closest biblical documents to our contemporary situation, allowing for the historical and cultural changes that have occurred between the first and the twenty-first centuries. There are differences, however, which the preacher should consider when seeking to apply the epistles today. For one thing, Paul was a member of a unique band whose office would never be repeated. He considered himself, on the basis of his calling and of his vision of Christ, to be one of the apostles. An apostle was among those who had known Jesus and were witnesses to his resurrection. They were the ones who were appointed by Jesus to give authoritative testimony to him before there was a canon of the New Testament. Now we have no such apostles, but we do have the New Testament as the result of the apostolic testimony.

If, then, the New Testament documents that are closest to our contemporary situation still have theological points of difference from us, how much more should we be aware of the differences of documents that are even further from us. One of the lively discussions that was revived in the 1960s involved the status of the book of Acts, and particularly the early chapters dealing with Pentecost and its immediate aftermath. The question raised was the extent to which Acts remains normative for the Christian Church today. Much of the confusion about this occurred because of a failure to apply any kind of biblical theology to the matter. One attempt to redress this failure was made by Frederick D. Bruner.[1] He showed that the subject of the coming of the Holy Spirit at Pentecost when put into the context of redemptive history took on a different significance from the one that the Neo-Pentecostal movement was giving it.

The essence of the theology of the first two chapters of Acts is one of transition from Jesus being here in the flesh to his being absent in the flesh but present by his Spirit. This transition could, and did, take place only once. The hermeneutical questions for preachers and for all Christian interpreters of these events involve understanding what are the elements of continuity and the elements of discontinuity between Pentecost and ourselves. This continuity-discontinuity, or unity-distinction, is at the heart of hermeneutics irrespective of what part of the Bible we are giving our attention to. While it is fairly obvious to most people that our relationship to the Old Testament involves continuity and discontinuity, when it comes to various parts of the New Testament this principle is easily overlooked.

The disciples of Jesus that are the subjects of the Pentecost experience as described in Acts 2 are caught up in a critical and unique time in the progress of salvation history. They, unlike us, had known Jesus in the flesh. They, unlike us, were Jews with certain expectations about what the coming of the Christ would mean for their nation and the world. They, unlike us, had witnessed the events that included the death of Jesus, and had seen him after his resurrection, or at least heard eyewitness reports of his appearances. They, unlike us, had received very special teaching from the risen Lord, culminating in the words recorded in Acts 1:5-8. This teaching was, in essence, the heart of the biblical theology that enabled them to place the events surrounding the death and resurrection of Jesus into context, and to understand how the kingdom would manifest itself from that point on. Thus, whatever we say about our continuity with Pentecost, there are some aspects of it that simply can never be repeated because there are no more disciples who knew Jesus in the flesh and who have to undergo this transition to knowing Jesus in the Spirit. It is important that we understand the Pentecost event in the wider context and, in effect, formulate a biblical theology of the Holy Spirit. This will help us to understand in what sense the disciples did not have the Spirit

1. Frederick D. Bruner, *A Theology of the Holy Spirit: The Pentecostal Experience and the New Testament Witness* (London: Hodder and Stoughton, 1971).

before Pentecost, and in what sense they did. Above all it will help us to understand that, in whatever sense Pentecost was a new experience, it was contingent not upon the faith or preparedness of the disciples but upon the finished work of Christ and his being glorified.

If the Pentecost experience characterizes the transition to the age of the gospel and Spirit, the period of the overlap of the ages, what can we say about the rest of Acts? The transition factor means that we should be at least ready to see other one-time or unique events. Certainly this would appear to be the situation in just those texts that have become contentious because of claims of normalcy. The cases of the Samaritans in Acts 8 and the disciples of John the Baptist in Acts 19 are good examples. In the former it is shown that the Samaritan believers cannot go it alone but require apostolic oversight. The perpetuation of the Samaritan schism with its roots going all the way back to Jeroboam I was thus averted. The case of the disciples of John the Baptist is simply one of the disciples needing to hear the full gospel of Jesus Christ. These events, along with the account of Cornelius and Peter in Acts 10–11, are part of the scene of transition from a focus on the Jews to the inclusion of the gentiles in the saving work of God.

Another area in Acts needs assessment in light of biblical theology: the prevalence of signs and wonders that accompany the ministry of the apostles. One approach has been to assess these as distinctive to the apostles so that once the apostles were gone such miracles no longer occurred.[2] This is probably a case of special pleading, but nevertheless we need to ask how and when signs and wonders figured in the bigger picture of salvation history. There are in fact three main clusters of miracles, though there are others that do not fit into these. The first is the cluster of signs and wonders accompanying the great redemptive event of the Exodus and the entry into the promised land. The second took place during the ministries of Elijah and Elisha, who call Israel back to covenant faithfulness at a time when the nation is on the verge of complete apostasy. The third cluster is found in the ministry of Jesus and the apostles. Outside of the Gospels and Acts references to signs and wonders are fairly scarce and mostly refer back to the apostolic ministry. The main exception is in Revelation, where lying signs from the beast, the demons, and the false prophet are referred to.[3] While it is difficult to say that signs and wonders do not happen after the apostles, it is noteworthy how relatively quiet the epistles are regarding the presence of such phenomena in the local congregations.[4] It seems to me that a biblical-theological approach will make us cautious about either trying to abolish miracles from the contempo-

2. Walter J. Chantry, *Signs of the Apostles* (Edinburgh: Banner of Truth, 1976).
3. Rev. 13:13-14; 16:14; 19:20.
4. Miracles are mentioned as happening in the congregation in 1 Cor. 12:10, 29, and Gal. 3:5.

rary scene or asserting their normality in the life of a congregation. I would have to say that being reserved about miracles while going all out to proclaim the gospel is far better than making miracles into the gospel. However, we must strive for the biblical norms, and no Christian can reflect upon his or her own conversion without believing in miracles.

The principal feature of the biblical theology that is expressed in the New Testament epistles, and that will affect the way we preach from these documents, is the relationship of Christian existence to the historic gospel event both in the past and in the future eschatological hope. In chapter 7 I discussed this in terms of the coming of the end for us, in us, and with us. It is the relationship of Christian living, or sanctification, to the gospel event. At the risk of being repetitious I say that the most serious problem that easily afflicts us all as preachers is the tendency to confuse this relationship. This happens when we expound Christian living on any other basis than the gospel. Sanctification is, as has been wisely said, our justification in action. James Buchanan expressed an important truth when he said, "Nothing can be more unscriptural in itself, or more pernicious to the souls of men, than the substitution of the gracious work of the Spirit in us, for the vicarious work of Christ for us, as the grounds of our pardon and acceptance with God."[5]

One is unlikely to assert that we are justified by sanctification, but, whether done intentionally or not, that is what happens when we allow the teaching of Christian living, ethical imperatives, and exhortations to holiness to be separated from and to take the place of the clear statement of the gospel. We can preach our hearts out on texts about what we ought to be, what makes a mature church, or what the Holy Spirit wants to do in our lives, but if we do not constantly, in every sermon, show the link between the Spirit's work in us to Christ's work for us, we will distort the message and send people away with a natural theology of salvation by works. Preaching from the epistles demands of the preacher that the message of the document be taken as a whole even if only a selection of texts, or just one verse, is to be expounded. Every sermon should be understandable on its own as a proclamation of Christ. It is no good to say that we dealt with the justification element three weeks ago and now we are following Paul into the imperatives and injunctions for Christian living. Paul wasn't anticipating a three-week gap between his exposition of the gospel and his defining of the implications of the gospel in our lives. Nor was he anticipating that some people would not be present for the reading of the whole epistle and would hear part of its message out of context.

5. James Buchanan, *The Doctrine of Justification* (Edinburgh: Banner of Truth, 1961), p. 401.

1. The Ascension and World Mission (Acts 1)

The ascension came before us in the treatment of the biblical theology of Jesus and the apostles in chapter 5. It will suffice, therefore, to remind us here that Acts 1 gives us an important insight into the structure of biblical revelation that results from the nature of the gospel event. In summary we note these following points. The disciples had accepted the generally held Jewish idea that the coming of the Messiah would mean the unambiguously final advent of the kingdom of God. Jesus' death disappointed them, but their hope was revived by the resurrection. Surely the kingdom would now appear, and hence the question to that effect in Acts 1:6, "Will you now restore the kingdom to Israel?" The answer that Jesus gives indicates that this question is misplaced. We must assume that his answer is not a put-down but a genuine answer to the question. He tells them, "You will receive power when the Holy Spirit comes upon you; and you will be my witnesses in Jerusalem, in all Judea and Samaria, and to the ends of the earth" (Acts 1:8). The kingdom of God is indeed being restored to Israel, but it will come about through the preaching of the gospel in all the world.

Some have used this statement to reinforce a view that Jesus was indicating that there are two different events to come: one is the restoration of the kingdom to Israel as a specifically Jewish salvation; the other is the world mission to the gentiles through the gospel. This, I suggest, does not fit the biblical facts, and we should understand Jesus to be saying that the kingdom is indeed being restored, but it will come to Jew and gentile alike through the preaching of the gospel.

The ascension, then, structures the age of the gospel and Christian experience. The ascension shows the nature of the overlap of the ages and creates the New Testament perspective of the "now" and the "not yet." It is a shame that the ascension is so neglected in preaching. I doubt if any Christian church would allow Easter Sunday to go by without some reference to the resurrection. Also, most Christians meet on Sunday with the rationale in the back of their minds that the first day of the week took the place of the Sabbath because Jesus rose that day. Every Sunday is a resurrection day, but ascension falls on a Thursday! Liturgically minded churches and those that follow the traditional ecclesiastical calendar may well observe Ascension Day. For most, I fear, it passes without notice, and usually without comment. Of course, we are not dependent on traditional ecclesiastical calendars for our preaching, and the ascension will not be neglected if we follow a gospel-centered program.

2. Pentecost in Biblical Theology (Acts 2)

If the Holy Spirit was given on the day of Pentecost as the fulfillment not only of certain Old Testament promises but also of the promises that Jesus made in his Last Supper discourse, in what way was he present before Pentecost? A quick summary of the Holy Spirit in biblical theology is called for. The Spirit was present and active at the creation and is the power of God by which life is breathed into human beings. The sin of man affects human relationships with God and therefore with the Spirit (Gen. 6:3). As salvation history unfolds, the role of the Holy Spirit is revealed mainly in conjunction with special saving ministries, including that of the judges and the kings.[6] As we come to prophetic eschatology, the Spirit's role becomes even more prominent as the agent of re-creation in the messianic age.[7] Through the Spirit, the servant of God will bring salvation to the nations (Isa. 42:1-3). He will gather God's people on the day of salvation, empower the word of the Lord as it goes out to achieve his purpose, and be the force behind the building of the new temple.[8] The day of the Lord will be marked by a pouring out of the Spirit on all God's people (Joel 2:28-32).

There are a few passages that indicate that the Spirit is involved in a more general way with the saving of the people of God,[9] but the main emphasis in the Old Testament is the Spirit's role in the saving work of God through the anointed savior figures. This role of the Spirit should prepare us for the Christological link between Spirit and word in the New Testament, and for the fact that we best understand the Spirit's work when we start with Jesus as the perfectly Spirit-endowed person. The Spirit's presence in the world is defined by the presence of the word of God. At Pentecost the Spirit is received in relation to the completed gospel and as the agent of the risen and exalted Christ in the world. In this sense there was a time when, as John says, "there was no Spirit . . . because Jesus was not yet glorified" (John 7:39). However we might assess the presence of the Spirit in the world before Pentecost, the emphasis is clear that the condition for the giving of the Spirit is the finished work of Christ.

We may assert that there are differences between the role of the Spirit under the old covenant and his role under the new. While the Old Testament is fairly muted about the place of the Spirit in lives of Israelite believers, we must surely believe that under the old covenant people were just as sinfully resistant and spiritually dead as under the new.[10] They were as much in need

---

6. Gen. 41:38; Exod. 31:3; Num. 11:29; Deut. 34:9; Judg. 3:10; 6:34; 11:29; 13:25; 14:6, 19; 15:14; 1 Sam. 16:13-14.

7. Isa. 11:1-9; 32:15-20.

8. Isa. 44:3; 59:21; 61:1; Ezek. 36:25-28; 37:14; 39:29; Zech. 4:6.

9. Ps. 51:10-12; Isa. 63:10-14.

10. The case for the Spirit's role in Old Testament believers is ably argued by Glenn

of the regeneration of the Spirit as we are if they were to receive the word of God by faith. Furthermore, we must believe that the Spirit is always the Spirit who is either present or not. So how does his Old Testament role differ from his role at Pentecost? The Spirit's role is to be the powerful agent of God's saving work and to apply the word of God, the word of the gospel, to the hearts of people. The distinctions in the Spirit's role are distinctions in the revelation of the gospel. The Spirit is active in the Old Testament, not only in the unique saving ways that foreshadow the Spirit of Christ in salvation, but also in the gospel revelation as it is at any given time.[11] This emphasis is continued into the Gospel narratives in that Jesus is above all the Spirit-endowed Israelite who fulfills all the roles of the Spirit-empowered figures of the Old Testament. In his perfect obedience, even unto death, Jesus establishes his right to share with all his people not only his righteous status as Son of God but also his endowment with the Spirit. That is why, once the transition to the period of the gospel and Spirit has taken place at Pentecost, the norm is that repentance and faith are accompanied by reception of the Spirit. Nothing further is predicated by way of the Spirit in the Christian life — no further baptism in the Spirit, only the life that is in step with the Spirit, which goes on being filled with the Spirit (Gal. 5:25; Eph. 5:18).

3. Cornelius and the Gentiles (Acts 10)

Placing this event in the context of biblical theology presents few problems. Once we have understood the eschatological nature of the gospel and the fact that the last days began with the first coming of Christ, we can see the expectations of the Old Testament coming to the fore in the way the gospel is proclaimed. The sticking point was that, even with the new hermeneutic of Luke 24, and even with the enlightenment of the Spirit at Pentecost, the human heart is slow to learn, as we all know from our own experience. The first Christians still seemed to have had difficulty in adjusting to the implications of the gospel for the gentiles. The Ethiopian and the Samaritans in Acts 8 press home the theology of the gospel for the non-Jew, and now in Acts 10 Peter is given an unforgettable lesson in the same truth.

Acts 10, then, where Peter learns not to call gentiles unclean, moves us

---

Davies, "The Spirit of Regeneration in the Old Testament," in *Spirit of the Living God*, ed. B. G. Webb, Explorations 5 (Homebush West, Sydney: Lancer, 1991).

11. John Goldingay ("Was the Holy Spirit Active in Old Testament Times? What Was New about the Christian Experience of God?" *Ex Auditu* 12 [1996]) correctly points out that many of the activities attributed to the Holy Spirit in the New Testament are described in the Old Testament without referring to the Spirit directly. Thus the New Testament makes it clear that the Spirit is responsible for such events and activities of God in the Old Testament.

closer to the all-out efforts of Paul to bring the gospel to the nations. The difficulties of circumcised believers at the news of the gentiles receiving the Holy Spirit illustrate the problems they were having in adjusting their views to the implications of the gospel. If anything, the inclusion of the gentiles forced a reevaluation of the way the law would function in the church. The other element shown in the way Luke has arranged his material is that this reevaluation would figure in the new thrust outward from Jerusalem, which was accelerated by the persecution of the Church after the death of Stephen. The Cornelius episode forms a significant part of a biblical theology of mission that enables us to understand the apparent change in perspective from the Old Testament ingathering of gentiles at the temple in Jerusalem, to the New Testament emphasis on outreach to the nations. The heart of this modification is expressed by Stephen as he indicates the need to move from a fixed temple made with hands (Acts 7:47-51). Jesus is now the temple that is both in heaven, where he sits at the right hand of God, and on earth through the Spirit and the gospel. The gentiles still flow in to the temple as Isaiah saw it, but the temple is now wherever the Spirit of Jesus gathers his people through the preaching of the gospel.

4. The Gospel and Christian Behavior (1 Cor. 6)

A few comments about this passage are in order because it illustrates so well the connection between the gospel indicative and the imperatives of sanctification. I have heard this passage expounded with great eloquence and yet without the gospel. The preacher seemed not to be aware, in his zeal to warn his hearers away from ungodly behavior patterns, that Paul gives a number of leads to the relationship of these stern injunctions to the gospel. The first is in v. 2, "Do you not know that the saints will judge the world?" Our relationship with Christ the judge has extraordinary eschatological consequences, and yet here are the Corinthian Christians behaving as if there were no consequences for the present.

When, in vv. 9-11, Paul comes to the list of those who will not inherit the kingdom, he is not saying simply that those who sin won't go to heaven, as true as that may be. Rather he reminds the congregation that these things are inconceivable for the one who is in Christ, who is washed, sanctified, and justified. The rationale and the motive for godliness is not law but gospel. Likewise, the exhortations to sexual purity are not based on naked law but on the gospel truth that the Spirit dwells in those who have been bought with a price (vv. 19-20). This should be obvious from even a cursory reading of the text, yet somehow and for some reason we are often unwilling, in our zeal to bring people into line, to follow the text and expound the gospel as the basis for sanctified behavior.

5. The Man of Sin (2 Thess. 2:1-12)

Leon Morris comments that "this passage is probably the most obscure and difficult in the whole of the Pauline correspondence."[12] From the perspective of biblical theology the problem is partly understanding what Paul is expecting and why. We have seen that there is a need to recognize the full eschatological implications of the gospel, that the end has come and prophecy has been fulfilled in the first coming of Christ. However, it is important that we don't allow that perspective to lead us into a full-blown realized eschatology so that we see nothing left to happen. In this passage Paul appears to counter this tendency. If Paul means by his man of lawlessness the same thing as John does when he speaks of the antichrist, then we have to believe both that many antichrists have gone out into the world, and that the man of sin, from Paul's perspective, was still to come.

When we place all the statements about the return of Christ in the Thessalonian epistles together, the eschatological theology is not as unclear as this one passage would seem to indicate. In 1 Thessalonians 4 Paul deals with the certainty of the resurrection of the dead when Christ returns. In chapter 5 he uses the image of a thief in the night to describe the coming. It is a call to vigilance and faithfulness so that we are not caught unawares. In 2 Thessalonians 1 he speaks of the certainty of judgment when Christ returns. In the light of these passages it would seem that 2 Thessalonians 2 is expressive of the reality of evil in these last days. His denial of the day of the Lord (v. 2) is a rejection of the realized eschatology of those who say it is all here now. There are still things that are yet to be resolved.[13]

As William Hendriksen shows, Paul's description of the man of lawlessness reflects a dependence on a number of passages in Daniel.[14] This being the case we have to understand Paul's statements in the wider context of the biblical theology of the victory of the Son of Man. If our biblical-theological analysis is correct, there is no conflict between the abomination that desolates, the apostasy and resistance to the kingdom of God, being given primary and starkest expression in the passion and death of Christ and the thought that these things are still to come. The emphasis in our passage is that the *status quo* has not yet been reached. Paul in no sense is going against the teaching of Jesus about the signs of the times. These were never intended to provide leverage for

---

12. Leon Morris, *1 and 2 Thessalonians,* Tyndale New Testament Commentaries (London: Tyndale Press, 1956), p. 123.

13. See William J. Dumbrell, *The Search for Order: Biblical Eschatology in Focus* (Grand Rapids: Baker, 1994), pp. 313-15; Gerrit C. Berkouwer, *Studies in Dogmatics: The Return of Christ* (Grand Rapids: Eerdmans, 1972), pp. 268-75.

14. William Hendriksen, *1 and 2 Thessalonians* (London: Banner of Truth, 1972). See Dan. 7:25; 8:9-14, 25.

those who like to predict times and seasons. They are there precisely to remind us that we are in the last days. With the certainty that God is going to act finally to consummate the kingdom, Paul exhorts the Thessalonian Christians to "stand firm and hold fast to the traditions that you were taught by us, either by word of mouth or by our letter" (2 Thess. 2:15).

Literary and Historical Considerations

The first consideration is that the epistles are mostly directed to a specific historical situation, yet they carry an authority that makes them generally applicable. The preacher's exegetical task is to try to understand first that historical situation. As important as this is, however, the preacher is always left with the task of trying to grasp the theological principles being expressed so that they might be transferred to our contemporary situation. As Scott Hafermann notes, "the truths expressed in the Epistles are all expressed in relation to and for the sake of the concrete situations and problems being addressed."[15] The theological significance of the epistolary text is illuminated by the situation that evoked it even if the data available are only what is in the content of the text itself. However, the specific situation, while illuminating the meaning of the text, is not in itself the message. In a sermon we need to hear more than an analysis of what Paul said to the Galatians in chapter 1 of the epistle, and what motivated him to say it. We need to have this translated into what God is saying to us today. Most of us have a favorite text that we apply over and over again with great fervor only to discover on closer examination that the wider context of the passage does not really allow this interpretation.

The literary characteristics of epistles have received much attention in recent studies.[16] The preacher needs to take these into account in the process of exegesis, and also when considering the form of the sermon. Scott Hafemann urges the preacher to consider at least five characteristics in the epistles that will affect our exposition of them. These are the theological character, the occasional nature, the discursive structure, the central thrust, and the imperative exhortations. With regard to the last, he comments:

> The danger in preaching the Epistles, therefore, is that the imperatives of the text will be separated from the indicative theological

15. Scott Hafemann, "Preaching in the Epistles," in *Handbook of Contemporary Preaching,* ed. Michael Duduit (Nashville: Broadman, 1992).

16. See Sidney Greidanus, *The Modern Preacher and the Ancient Text* (Grand Rapids: Eerdmans, 1988), chapter 12.

statements upon which they are inseparably based, or from the fulfillment of the promises to which they inevitably lead.[17]

Because we are dealing with letters written for particular situations, it is not safe to assume that they will contain systematic arguments — although, as Leland Ryken suggests, Romans and Hebrews would be exceptions.[18] Ryken also proposes that the points emphasized in the epistle are not necessarily those that are theologically the most central. These may be assumed by the writer while he turns his attention to the specific occasion for the letter.[19]

Planning Sermons from Acts and the Epistles

The implications of the foregoing discussion for planning sermons on these books should be fairly clear by now. Our task is to proclaim Christ and him crucified. All our ethical or sanctificational exhortations must not only stem from the gospel but be seen to stem from the gospel. In dealing with Acts there is great scope here for providing a biblical-theological panorama of the New Testament since the book embraces the whole transition from the present Jesus to the absent Jesus who comes among his people by his word and Spirit. It moves from this transition into the early stages of world mission, including the establishment of both Jewish and gentile churches. Because of this critical development that takes place within the scope of this one book, no sermon or series of sermons on Acts should be attempted without some measure of theological contextualizing. The temptation to deal with Paul and the other apostles only as missionary heroes is strong but must certainly be resisted. Character studies of these people should be carried out in much the same way as character studies of any of the great figures of biblical narrative. They are ultimately subservient to the wider theological question of what God is doing in his great mission to lost humanity.

Any series of sermons on the epistles should allow the theological structures of the epistles to come through. From the point of view of biblical theology the main consideration is that the function of the epistles in general terms be understood and brought out. They apply the subject of the grace of God in the gospel to Christian existence. The best preventative against legalism is systematic expository preaching, with this one proviso: no one sermon should ever be allowed to stand apart from the whole gospel-based thrust of the epistle.

17. Hafemann, "Preaching in the Epistles," p. 372.
18. Leland Ryken, *Words of Life: A Literary Introduction to the New Testament* (Grand Rapids: Baker, 1987), p. 90.
19. Ryken, *Words of Life,* p. 90.

CHAPTER 18

Preaching Biblical Theology

The Place of Thematic Sermons
and Series in Preaching Programs

Having endeavored to establish the place of biblical theology in preaching any sermon, I want now to turn to a consideration of the place of the sermon and series of sermons specifically aimed at teaching biblical theology. Mostly these will be thematic sermons in which a certain important theme is followed through the structures of biblical revelation. This approach demonstrates the principle that has informed, it is to be hoped, all of our preaching. In chapter 11 I gave the illustration of the ceremonial directive for the trumpets in Numbers 10:1-10. When I preached on this passage I raised the question of whether there is a biblical theology of trumpet blowing. I answered in the affirmative and went on to expound on this passage. This probably would not fit some definitions of expository preaching, but it seemed to me that it did. The aim was to clarify the significance of the trumpets and their use. However, as with any ceremonial directive in the Old Testament, the question is, What does it mean for us today? The principle at work here is that any text, event, or person is part of the unity that testifies to Christ.

The Thematic Approach to Biblical Theology

Biblical theology is of great value in helping us to understand the real context, basis, and texture of some New Testament concept or theme that impinges on our Christian experience. Alternatively, we may come upon some prominent theme or motif in the Old Testament that we want to follow through to see how it testifies to Christ and, thus, how it edifies us. I want to conclude this study of biblical theology in preaching by summarizing the structure of revelation as it affects the understanding of key characters and themes in the Bible. Between the two extreme parameters of creation and new creation we have a marvelous, divinely crafted structure or plan of salvation that centers in the person and work of Jesus of Nazareth. The focus of salvation history is the people of God and the dealings of God with them to bring them to himself. As we have seen, the main characters who define the plan of God are: Abraham, David (with Solomon), and Jesus Christ. We have also seen how the revelation of the saving work of God and the coming of his kingdom occurs principally in three epochs or blocks of biblical revelation. I have designated these in the various diagrams as A, B, and C. These refer respectively to the kingdom revealed in Israel's history, the kingdom revealed in prophetic eschatology, and the kingdom revealed and fulfilled in Christ.

Thus, in A (the kingdom revealed in Israel's history) we include the whole history of God's activity outside of Eden up to and including David and the first part of Solomon's reign. The key figures are Abraham as recipient of the promises of God, and David as the one to whom a certain measure of the fulfillment of these promises comes. This epoch becomes the first anchorage for the doing of biblical theology. The second epoch, B, takes in the historic decline of Israel, including the exile and beyond, but the major impetus in revelation is the prophetic promise of a future perfect salvation. The third epoch, C, is the fulfillment of the historic promises to Abraham and his descendants, and of the prophetic hope, in Jesus Christ.

Our three epochs, then, become for us the three main anchorages for our biblical theology. We can follow the theological significance of persons and events through these epochs and so relate them first to their fulfillment in Christ and then to ourselves.

Here are some suggestions for procedure:

1. If starting with a New Testament theme, look for its relationship to the central facts of the gospel. It may be the links made by Jesus or the apostles with the Old Testament that give us a starting point. If starting with an Old Testament theme or text, see if there are any direct links made through quotations or allusions in the New Testament.
2. Do some creative thinking and write down all the words and themes that are conceivably expressive of the matter to be investigated. As you work with a concordance you will probably discover related words or concepts that bear following up. Don't stray too far from the central idea you started with, or you are likely to be there forever.
3. Now deal with the texts you have uncovered in their specific biblical-theological contexts. There is room for further differentiation within the

fundamental framework of the three epochs. What you are looking for is the way these concepts under investigation function theologically against their horizon in each epoch. Ask yourself what contribution a concept makes to the bigger picture of the revelation of salvation and the kingdom of God in that epoch. Thus, you might follow up a theme in any of the relevant texts by identifying its place in the overall scheme or framework of things. This framework might be represented thus:

A. *Historical epoch*
creation
prepatriarchal period
patriarchal period
the Exodus and wilderness
the entry to the establishment of the kingship
Israel's ongoing faith (wisdom, Psalms)
decline and fall
exile and restoration

B. *Prophetic eschatology*
preexilic prophets
exilic prophets
postexilic prophets

C. *New Testament fulfillment*
fulfillment in Christ
fulfillment in the people of God
fulfillment in the consummation

Warning: do not confuse a given word with a concept or theme. Doing biblical theology involves a great deal more than keying a specific word into your computer concordance. On the one hand, the one word may be used for a number of quite distinct concepts. On the other hand, the concept or theme may be represented by a number of different words. This is certainly not to say that words are unimportant. In fact, one of the main stimuli to doing biblical theology is the use of technical words or phrases in the New Testament in a way that seems to assume something about the history of these terms in the Old Testament. It is this New Testament presupposition that its message comes out of the Old Testament that gives biblical theology its dynamic.

The Single Sermon on Biblical Theology

The major emphasis of this study has been the need to deal with any chosen text in its context of biblical theology. We do this for the important reason that the text is part of the whole and takes its meaning from the whole unified message of Scripture. This is not an optional extra or one choice out of many. No text can yield its true meaning if it is removed from its context in the one revealed message of the Bible. Every sermon should be prepared with this in mind. I cannot think of any reason why there should be a single exception to this principle. The Bible is what it is, and if we are going to be faithful proclaimers of the Bible's message, we must allow the nature of the Bible as a whole to dictate the way we teach and preach.

However, it is one thing to recognize the place of biblical theology in the preparation of a sermon so that the way we explain a text and apply it is shaped by the way that text fits into the grand scheme of biblical revelation. It is another thing to actually preach a sermon that demonstrates the method and results of approaching the Bible in this way. This is really a matter of emphasis and not a complete separation of the two approaches. Every sermon without exception should contain the results of doing biblical theology. Sometimes we might want to demonstrate the way it is done. In other words, sermons can teach people how to read and understand the Bible. Every sermon should do that to some degree, but sometimes we should make it the main theme.

1. Salvation History and the Messiah

There are at least two ways that a sermon can teach the principles of biblical theology. One is to take a passage that actually has some expression of biblical theology in it. A sermon on Matthew 1 would be a case in point, and it has the added advantage that, at least for the first ten minutes, you will have the congregation on the edge of their pews waiting to see what on earth you are going to do with a boring old genealogy! A possible structure for such a sermon could be something like the following example.

Sermon 1: Salvation history and the Messiah.
Text: Matthew 1.
    a. Abraham, the father of the Messiah.
    b. David, the forerunner to the Messiah.
    c. The exile and the need for the Messiah.
    d. Jesus the Messiah.

248

There is of course material enough for a series of three or four sermons in this, but one of the great things about biblical theology is that it is flexible enough to expand or contract to fit the need. I have conducted studies on the complete outline of biblical theology in one hour and in courses of fifty hours. Be patient but consistent in leading your congregation into a biblical-theological understanding of the Scriptures.

2. Jesus in All the Scriptures

Another single sermon on biblical theology could follow the text of Jesus' postresurrection discourses in Luke 24. The focal points would be verses 27 and 44, with the fruit of this exposition in v. 45.

> **Sermon 2: Jesus in all the Scriptures.**
> Text: Luke 24.
>   a. Moses writes of Jesus.[1]
>   b. The prophets write of Jesus.[2]
>   c. The psalms are about Jesus.[3]
>   d. Jesus is the key to understanding Scripture.

Another passage that contains the outline of a biblical theology is Peter's Pentecost sermon (Acts 2:22-36). This could include an exposition of Peter's use of Joel 2 as a preamble to his sermon, but this probably ought to be dealt with at another time. Paul's sermon in Acts 13 and Stephen's apology in Acts 7 are also structured as biblical theology.

Using Themes in Biblical Theology

The second approach to a single sermon on biblical theology is to focus on a prominent theological theme that may be a concept or a significant character in redemptive history. In addition, the theme or person may link with another theme or person to provide continuity. It is the theological concept that counts, not the specific manifestation of it that often undergoes modification.

---

1. Moses would be a reference to the whole Pentateuch.
2. The prophets include the Former Prophets (Joshua, Judges, Samuel, and Kings) and the Latter Prophets (the writing prophets).
3. The psalms almost certainly here is used inclusively for the whole third section of the Hebrew canon, the Writings, which contain Psalms, the wisdom books, and the other works not included in Moses or the prophets.

This, by the way, is where a rigidly literalistic interpretation becomes unstuck. Such an interpretation simply cannot cope with the way the Bible rings the changes on the external forms while maintaining the theological significance. Furthermore, what we have seen regarding unity and distinction applies to the way one thing can represent another, and one person can represent a whole nation.

One example of these modifications will suffice. The Garden of Eden is lost to human experience due to sin, but in its place is the promise of a land flowing with milk and honey. In the Old Testament the theme of the land is prominent, yet when we come to the New Testament it is much harder to find. The mystery of the disappearing promised land is resolved when we see that certain institutions begin to represent its reality as the place where God and his people dwell together in fellowship. Thus: Eden →promised land → Zion →temple →new temple (in the prophets) →Christ, the new temple. Only then can we move to the new Eden or the new heaven and earth. The promises of the land and a return to Eden are incorporated into the theology of the temple as the place where God dwells with his people. The physical nature of the land reappears in the prospect of a new creation that, contrary to some forms of popular piety, is not a nonmaterial and purely spiritual concept. The whole creation will be remade. It will be different but have some continuity with the world. The melding of the temple and Eden images, which occurs in the eschatology of Ezekiel 47, is found again in Revelation 21:22–22:5.

The Series of Sermons on Biblical Theology

Much more challenging is the series of sermons that aims to describe some theme of biblical theology. The challenge is not so much in deciding on a theme, for there is an endless supply of topics in Scripture. The challenge lies more in the crafting of a series that will allow the preacher to move toward a climax in the whole series while at the same time preaching complete Christian sermons each time. It would seem that we must sacrifice the surprise element of the series in order to bring each individual sermon in the series to a satisfactory resolution in Christ. This is where the creative imagination of the preacher comes in, not in the sense of making up some fiction, but in the management of the series so that the many facets of the theme are shown to come to their fulfillment in the various dimensions of the gospel. Here are a couple of suggestions from among the more obvious and productive themes. It would be wise to deal with those that are most central to the story of salvation history and the gospel rather than becoming too bold in looking for obscure themes. You will notice that in the following series the basic structure of biblical theology is followed starting with the gospel, then going back to the historical epoch, then the prophetic eschatology, and finally returning again to the fulfillment in Christ. This structure can be varied and expanded at will provided that the essential relationships are made visible.

1. A Biblical Theology of Mission

Sermon 1: Mission means the kingdom of God has come with Jesus.
Text: Acts 1:1-11.
  a. The resurrection and the kingdom (vv. 1-3).
  b. The Holy Spirit and the kingdom (vv. 4-6).
  c. The kingdom and mission (vv. 7-8).
  d. Mission and the return of Christ (vv. 9-11).

Sermon 2: Mission means Jesus has been given authority over all things.
Text: Matthew 28:16-20.
  a. Jesus is the victorious Son of Man (vv. 16-18).
  b. Jesus takes charge of the nations (v. 19).
  c. Jesus is the evangelist (v. 20).

Sermon 3: The promise of God for the nations.
Text: Genesis 12:1-3.
  a. Abraham is called from the nations (v. 1).
  b. Abraham is the object of God's blessing (v. 2).
  c. Abraham's descendants are the source of world blessing (v. 3).
  d. The descendant of Abraham is Christ (Galatians 3:6-9).

Sermon 4: The ingathering of the nations.
Text: Isaiah 2:1-4.
  a. The failed kingdom (Isaiah 1).
  b. The promise of restoration for Zion (vv. 1-2).
  c. The promise of the nations (vv. 2d-3).
  d. The healing of the nations (v. 4).
  e. The Lamb and the new temple (Rev. 21:22–22:2).

Sermon 5: Israel's outreach to the nations.
Text: Acts 13:44-52.
  a. The new temple not made with hands (John 2:19-22; Acts 7).
  b. The apostasy of Israel (vv. 44-45, cf. Isa. 1).

  c. A light to the gentiles (vv. 46-47, cf. Isa. 2:1-4).
  d. The gentiles come to the new temple (vv. 48-49).

2. A Biblical Theology of Resurrection

A central theme that stretches our biblical-theological skills is that of the resurrection. There are few references to anything like a bodily resurrection in the Old Testament that we might see as the antecedent to the New Testament doctrine. Are we simply looking at a developing notion of life after death or is there something more significant about the way the doctrine is presented? There can be no disputing that the resurrection of Jesus is at the heart of the gospel as proclaimed by the apostles and the New Testament writers. While Paul, in 1 Corinthians 15:3-4, can summarize the gospel as the death and resurrection of Christ, "according to the Scriptures," these Scriptures contain very little by way of explicit reference to resurrection.[4] Life after death in the Old Testament is a very shadowy and undefined reality incorporating ideas of "sleep," "the pit," and an ambiguous reality known as "sheol." What can we do to arrive at a biblical theology of resurrection when it seems to be a notion that develops among Jews almost entirely during the intertestamental period? The answer is that we allow the exposition of the gospel in the New Testament to guide us. When we examine the New Testament references to resurrection, we come up with a number of concepts or themes that are linked to the significance of the resurrection and that we can follow up in the redemptive-historical revelation. For example:

  1. Life after death (Matt. 22:23-33; Luke 14:14; 1 Cor. 15).
  2. David's covenant (Acts 2:30-31).
  3. The fulfillment of God's promises to Israel (Acts 13:30-33).
  4. The son of God (Rom. 1:4).
  5. The justification of God's people (Rom. 4:24-25).
  6. Judgment (John 5:29; Acts 17:29-34).
  7. Regeneration or new birth (1 Pet. 1:3-5).
  8. Son of Man (Matt. 17:9).
  9. The new temple (John 2:19-22).

Every one of these themes is traceable back into the Old Testament. Every one of them contributes to the meaning of the resurrection of Jesus. Every one of them is capable of being developed into a sermon that traces the

---

4. The clearest references are Isa. 26:19; 52:13; Dan. 12:2; and possibly Job 19:26 (which is disputed on textual grounds by many scholars).

theme through the three epochs leading to some aspect of the gospel. So significant is the resurrection that we see the reasonableness of our understanding Paul to mean that ALL the promises of God are fulfilled in it (Acts 13:32-33).

Sermon 1: The resurrection shows that Jesus is Lord.
Text: Acts 2:22-36.
    a. The death of Jesus in the plan of God (vv. 22-23).
    b. The resurrection shows he is God's holy one (vv. 24-28).
    c. The resurrection shows he is the son of David (vv. 29-35).
    d. The resurrection shows he is Lord and Christ (v. 36).

Sermon 2: The resurrection shows that Jesus is the true humanity.
Text: Romans 1:1-4.
    a. The gospel is God's solution to the problem (v. 1).
    b. The gospel is the message of the Old Testament (v. 2).
    c. Jesus is the son of David, the Messiah (v. 3).
    d. Jesus is the son of God, the true Israel (v. 4).
    e. The resurrection is the justification of Jesus and of all who are in him (Rom. 4:24-25).

Sermon 3: The resurrection is the fulfillment of all prophecy.
Text: Acts 13:16-39.
    a. Biblical theology from Abraham to David (vv. 16-22).
    b. From David, through the prophets, to Christ (vv. 23-29).
    c. The resurrection fulfills prophecy (vv. 30-37).
    d. The resurrection and forgiveness of sins (vv. 38-39).

Anchor Points for Major Characters and Themes

1. Biblical-Theological Character Studies

Historical Epoch	Prophetic Eschatology	Jesus Christ
Adam, Abraham, Abraham's seed	New Israel, new David, new Davidic prince	Last Adam, Christ the seed of Abraham
Jacob, Israel	New Israel	True Israel, Christ
David, David's son	New Davidic prince	Jesus, son of David

Psalmist as Israelite	New Israel	True Israel
Psalmist as king	New David	Son of David
Elijah	New prophet, new Elijah	John the Baptist, Jesus the true prophet

2. Biblical-Theological Theme Studies

Historical Epoch	Prophetic Eschatology	Jesus Christ
Creation	Land, new heavens and earth	Christ as new creation, new heavens and earth
Abraham's seed given the promises of the covenant	New Israel	Abraham's seed is Christ
Eden, promised land	Return to the land	New creation, new earth
Exodus from Egypt	Second exodus from Babylon	Jesus' exodus, Christ our Passover
Tabernacle-temple	Restored temple	New temple in Jesus' body, temple in heaven
Covenant: Abraham, Moses, David	New covenant on the heart	New covenant in Christ

Some Examples of Concepts in Biblical Theology

1. The Kingdom of God

This is a New Testament phrase, and although the actual name is not found in the Old Testament, the concept is everywhere in the Bible. This involves us in a process of getting behind the phrase to its theological reality. Sometimes this requires a little creative or lateral thinking and some trial and error. We find that the New Testament, in using the phrase, is speaking of a central reality involving God ruling his people in time and space. Thus, we have been able to follow it through as a central unifying theme in biblical theology.

2. Regeneration

This is another theme that we have sought to relate to the broad picture. If the kingdom of God took us to creation, creation points us to the new creation. This provides the proper context for thinking about specific aspects of the theme: for example, what it means for a Christian to be regenerated and to be a new creation in Christ. Our biblical-theological perspective places personal regeneration squarely into the framework of Christ as the representative new man and the regeneration of the heavens and the earth at the consummation.

3. Covenant

The covenant emerges as a way of speaking about God's commitment to his creation and, specifically, to his people. It too has its origins in creation and in the eternal purposes of God. Biblical theology is concerned with taking the various ideas of covenant and examining the diversity as well as the unity behind them. The diversity is a function of progressive revelation (the covenants with Noah, Abraham, Moses, and David, Jeremiah's new covenant, the new covenant in Christ). The unity lies in the fact that we observe the one work of the one God leading to one consummation.

Applying Typology

A practical application of the principles enunciated in chapter 8 can now be summarized. The principal presuppositions governing the recognition of the typological structure of the Bible are:

a. The inspiration and authority of the Bible as the word of God.
b. The unity and diversity of the biblical message.
c. The structure of the "big picture" of the Bible involving the three major epochs of revelation of the kingdom of God.
d. The centrality of the person and work of Jesus Christ as the one to whom all Scripture testifies.

Typology is based on the recognition that the three major epochs of revelation have the same basic structure of the way God brings sinners into his kingdom by means of his saving acts. It recognizes that, in God's economy of salvation, he has revealed these fundamental truths, first by a shadow or type, and then in the solid reality or antitype.

255

1. Explicit Typology

This exists where an event or person in the historical epoch is deliberately taken up in the New Testament as a way of understanding the New Testament message. The relationship may be parallel or a reversal, or both. That is, the *antitype* in the New Testament may be expressed as corresponding positively with the *type* in the Old Testament, or it may answer it by providing what was lacking in the type. Thus, positively Jesus is the last Adam as the federal head of the new human race. As a reversal, Jesus provides what Adam failed to provide: in Adam all die; in Christ all shall be made alive. In explicit typology the historical event may also figure in the prophetic eschatology in a way that confirms the nature of the type. But even if it is not there, it will be taken up in the New Testament.

2. Implicit Typology

When a person or event in the Old Testament, either in history or prophecy, is given no explicit reference in the New Testament, the typology is implicit. How are we to interpret its significance and apply it to ourselves? To answer this we have to be able to perceive the theological significance of this event in its own epoch. If the person or event is so incidental to the main narrative that it is difficult to do this, there is probably not a lot to be gained. However, we must not fall into the trap of saying that something has no significance at all. We may need to look at it as part of a larger whole before we can say what its significance is.

Implicit typology is the recognition that the whole of the Old Testament is the testimony to Christ. While some texts may be more peripheral to the main message, no text is totally irrelevant. Thus, an event or person in the historical narratives of the Old Testament may never be specifically mentioned again. But it functions theologically within its own epoch, even if only to be one of the less prominent events or people in the outworking of God's plan. It will always be part of a larger whole whose theological significance can be determined. Typology simply means that this event or person functions as part of the larger foreshadowing of the later theological function as it comes to have its fuller significance in Christ.

*   *   *

Then he opened their minds to understand the scriptures.
(Luke 24:45)

Bibliography

Achtemeier, Elizabeth. *Preaching Hard Texts of the Old Testament.* Peabody, Mass.: Hendrickson, 1998.

Adam, Peter. *Speaking God's Words.* Leicester: IVP, 1996.

Alexander, T. D. *From Paradise to the Promised Land: An Introduction to the Main Themes of the Pentateuch.* Carlisle: Paternoster, 1995.

Allison, C. FitzSimons. *The Cruelty of Heresy.* London: SPCK, 1994.

Athanasius. "Athanasius' Letter to Marcellinus on the Interpretation of the Psalms," printed as an appendix to *St. Athanasius on the Incarnation: The Treatise de Incarnatione Verbi Dei.* London: Mowbray, 1953.

Baker, David L. *Two Testaments, One Bible,* rev. ed. Leicester: Apollos, 1991.

Baldwin, Joyce. *Daniel,* Tyndale Old Testament Commentaries. Leicester: IVP, 1978.

Barton, John. *Reading the Old Testament: Method in Biblical Study,* 2nd ed. London: Darton, Longman, and Todd, 1996.

Berkhof, Hendrikus. *Christ the Meaning of History.* Grand Rapids: Baker, 1979.

Berkouwer, Gerrit C. *Studies in Dogmatics: The Return of Christ.* Grand Rapids: Eerdmans, 1972.

Blomberg, Craig L. *Interpreting the Parables.* Leicester: Apollos, 1990.

Bolt, Peter. "Mark 13: An Apocalyptic Precursor to the Passion Narrative." *Reformed Theological Review* 54.1 (1995).

Bright, John. *The Kingdom of God.* New York: Abingdon, 1955.

———. *Early Israel in Recent History Writing.* London: SCM, 1956.

———. *The Authority of the Old Testament.* London: SCM, 1967.

———. *A History of Israel,* 2nd ed. Philadelphia: Westminster, 1972.

Brueggemann, Walter. *The Message of the Psalms.* Minneapolis: Augsburg, 1984.

Bruner, Frederick D. *A Theology of the Holy Spirit: The Pentecostal Experience and the New Testament Witness.* London: Hodder and Stoughton, 1971.

Bryson, Harold T. *Expository Preaching.* Nashville: Broadman, 1995.

Buchanan, James. *The Doctrine of Justification.* Edinburgh: Banner of Truth, 1961.

Bultmann, Rudolf K. *History and Eschatology: The Presence of Eternity.* Edinburgh: Edinburgh University Press, 1957.

Carson, Donald A. *Exegetical Fallacies.* Grand Rapids: Baker, 1984.

Chantry, Walter J. *Signs of the Apostles.* Edinburgh: Banner of Truth, 1976.

Childs, Brevard S. *Biblical Theology in Crisis.* Philadelphia: Westminster, 1970.

———. "Reflections on the Modern Study of the Psalms." In *Magnalia Dei: The Mighty Acts of God,* edited by F. M. Cross et al. New York: Doubleday, 1976.

———. *Biblical Theology of the Old and New Testaments.* London: SCM, 1992.

Clowney, Edmund P. *Preaching and Biblical Theology.* London: Tyndale Press, 1962; Grand Rapids: Eerdmans, 1961.

Collins, J. J. "Towards the Morphology of a Genre." *Semeia* 14 (1979).

Conzelmann, Hans. *An Outline of the Theology of the New Testament,* translated by John Bowden. London: SCM, 1969.

Craigie, Peter C. *The Book of Deuteronomy,* The New International Commentary on the Old Testament. Grand Rapids: Eerdmans, 1976.

———. *Psalms 1–50,* Word Biblical Commentary. Waco: Word, 1983.

Cullmann, Oscar. *Christ and Time.* London: SCM, 1951.

Currid, John. "Recognition and Use of Typology in Preaching." *Reformed Theological Review* 53.3 (1994).

Daane, James. *Preaching with Confidence.* Grand Rapids: Eerdmans, 1980.

Davies, Glenn. "The Spirit of Regeneration in the Old Testament." In *Spirit of the Living God,* edited by B. G. Webb. Explorations 5. Homebush West, Sydney: Lancer, 1991.

Dodd, C. H. *According to the Scriptures.* London: Nisbet, 1952.

Dumbrell, William J. *Covenant and Creation: An Old Testament Covenantal Theology.* Exeter: Paternoster, 1984.

———. *The Faith of Israel.* Grand Rapids: Baker, 1988.

———. *The Search for Order: Biblical Eschatology in Focus.* Grand Rapids: Baker, 1994.

Foulkes, Francis. *The Acts of God: A Study of the Basis of Typology in the Old Testament.* London: Tyndale Press, 1958.

Frei, Hans W. *The Eclipse of Biblical Narrative.* New Haven: Yale University Press, 1974.

Friesen, Gary. *Decision Making and the Will of God.* Portland: Multnomah, 1980.

Goldingay, John. "Was the Holy Spirit Active in Old Testament Times? What Was New about the Christian Experience of God?" *Ex Auditu* 12 (1996).

Goldsworthy, Graeme. *Gospel and Kingdom: A Christian Interpretation of the Old Testament.* Exeter: Paternoster, 1981.

———. *The Gospel in Revelation.* Exeter: Paternoster, 1984. Published in U.S.A. as *The Lamb and the Lion.* Nashville: Thomas Nelson, 1985.

———. " 'Thus Says the Lord,' the Dogmatic Basis of Biblical Theology." In *God Who Is Rich in Mercy: Essays Presented to Dr. D. B. Knox,* edited by P. T. O'Brien and D. G. Peterson. Homebush West, Sydney: Lancer, 1986.

———. *Gospel and Wisdom: Israel's Wisdom Literature in the Christian Life.* Exeter: Paternoster, 1987.

———. *According to Plan: The Unfolding Revelation of God in the Bible.* Leicester: IVP, 1991.

———. "The Pastor as Biblical Theologian." In *Interpreting God's Plan: Biblical Theology and the Pastor,* edited by R. J. Gibson. Explorations 11. Carlisle: Paternoster, 1997.

———. "Is Biblical Theology Viable?" In *Interpreting God's Plan: Biblical Theology and the Pastor,* edited by R. J. Gibson. Explorations 11. Carlisle: Paternoster, 1997.

——. "'With Flesh and Bones': A Biblical Theology of the Bodily Resurrection of Christ." *Reformed Theological Review* 57.3 (1998).

——. "The Gospel." In *The New Dictionary of Biblical Theology,* edited by B. Rosner and T. D. Alexander. Leicester: IVP, forthcoming.

——. "The Gospel and the End of History." Explorations 13. Carlisle: Paternoster, forthcoming.

——. "The Kingdom of God." In *The New Dictionary of Biblical Theology,* edited by B. Rosner and T. D. Alexander. Leicester: IVP, forthcoming.

——. "The Relationship of the Old Testament and the New Testament." In *The New Dictionary of Biblical Theology,* edited by B. Rosner and T. D. Alexander. Leicester: IVP, forthcoming.

Gooding, D. W. "The Literary Structure of the Book of Daniel and Its Implications." *Tyndale Bulletin* 32 (1981).

Goppelt, Leonhard. *Theology of the New Testament,* vol. 1, translated by J. Alsup. Grand Rapids: Eerdmans, 1981.

——. *Typos.* Grand Rapids: Eerdmans, 1982.

Gow, M. D. *The Book of Ruth: Its Structure, Theme and Purpose.* Leicester: Apollos, 1992.

Gowan, Donald E. *Reclaiming the Old Testament for the Christian Pulpit.* Atlanta: John Knox, 1976.

Green, E. M. B. *The Authority of Scripture.* London: Falcon, 1963.

Greidanus, Sidney. *Sola Scriptura: Problems and Principles in Preaching Historical Texts.* Toronto: Wedge, 1970.

——. *The Modern Preacher and the Ancient Text.* Grand Rapids: Eerdmans, 1988.

——. "Preaching in the Gospels." In *Handbook of Contemporary Preaching,* edited by Michael Duduit. Nashville: Broadman, 1992.

Gruenler, Royce. *Meaning and Understanding.* Foundations of Contemporary Interpretation 2. Grand Rapids: Zondervan, 1991.

Hafermann, Scott. "Preaching in the Epistles." In *Handbook of Contemporary Preaching,* edited by Michael Duduit. Nashville: Broadman, 1992.

Harrisville, Roy A., and Walter Sundberg. *The Bible in Modern Culture.* Grand Rapids: Eerdmans, 1995.

Hasel, Gerhard F. "The Future of Old Testament Theology: Prospects and Trends." In *The Flowering of Old Testament Theology: A Reader in Twentieth-Century Old Testament Theology, 1930-1990,* edited by B. Ollenberger, E. Martens, and G. Hasel. Winona Lake, Ind.: Eisenbrauns, 1992.

——. "Proposals for a Canonical Biblical Theology." *Andrews University Seminary Studies* 34.1 (1996).

Heinisch, Paul. *Theology of the Old Testament.* Collegeville: Liturgical Press, 1955.

Hendriksen, William. *1 and 2 Thessalonians.* London: Banner of Truth, 1972.

Henry, Carl F. H. *Toward a Recovery of Christian Belief.* Wheaton: Crossway, 1990.

Hoekema, Anthony A. *The Bible and the Future.* Grand Rapids: Eerdmans, 1978.

Holbert, John C. *Preaching Old Testament: Proclamation and Narrative in the Hebrew Bible.* Nashville: Abingdon, 1991.

Hooker, Morna. *The Son of Man in Mark.* London: SPCK, 1967.

Jacob, Edmund. *Theology of the Old Testament.* London: Hodder and Stoughton, 1955.

Jensen, Peter F. *At the Heart of the Universe.* Leicester: IVP, 1994; Wheaton: Crossway, 1997..

Jensen, Phillip D., and Anthony J. Payne. *The Last Word on Guidance.* Homebush West, Sydney: Anzea Press, 1991.

Kline, Meredith G. *Treaty of the Great King: The Covenant Structure of Deuteronomy.* Grand Rapids: Eerdmans, 1963.

König, Adrio. *The Eclipse of Christ in Eschatology.* Grand Rapids: Eerdmans, 1989.

Kraus, Hans-Joachim. *Die Biblische Theologie: Ihre Geschichte und Problematik.* Neukirchen-Vluyn: Neukirchener Verlag, 1970.

Ladd, George Eldon. *A Theology of the New Testament.* Grand Rapids: Eerdmans, 1974.

Lampe, G. W. H., and K. J. Woollcombe. *Essays on Typology.* London: SCM, 1957.

Leith, John H., ed. *Creeds of the Churches: A Reader in Christian Doctrine from the Bible to the Present,* rev. ed. Richmond: John Knox, 1973.

Lindsey, Hal, with C. C. Carlson. *The Late Great Planet Earth.* Grand Rapids: Zondervan, 1970.

Lloyd-Jones, D. Martyn. *Authority.* London: Inter-Varsity Fellowship, 1958.

Long, Thomas G. "Shaping Sermons by Plotting the Text's Claim Upon Us." In *Preaching Biblically,* edited by Don M. Wardlaw. Philadelphia: Westminster, 1983.

Long, V. Philips. *The Art of Biblical History.* Foundations of Contemporary Interpretation 5. Grand Rapids: Zondervan, 1994.

Lowry, Eugene L. "The Revolution of Sermonic Shape." In *Listening to the Word: Studies in Honor of Fred B. Craddock,* edited by G. R. O'Day and T. G. Long. Nashville: Abingdon, 1993.

———. *The Sermon: Dancing the Edge of Mystery.* Nashville: Abingdon, 1997.

Mayhue, Richard L. "Rediscovering Expository Preaching." In *Rediscovering Expository Preaching,* edited by John MacArthur, Jr. Dallas: Word, 1992.

McCarthy, D. J. *Old Testament Covenant: A Survey of Current Opinions.* Richmond: John Knox, 1972.

McComiskey, Thomas Edward. *The Covenants of Promise.* Nottingham: IVP, 1984.

McIntosh, John. "Biblical Exclusivism: Towards a Reformed Approach to the Uniqueness of Christ." *Reformed Theological Review* 53.1 (1994).

McLuhan, Marshall. *The Medium Is the Massage.* Harmondsworth: Penguin, 1967.

Miller, Calvin. "Narrative Preaching." In *Handbook of Contemporary Preaching,* edited by Michael Duduit. Nashville: Broadman, 1992.

Miller, Donald. *The Way to Biblical Preaching.* Nashville: Abingdon, 1957.

Morgan, Donn F. *Wisdom in the Old Testament Traditions.* Atlanta: John Knox, 1981.

Morris, Leon. *1 and 2 Thessalonians,* Tyndale New Testament Commentaries. London: Tyndale Press, 1956.

———. *I Believe in Revelation.* London: Hodder and Stoughton, 1976.

Motyer, J. A. *The Prophecy of Isaiah.* Leicester: IVP, 1993.

Noth, Martin. *The Deuteronomistic History,* translated from the 2nd German ed. of 1957. Sheffield: JSOT, 1981.

O'Day, Gail. "Toward a Biblical Theology of Preaching." In *Listening to the Word,* edited by G. O'Day and T. G. Long. Nashville: Abingdon, 1993.

Packer, James I. *Fundamentalism and the Word of God.* London: Inter-Varsity Fellowship, 1958.

———. *Evangelism and the Sovereignty of God.* London, Downers Grove: IVP, 1961, 1991.

———. "The Preacher as Theologian." In *When God's Voice Is Heard: Essays on Preaching Presented to Dick Lucas,* edited by C. Green and D. Jackman. Leicester: IVP, 1995.

Peterson, David G. *Possessed by God: A New Testament Theology of Sanctification and Holiness.* Leicester: Apollos, 1995.

Poythress, Vern. *The Shadow of Christ in the Law of Moses.* Brentwood, Tenn.: Wolgemuth and Hyatt, 1991.

Psalter Hymnal. Grand Rapids: CRC Publications, 1987.

Rad, Gerhard von. "Typological Interpretation of the Old Testament." In *Essays on Old Testament Hermeneutics,* edited by Claus Westermann. Richmond: John Knox, 1964.

————. *Old Testament Theology.* Edinburgh: Oliver and Boyd, 1965.

————. *Wisdom in Israel.* London: SCM, 1972.

Radmacher, Earl D., and Robert D. Preus, eds. *Hermeneutics, Inerrancy, and the Bible.* Grand Rapids: Zondervan, 1984.

Ramm, Bernard. *The Evangelical Heritage.* Waco: Word, 1973.

Reddish, M. G., ed. *Apocalyptic Literature: A Reader.* Nashville: Abingdon, 1990.

Richardson, Alan. *An Introduction to the Theology of the New Testament.* London: SCM, 1958.

Robertson, O. Palmer. *The Christ of the Covenants.* Phillipsburg: Presbyterian and Reformed, 1980.

Robinson, Donald W. B. *Faith's Framework: The Structure of New Testament Theology.* Sydney/Exeter: Albatross/Paternoster, 1985.

Robinson, Haddon W. *Expository Preaching.* Leicester: IVP, 1986.

Runia, Klaas. *The Sermon Under Attack,* The Moore College Lectures, 1980. Exeter: Paternoster, 1983.

Rushdoony, Rousas J. *The One and the Many: Studies in the Philosophy of Order and Ultimacy.* Fairfax, Va.: Thoburn Press, 1978.

Ryken, Leland. *Words of Life: A Literary Introduction to the New Testament.* Grand Rapids: Baker, 1987.

Sailhamer, John. *The Pentateuch as Narrative: A Biblical-Theological Commentary.* Grand Rapids: Zondervan, 1992.

Sandys-Wunsch, J., and L. Eldredge. "J. P. Gabler and the Distinction between Biblical and Dogmatic Theology: Translation, Commentary, and Discussion of His Originality." *Scottish Journal of Theology* 33 (1980).

Schaeffer, Francis. *He Is There and He Is Not Silent.* London: Hodder and Stoughton, 1972.

Senarclens, Jacques de. *Heirs of the Reformation.* London: SCM, 1963.

Shires, Henry. *Finding the Old Testament in the New.* Philadelphia: Westminster, 1974.

Sire, James W. *Scripture Twisting.* Downers Grove: IVP, 1980.

Strickland, Wayne, ed. *Five Views on Law and Gospel.* Grand Rapids: Zondervan, 1996.

Thielicke, Helmut. *The Evangelical Faith.* Vol. 1, *Prolegomena.* Grand Rapids: Eerdmans, 1974.

Thompson, John A. *The Ancient Near Eastern Treaties and the Old Testament.* London: Tyndale Press, 1964.

Torrance, Thomas F. *Space, Time and Resurrection.* Grand Rapids: Eerdmans, 1976.

Tucker, Gene M. *Form Criticism of the Old Testament.* Philadelphia: Fortress, 1971.

Unger, Merrill. *Principles of Expository Preaching.* Grand Rapids: Zondervan, 1955.

Van Til, Cornelius. *The Reformed Pastor and Modern Thought.* N.p.: Presbyterian and Reformed, 1974.

VanGemeren, Willem. *The Progress of Redemption.* Grand Rapids: Zondervan, 1988.

Vanhoozer, Kevin. *Is There a Meaning in This Text?* Grand Rapids: Zondervan, 1998.

Vos, Geerhardus. *Biblical Theology: Old and New Testaments.* Grand Rapids: Eerdmans, 1948.

Waltke, Bruce K. "A Canonical Process Approach to the Psalms." In *Tradition and Testament,* edited by J. Feinberg and P. Feinberg. Chicago: Moody, 1981.

Webb, Barry G. "The Song of Songs as a Love Poem and as Holy Scripture." *Reformed Theological Review* 49.3 (1990).

———. "Zion in Transformation: A Literary Approach to Isaiah." In *The Bible in Three Dimensions,* edited by D. Clines et al. Sheffield: JSOT, 1990.

———. *The Message of Isaiah.* Leicester: IVP, 1996.

Weiser, Artur. *The Psalms.* London: SCM, 1962.

Wenham, Gordon J. *The Book of Leviticus,* The New International Commentary on the Old Testament. Grand Rapids: Eerdmans, 1979.

Westermann, Claus. *Praise and Lament in the Psalms.* Edinburgh: T. & T. Clark, 1981.

Wilson, Gerald H. "The Shape of the Book of Psalms." *Interpretation* 46.2 (1992).

Wright, Christopher. *Living as the People of God.* Leicester: IVP, 1983.

Wright, George Ernest. *God Who Acts: Biblical Theology as Recital.* London: SCM, 1952.

Wright, J. Stafford. *The Date of Ezra's Coming to Jerusalem.* London: Tyndale Press, 1947.

Index of Authors

Index of Subjects

Index of Scripture References